RENEWALS 458-4574

DATE DUE

On Borrowed Time

On Borrowed Time

THE ART AND ECONOMY OF
LIVING WITH DEADLINES

Harald Weinrich

TRANSLATED BY
Steven Rendall

The University of Chicago Press   Chicago and London

HARALD WEINRICH is the author of many books, among them *Lethe: The Art and Critique of Forgetting* and *The Linguistics of Lying and Other Essays*.
STEVEN RENDALL was a professor of romance languages at the University of Oregon, and now enjoys a second career as a translator, having translated over three dozen books from German and French.

. . .

The University of Chicago Press, Chicago 60637
The University of Chicago Press, Ltd., London
© 2008 by The University of Chicago
All rights reserved. Published 2008
Printed in the United States of America
17 16 15 14 13 12 11 10 09 08   1 2 3 4 5
ISBN-13: 978-0-226-88601-5 (cloth)
ISBN-10: 0-226-88601-8 (cloth)

Originally published in German as *Knappe Zeit: Kunst und Ökonomie des befristen Lebens*
© Verlag C.H. Beck oHG, München 2005

Library of Congress Cataloging-in-Publication Data
Weinrich, Harald. [Knappe Zeit. English]
On borrowed time : the art and economy of living with
deadlines / Harald Weinrich ; translated by Steven Rendall.   p. cm.
Includes bibliographical references and index.
ISBN-13: 978-0-226-88601-5 (cloth : alk. paper)
ISBN-10: 0-226-88601-8 (cloth : alk. paper)
1. Time in literature. 2. Time—Philosophy. I. Title.
PN56.T5W4513 2008
115—dc22   2008006399

♾ The paper used in this publication meets the minimum
requirements of the American National Standard for
Information Sciences—Permanence of Paper for Printed
Library Materials, ANSI Z39.48-1992.

For D.
and U.
and L.

Contents

1

Life Is Short, Art Is Long

MEDICAL APHORISMS AND THE MOVEMENT OF TIME
Hippocrates, Aristotle, Theophrastus

We all know intuitively that human life is short, at least when we get older and have to recognize that we have significantly less time ahead of us than behind us. Physicians are most aware of this, since their task, which they often strive in vain to fulfill, is to make people's lives as long as possible. It was a great physician, Hippocrates, who first formulated the famous saying "Life is short and art is long."

Hippocrates, a contemporary of Socrates, lived on the Aegean island of Kos, around 400 BC. Plato also knew and admired him. In history, he is considered the "father of medicine." For many centuries physicians in the Western world have sworn by the "Hippocratic oath" to help their patients as much as they can and in no case to do them harm. Only recently has this oath—but not, I hope, its ethical content—fallen into disuse.

Among the writings of Hippocrates (the so-called "Corpus Hippocraticum") that have come down to us, the "Aphorisms," a collection of eighty-seven brief maxims that runs to about thirty-five pages in modern editions, is of special importance for the history of medicine. The first of these aphorisms—or more precisely, the first sentence of the first aphorism—is the one about the shortness of life and the length of art. It soon became widely known through numerous quotations, and it has been a frequent subject of commentary and discussion by physicians, philosophers, and writers ever since.[1]

It is not hard to see what the first half of the aphorism means. Historical demography has taught us well enough how short life expectancy was in premodern times. Most children did not even live into adulthood; for instance, of Goethe's five children, only one, his son August, "came through." But even August died at the age of forty-one, two years before his father's death. Thus more than two millennia earlier no physician needed to offer a justification for saying that human life was "short." However, Hippocrates himself lived on well into his eighties, so that one of Molière's doctors calls him, with wonderment, "the divine old man." This is one of the few exceptions that confirm the rule.[2]

The second half of the Hippocratic aphorism requires a more detailed justification, at least for modern readers. What does it mean to say that "art is long"? Here we must not think of the modern concept of art, as it was developed in the cult of genius in the late Enlightenment and in early Romanticism. We must also avoid all the ideas of inspiration, spontaneity, and creativity that are associated with this concept. Art in the Hippocratic and especially in the premodern sense of the word (*technē* in the Greek text) must be understood instead as "a way of knowing" (Heidegger), that is, as a complex object of knowledge formulated in rules that can be taught and learned; this is the meaning given the term today in many scientific disciplines.[3] Above all it refers to the medical art (Greek *iatrike technē*, Latin *ars medica*) itself. Such an art is naturally "long," since considerable time is required to achieve "competence" in it. And in relation to it, life is discouragingly short. Following the Fates and Hans Blumenberg, I will call this incongruity the Hippocratic time-shear (*Zeitschere*).[4]

It would, however, be inappropriate to quote Hippocrates' first aphorism only in the abbreviated form it has developed in the tradition, generation after generation. In fact, in its full form, the text of this aphorism reads as follows:

> Life is short, art is long, opportunity fleeting, experience deceptive, judgment difficult. For (as a physician) one must not only do the right thing, but also see to it that the patient, the people around him, and the whole context collaborates with him.

In this complete version, the two clauses about the shortness of life and the length of art constitute only the prelude (though a brilliant one) to a longer series of maxims based on experience and professional advice addressed to other physicians. Only the manifest incongruity of the first two clauses has resulted in their being, in later reception, separated from the rest of the aphorism and seen as antithetical to each other, and even as opposite poles. Out of this "prelude" was extracted "the" first Hippocratic aphorism, whose asymmetry of content (life/art, long/short) is contrasted with a powerful symmetry of form and thereby made into a ringing phrase. This is even clearer in some other languages, especially in the classical languages. In an interlinear version, the Greek original goes like this:

> Ho bios brachys, hē de technē makrē.
> Life short, (whereas) art long.

In "gnomic" maxims of this kind, Greek can omit the verb when it is in the present tense. Thus here we find on each side of the antithesis only three words, whose asymmetry in content sharply contrasts, however, with their formal symmetry. Only the weakly accented particle *de* in the second half of the maxim deviates from the formal symmetry, but merely in order to further emphasize, through its adversative sense ("whereas"), the aphorism's asymmetry in content.

Regarding the precise meaning of the second half of the maxim in its Greek formulation, we should also note that the adjective *makrē* (masculine *makros*) could also be rendered as "large" (cf. *mikrokosmos/ makrokosmos*). From this it follows that the "length" of art refers to a "height." Thus we find ourselves in the vertical dimension of growth. Short life and long art differ not in gigantic but rather in human proportions, in more or less the same way that a short man (e.g., King Pepin III the Short of France) differs from a tall one, that is, one who has grown tall (we may think here of King Friedrich Wilhelm of Prussia, who required that all members of his Guard be "tall men"). Thus the art Hippocrates has in mind is indeed long, but not incalculably and certainly not "endlessly" long. So for him life is perhaps not so terribly short after all.

Already in antiquity, the Hippocratic aphorism was formulated in Latin translation as "vita brevis, ars longa." Latin, whose very structure suits it for laconic maxims, translates the Hippocratic aphorism with only four words, arranged in opposed pairs. This brevity pushes to the extreme the contrast between the asymmetry of content and the symmetry of form. In this form the maxim is also especially easy to memorize.

From English literature, I cite here only two translations that give the concept of "art" a popular and a learned form. Chaucer: "the lyf so short, the craft so long to lerne." Francis Bacon: "that Life is short, and art long."

Among German writers on medicine and philosophy the maxim is usually translated as "Kurz ist das Leben, lang (ist) die Kunst." Like English, German is not quite so economical as classical Greek and Latin, and requires seven or eight words. Yet a translation that prominently foregrounds the adjectives "kurz" and "lang" gives the maxim a stylistic profile in which the asymmetry of the two adjectives strikingly contrasts with their formally emphasized symmetry.

Among the numerous commentators on the Hippocratic aphorisms we should single out the Greek physician Galen, who practiced his art in Rome in the second century AD.[5] He greatly admired Hippocrates and helped his teaching gain wider recognition in Greco-Roman culture. Galen's own reflections confirmed the Hippocratic time-shear. He was convinced that no individual could in his short lifetime completely master a "long" art such as the art of medicine, even if the conditions in which he lived were favorable. Galen was the first to wonder why the great Hippocrates had handed down his experience in the medical art in such concise, aphoristic form, thereby creating the literary genre of the aphorism. He suggests that the reason was that because life is short, time is limited for anyone who has to master a long art. No time is left for reading lengthy books. So a wise teacher keeps the time-shear in mind and expresses himself as concisely as possible, preferably with aphoristic brevity. In this way a long art seeks to accommodate a short life. The Hippocratic time-shear is set aside here, but of course never for long enough.

The Father of Medicine may have thought one thing through less deeply than his Greco-Roman commentator could imagine more than half a millenium later. When an author seeks extreme brevity of expression, as Hippocrates did in his eighty-seven aphorisms, his less informed readers feel a greater need for the most comprehensive explanations possible, such as are found, for example, in Galen's commentaries. In this way brevity produces new lengths, and so far as art and knowledge are concerned, if we consider not only the seductively brief aphorisms but also the many thick volumes of commentaries that have been elicited by them over the centuries, this becomes, to put it in modern terms, a zero-sum game in which the fatal time-shear is just as threatening at the end as it was at the beginning.

However short the first sentence of the Hippocratic aphorism may be, hidden within it lies an unspoken problem that also explains its intensive after-life. If life is short and art is long, what does this mean for all those who want to act responsibly in the public sphere? Do they have to accept the brevity of life and the length of art as a matter of fate? Or can the asymmetrical conditions of the Hippocratic time-shear perhaps be altered by purposeful action?

We will be concerned with the ways that have been devised, in the course of history, to escape the fatality of this time-shear. There are two basic methods. Either we can attempt to lengthen all-too-short life or to shorten all-too-long art. Both methods can of course be combined, and Hippocrates himself already had this possibility in mind. As a physician and teacher, he was the first to have set for himself the task of keeping his patients healthy and in this way prolonging their lives. The ten volumes of the "Corpus Hippocraticum" (much of which was not, however, written by him) offer a clear idea of the many therapeutic procedures that were used by Hippocrates and his school in their "soft" art of medicine, many of them still sound.

■　■　■

If we now turn from the physician Hippocrates to the philosopher Aristotle (384–22 BC), we find a very different conception of time. Aristotle was born more than half a century after Hippocrates and lived on the other side of the Aegean, in Athens, where he founded his Peripatetic school, whose name (Greek *peripetos* = promenade) already suggests movement in space.

Aristotle's philosophy of time has come down to us mainly in the form of a short treatise "On Time" (*Peri chrōnou*, whose fifteen pages correspond to chapters 10–14 of part 4 of his *Physics*). This section is preceded by a somewhat longer treatise, "On Space" (*Peri topou*).[6]

The order in which the two subjects are taken up reflects the philosopher's way of thinking, since he conceives of time entirely on the basis of space. This seemed wholly plausible to Aristotelians for two millennia. Only at the beginning of the twentieth century did the

French philosopher Henri Bergson formulate the critical notion that Aristotle's spatialization of time might have led him down a mistaken path. Can the role of space as a model in philosophers' thinking about time be undone—by introducing a genuinely temporal basic concept such as "duration" (*durée*), for example? We will return to this question in the epilogue to this book.

Thus Aristotle, who judges everything temporal on the basis of the spatial, thinks of time as being fundamentally a measurable movement in space. Consequently, his thought constitutes an image-field (*Bild-feld*) that includes a considerable number of congruent metaphors—for example, change (*metabolē*), locomotion (*phoras*), path (*hodōs*), and walking (*poreia*)—and all these metaphors serve us as models. The corresponding adjectives and adverbs appear chiefly in pairs and are given in the text as short (*brachys*) and long (*makrōs*), slow (*bradys*) and rapid (*tachys*), backward (*hysteron*) and forward (*prōteron*)—and they are all organized by the schema less (*ēlatton*)/more (*plēion*).

The well-known Aristotelian definition of time also finds its place in this image field: "Time is 'number of movement in respect of the before and after'" (*Touto gar estin ho chrōnos, arithmos kinēseos kata to prōteron kai hysteron*).[7] The translation given here is problematic, because it silently interprets in temporal terms the Greek pair of opposites *prōteron/hysteron*, which clearly belongs to the spatial image field outlined above. Given the primarily spatial context, a congruent spatial translation, "in respect of an anterior position and a posterior position," would be more plausible. These were the terms chosen by Henri Carteron, a French translator of Aristotle.[8] According to Carteron, in Aristotle we have a consistent spatially conceived idea of time, a view Heidegger explicitly endorses: "[in Aristotle,] time goes with 'place' and 'movement.'"[9]

Movement in space, in relation to which Aristotle's thinking about time is oriented, proceeds in his treatise either in a linear fashion ("walking" along a "path" or in a peripatetic lobby) or in a cyclical one (the circular movement of the stars in the first sphere of the heavens). In both places time can be measured, either with a water clock (clepsydra) or with a sundial, so that more or less reliable numerical measurements are available for both short-term and long-term movements. For linear forward movement, in the case of running, there is in addition the relative comparative measure of the footrace, which was one of the ancient Greeks' favorite athletic events. No doubt philosophers were among the spectators, especially when Achilles raced against a tortoise.

The most striking difference between Hippocrates' and Aristotle's ways of thinking about time consists in their having different forms and dimensions of movement before their eyes and in their minds. When the physician from Kos opposes the shortness of life to the length of art, he is thinking in the vertical dimension where only the very slow movement of growth (trees, humans, . . .) can be observed. That is the kind of movement, as its long-term result shows, in which a given person—a small (that is, short, *brachys*) child, for instance, shoots up to become a large (that is, tall, *makrōs*) adult. In his treatise on time, Aristotle does not consider this vertical dimension at all. Neither does it find a place in his physics. It could also be said that in order to make change more conspicuous, he transferred the vertical dimension of growth to the horizontal dimension, in which goal-directed linear movement can be given an easily measurable speed. On the other hand, he bent it into the circular movement of the spheres, whose observation in the heavens, while it is supposed to be measurable with instruments, is reserved for competent astronomers and philosophers alone. In this way, time is, at least virtually, given winged racing shoes with which it can make itself manifest in the world, understood as an arena of speed.

In the following chapters of this book the Aristotelian way of conceiving time, along with every other kind of spatially oriented theory of time, will not be considered. Instead, I will attempt, in reflecting on the nature, essence, and sense of time, to make use of the stimuli of the "Hippocratic method" (Goethe), even if the latter may at first seem, in its aphoristic concision, far inferior to any theoretically formulated doctrine.[10] This shortcoming, if it is one, can already easily be countered. It is not very difficult to translate into theoretical terms the Hippocratic aphorism on which I am basing myself here. We need only define time in the Aristotelian manner as "the quantitative measure of human life with respect to the shorter (smaller) and the longer (greater)." Translated back into Aristotelian Greek, the definition might go like this: "*Touto gar estin ho chronos, arithmos tou biou kata to brachyteron kai makroteron.*" In the framework assumed by the Hippocratic contrast between life and art, this quantity (*arithmos*) of time seems to be in principle to be short. It therefore underlies the basic law of economy (*oikonomia*), which requires that humans seek a maximum of effect with a minimum of means.

. . .

Aristotle's first successor as head of the Peripatetic school of philosophy in Athens was Theophrastus (371–287 BC).[11] In the history of philosophy and literature, Theophrastus is known chiefly for a small work about thirty-five pages long, the *Characters*. This is a series of short character studies, for example of the chatterbox, the flatterer, the boor, the skinflint, the over- and underachiever, and other types. Two thousand years later, Theophrastus became almost a classical author in France, where the moralist Jean de la Bruyère (1645–98) translated his work and used it as a prelude to his own work of the same title (*Les Caractères*). To accompany his translation, La Bruyère also wrote a "Discourse on Theophrastus," in which he collected from Diogenes Laertius and Cicero all the information he could find regarding the Greek author.[12]

In this discourse, La Bruyère is mainly interested in the philosopher's memorable sayings (he calls them "maxims"). Thus even on his deathbed the aged philosopher lamented the brevity of life (Cicero: "tam exiguam vitam"): "Hardly has one begun to live, and one must already die." In another maxim Theophrastus is said to have complained that it was only as an old man that he had begun to grow wise. However, La Bruyère gives most attention to a mental image that was coined by Theophrastus and that has proven to be one of the most long-lived creations of (Western!) reflection on time: the metaphor that compares time to money, according to whose logic time should be "spent" as sparingly and carefully as money. In Diogenes Laertius's version, this report reads as follows: "He was accustomed to say that no expenditure was costlier than an expenditure of time."

We can ask why a man with such reasonable views on life and our life span lived to be "only" 85 and not 107, as Saint Jerome claimed. Once again, Diogenes Laertius knows why. In great age, Theophrastus allowed himself somewhat more peace and quiet in which to carry out his intellectual work. This caused his death. Theophrastus' biographer deemed his remarkable case worthy of a few lines of verse:

> Believe this, wisdom's bow breaks if not strung tight!
> That's the apt saying of an intelligent man.
> So long as Theophrastus labored on, full of enthusiasm,
> He was happy and healthy, but once he relaxed he died, burdened
>   with ills.

We can also see in these lines which article of athletic or military equipment inspired the metaphor of life's arc (cf. below, chap. 3, sec. 2).

Hippocrates' aphorism has left a deep mark on subsequent thought. Perhaps the most well known and influential challenge to his view in Roman times—before Galen—can be found in the treatise *On the Shortness of Life* (*De brevitate vitae*) by the philosopher Lucius Annaeus Seneca (probably 4 BC–65 AD).

The philosopher and poet Seneca—not to be confused with his father, an orator and teacher of rhetoric who bore the same name—came from Cordoba, in Spain. He was close to the Stoic school of philosophers, and already as a youth he was ready to assume the responsibilities of public office. Nonetheless, the outlook for his other plans seemed dim when, at the age of forty-five, he was exiled (why, we do not know precisely) to the island of Corsica. There he had to wait for eight years, until he was pardoned in 49 AD and immediately called, as a result of favorable or unfavorable circumstances, to the highest state offices. Here we will leave his biography for a moment, for it was in 49, at the end of his exile or shortly afterward, that Seneca composed his work on the shortness of life. It became one of the most frequently read works of Roman antiquity.[13]

In view of its subject, it is fitting that Seneca devoted a short work to the shortness of life. In print, it runs to about thirty-five pages and is thus hardly longer than Hippocrates' collection of aphorisms. Seneca also took Hippocrates, whom he considered the "greatest of physicians" (*maximus medicorum*), as the starting point for his philosophical reflections. He concedes at the outset that the Greek physician was surely correct in making the lapidary observation, in his *Aphorisms*, that life is short and art is long (*vitam brevem esse, longam artem*). But what are the consequences of this for the philosopher's doctrine of wisdom? How should a man live, if he knows that life is short?

In answering this question, Seneca himself draws on a Greek philosopher, the previously mentioned follower of Aristotle, Theophrastus. From the latter Seneca borrows the comparison between time and money, which has become famous in later thought chiefly in Seneca's version.[14] A man's life span, Seneca says, is a great good that is comparable to money and of at least equal value. However, time differs from money in that it is materially intangible, it is a *res incorporalis*, which does not strike the eye with the same force as a coin minted in a precious metal. Thus it is not surprising that people do not recognize the value of time and consider it as almost nothing (*quasi gratuito*), even though time is in reality the most precious good in the world: *res omnium pretiosissima*. Therefore it should actually be obvious to everyone that time must be handled with as much care as money.

In many other passages in Seneca's treatise, the comparison of time with money—which already anticipates Benjamin Franklin's famous maxim, "Time is money" (see below, chap. 3, sec. 3)—becomes an argument in moral philosophy, sometimes in conjunction with very specific financial metaphors, as when the author advises his readers to invest (*collocare*) their precious life-time[15] as profitably as possible, to credit (*imputare*) it with care to their time account, and to draw up a balance sheet (*ad computationem revocare*) for every expenditure of time to see if it really yields the expected return (*in reditu est*). Here we must recall that Seneca obviously knew a great deal about the financial system; at the apex of his political career he was one of the richest men in the Roman Empire.

However, as a Stoic philosopher, it was less important to him to be rich in money than rich in time. In the restless city of Rome, he could see every day how carelessly people spent their time and how they squandered this precious good (*vitam perdere*) on futile ends. Being constantly busy (*occupati*) was what made their lives slip through their fingers, so that for them, but not only for them, life was in fact short, and precisely because they themselves made it so short (*brevissimam esse occupatorum vitam*).

On the other hand, if we set aside the misconceived life of people who are always busy, in Seneca's view the first sentence of Hippocrates' aphorism is only partially valid. For all men who follow the advice of philosophers and the demands of reason, the human life span is "long enough" (*satis longa*), and for some people even "excessively long" (*longissima*). They must, however, have learned to live their lives "forward" (*protinus*), making use of every day as though it were the last.

How this ideal is to be realized in everyday life was the subject of much reflection and debate in antiquity. In this respect, the Epicurean and Stoic schools of philosophy offer different advice. The neo-Epicureans, for example the poet Horace, taught and practiced the art of enjoyment. It is true that the latter does not make life longer, but it does make it more pleasant, in accord with Horace's maxim: "Live happily, live and consider how short your life span is!" ("Vive beatus, vive memor quam sis aevi brevis").[16] In contrast, to Stoicism's adherents, for example Seneca, to have a happy life it seemed more important to practice strict virtue and especially to assume public responsibilities, although never to excess. They thought they would be making poor use of their time if the demands of their offices caused them to forget to live their lives, as had already been seen in the cases of the emperor Augustus, the politician and writer Cicero, and countless other people who were always busy. For the whole of one's life must not be given over to public service, but only part of it—even if it was a very considerable part. Everyone should reserve a certain proportion of time for private life, for his own needs and pleasures. Seneca calls this time "one's own time" (*tempus suum*).[17]

By this Seneca means leisure time (*otium*), which he is moreover convinced is best used in enjoying the fine arts (*bonae artes*) and studying philosophy (*sapientia*). However, for Seneca "quality of life" (*qualitas vitae*) includes living in a meaningful way, and also, on an equal footing, the art of dying well.

Lucius Annaeus Seneca must have needed both these arts in his own life. For it was deemed fitting, shortly after his return from his Corsican exile, for Seneca to serve as tutor to the young Nero, who proved to be, as Racine put it, a "nascent monster" (*monstre naissant*).[18] For eight years, Seneca served Nero (one wonders why) as a kind of prime minister of the Roman Empire, with only limited opportunities, to be sure, to preserve his "own time" alongside his official responsibilities. Thus the philosopher finally hoped, when he had already passed his sixtieth year, to have, at least in his old age, more leisure and time for reading and writing. But in 62 AD Nero refused his request for "early retirement." Nevertheless, without any express permission, Seneca withdrew from the imperial court, and in the course of the three subsequent years wrote a series of his best works, including his *Moral Letters to Lucilius*. In the latter Seneca explains once again, this time with the acquired authority of age and experience, the incomparable value of time, and warns his (younger) correspondent to organize his time carefully and plan it on a daily basis, so that no hour might go unused. Clearly at this time Seneca already sensed how little time he himself had left to live. Though far away, Nero had kept an eye on his former tutor and minister. When Seneca was suspected of taking part in a conspiracy against the imperial tyrant's regime, Nero forced Seneca to take his own life. Seneca died with dignity, as a Stoic philosopher.

DOMESTIC ECONOMY AND TIME MANAGEMENT
Leon Battista Alberti

The concept of economy, which originally meant "domestic economy," comes down to us from Greek antiquity. In the form *oikonomia* it is derived from *oikos* (household). Early on, the concept was borrowed by Latin in the form *oeconomia*, and for the Romans it meant "care for domestic matters" (Quintilian: *cura rerum domesticarum*). Aristotle—if he was in fact the author—devoted one of his own works to domestic economy. This work is still cited today by supporters of a paternalistic economy. It is nevertheless of no use to us in our investigation into an economy of time.[19]

However, since the most ancient times (Hermagoras, second century AD), Greek rhetoric has had another conception of economy. This conception has to do with the ordering of the arguments in a forensic oration, and it was later also transferred to the thematic structure of longer literary texts. In this area, the concept of *oikonomía/oeconomia* competes with more frequently used technical terms referring to the same subject, Greek *taxis* and Latin *dispositio*. In this special meaning the rhetorical-literary concept of economy has a temporal component. For this (second) part of rhetoric is concerned with the art of arranging themes (*topoi*)—the latter having been collected in the first part of rhetoric, invention (Greek *heuresis*, Latin *inventio*)—in a temporal sequence, which is required for the delivery of the speech or for organizing a text. This sequence can be an order corresponding to the nature of the subject matter (*ordo naturalis*) or an artificial one deviating from it (*ordo artificiosus*). The proper length of a rhetorical or literary text—not too short, not too long—is also subject to the rules of this economy.[20]

After this rather brief sketch of ancient authors' efforts to deal with the problems of a temporal economy (which in this respect are not surpassed by St. Augustine's remarkable philosophy of time), we record a long period during which the idea of economy remained latent. Finally, in the middle of the fifteenth century, in northern Italy, it re-emerged, and in its new version immediately showed that the use of mechanical clocks since about 1300 had initiated a cultural revolution of significant proportions.[21] For over two centuries, the best technologists in Italy, and later in other European countries as well, had been competing to produce steadily improved mechanical clocks, which were prominently placed on the towers of churches and city halls, and which prescribed ever more imperiously the rhythm of life, and especially of economic life. Clock-time is a fundamentally limited time, because clocks can measure only relatively short lengths of time.

These temporal relationships are illustrated in an exemplary way in the life of a man whom Jacob Burckhardt praised as the prototypical *uomo universale* of this historical period: Leon Battista Alberti (1404–72). For Burckhardt, Alberti was one of the greatest stimulators and shapers of the early Italian Renaissance. Burckhardt considers him one of the "truly all-around" people of this period.[22] As a humanist and theorist of art, Alberti's fame was based mainly on his Latin works on painting (*De pictura*) and architecture (*De re aedificatoria*), with which he gave these arts a prominent place in the humanistic cultural canon. But in his social activity this "artist-engineer" and "first urban planner of the modern age" (Friedrich Kittler) also left his beneficent mark on many places in Italy.[23]

Alberti interests us here chiefly as a humanist and the author of a dialogue *On the Family* (*Della famiglia*, 1437–41).[24] The thematic framework of this work seems to have been borrowed from Aristotle, but as the first author of the European age of clock-time—with a humanistic glance back to Seneca as well—Alberti broadened Aristotle's "economics" to make it the central point of view of the economy of time. In his work, careful money management plays for the first time an important role in the domestic economy. In people's activity in family and professional relationships, time henceforth rivals in importance the old anthropological coordinates of body (*corpo*) and spirit (*animo*). Alberti considers time almost more important for human beings than their eyes and hands, and thus he calls it, using almost exactly the same words as Seneca, a "precious thing" (*cosa preziosissima*). Time is at least as much a substantial part of human nature as are these organs and parts of the body, insofar as Alberti wants to regard the latter as only his own (*cosa propria*).

But how can that happen, if time, as is well known, slips away from us in every instant and cannot be held back with either eyes or hands? This question is asked by Giannozzo, the author's spokesman in the dialogue mentioned above, and answered in a manner that recalls Seneca: the art of correctly using time consists in never wasting it (*non perdere tempo*). But now Alberti, as an author of the early modern age, constantly has his eye on the clock, which counts the hours "one by one," to see if time has been rightly or wrongly employed. Even the leisure time still so highly prized by Seneca is now subjected to a strict time control: "This is what I do: I flee sleep and leisure, always doing something" ("Cosí adunque fo: fuggio il sonno e l'ozio, siempre faccendo qualche cosa"). The object of this chrono-economy is only the time in which one can act (*la stagione della faccenda*).

Can it happen that in the confusion of his many activities, a person loses his bearings and gives the worse precedence over the better? This dangerous mistake is in any case to be avoided, and for that reason the time-economist Giannozzo follows the following daily plan:

> When I get up in the morning, I first think about what I have to do that day. There is so much to do, so I order everything, evaluate it, and assign everything its own time, one for the morning, another for the afternoon, and still another for the evening. And in this way everything gets done in the right order, almost without any stress whatever.

> La mattina, prima, quando io mi levo, cosí fra me stessi io penso; oggi in che arò da fare? Tante cose: annòverole, pensovi, e a ciascuna assegno il tempo suo: questo stamane, quello oggi, quell'altra stasera. E a qeullo modo mi viene fatto con ordine ogni faccenda quasi con niuna fatica.

The day is thus passed purposefully and laboriously, yet without stress. Finally, in the late evening, before Giannozzo goes to bed, he once again thinks over, self-critically, everything he has done or left undone.

Thus in the middle of the fifteenth century, domestic economy is in easy relation with the rhetorical art of organizing a discourse, and from it first the Italians and soon other peoples learn "how to organize things in accord with time" (*secondo il tempo distribuire le cose*).

In concluding this chapter, let us ask once again why it happened to be precisely the spatial artist Alberti who wrote down such forward-looking thoughts regarding time management. What moved him to pay so much attention to the economy of time, not only theoretically but obviously also in the practice of everyday life? This may have to do with the ups and downs of his own life.[25] Alberti came from an old family of the Florentine nobility that had acquired considerable wealth through maritime trade while living in exile in Genoa. But he lived in this family as an illegitimate son. And so it happened that when his father died prematurely, Leon Battista, as a bastard, received no legacy. Deprived of the support that the economic power of a rich family could provide, the young man had to seek his own way in early capitalist society, more or less as a "self-made man." Thus he became, through the force of circumstances, a brilliant "artist of self-creation" (Anthony Grafton). Part of this artistic self-creation doubtless consisted in the strict control over time and the economy of time that helped Alberti derive from his brief years of study so rich a profit for his later life as a humanist in Italian Renaissance society.

TEACHING TIME MANAGEMENT IN LONDON AND PARIS
Chesterfield, Rilke

In the fifteen years between 1739 and 1754, Philip Dormer Stanhope, Earl of Chesterfield (1694–1773), wrote a large number of letters to his son Philip (aged only eight at the beginning of the correspondence), who attended various schools and later universities on the continent (*Letters to his Son*, 1774).[26] These letters tell us how a British gentleman of the mid-eighteenth century imagined educating his son to be a man of the world and of culture. An important part of this education consists in training him to make reasonable use of his life-time.

Not that Chesterfield, as a member of the British high aristocracy, wanted to make his son into a model of erudition. He is not greatly concerned with how seriously his son takes his studies in Rome or Leipzig, and in various passages in his letters we can even sense that he sees no need for his son to forego the pleasures of life—any more than he himself did when he was a boy. But time for such things must not be taken away from the education his son is to acquire.

So a time management plan is necessary, and Chesterfield takes the opportunity to demand that his son draw up a daily or even a weekly plan. "For since time is precious, but life is short, one must not squander it" (September 30, 1738). In no case should the young man give himself over to idleness and laziness. That would be unworthy of a scion of this family. And the son should certainly not spend his time on trifles, since he can lend it at much higher interest, so that it may after a suitable time represent "an immense capital" (January 1, 1748). Put concretely, this art of time management means above all that in one's youth, when the memory is still malleable, one should acquire a broad acquaintance with culture that will later be of service in every situation, and especially in conversation.

But where is one to find the time for this, if studying and the indispensable pleasures consume a huge amount of time? Chesterfield has a recipe at hand in which he puts great stock, since he has tested it throughout his own life. Its chief recommendation is this: never sleep too long (six to seven hours), rise early, be sure to make good use of the precious morning hours, but during the rest of the day as well do not neglect the short intervals that often remain free alongside one's main business. These intervals often provide enough time to read interesting passages from a book that is close at hand, or, if necessary, from an encyclopedia, and so one always has something to ponder or think about. In this way one can introduce into the daily time management plan a quarter of an hour here, a few minutes there, in which the mind can be kept in movement, just as true thriftiness begins with the careful management of small change. A more important part, perhaps even the most important part, of education thus culminates in this maxim: "Learn to recognize the true value of time!"

Did this yearlong education by correspondence yield fruit in the young Philip Stanhope? Apparently not. The young man was by nature clumsy in social situations and little given to conversation, but above all he was hopelessly shy. In such a case the splendid prose of his father, who was himself brilliant in society, could work no wonders. But since their publication in book form, grateful readers have found in these classic letters counsels that can encourage them to gain a modest intellectual profit from even the briefest reserves of time.

. . .

That, if necessary, one can educate oneself in matters of the economy of time—although with equally problematic results—we learn two centuries later from the works of a man named Nikolai Kusmitsch. This minor official from Russia, whom one can hardly imagine having read Benjamin Franklin or Max Weber, makes a brief appearance in *The Notebooks of Malte Laurids Brigge*, by Rainer Maria Rilke (1875–

1926).[27] The scene is Paris. The hero of this episode is about thirty, and one leisurely Sunday he calculates that if all goes well, he probably still has fifty years of life before him, which amounts to a fabulous time capital if it is converted into minutes and seconds and spent only as small change. Since he has always heard that time is precious, using this method he drastically reduces his expenditures of time, sleeps less, and drinks his morning tea standing up. This does not help. Just as earlier, when he had not yet reflected on the interchangeability of time and money ("as if they were inseparable!"), the "paltry seconds" run through his fingers at a breathtaking pace. He feels dizzy. If only there were a "time bank," where one could exchange the small change of "seconds" for ten-year bills! But this matter that is so painful for him cannot be resolved so easily. Another method is necessary.

How does Nikolai Kusmitsch solve his time problem? Art must come to the aid of life. So our hero artificially prolongs his life-time by reciting to himself long poems by Pushkin and Nekrassov, as slowly as possible and with equal stress on the end-rhymes, "the way children recite poems when they are asked to do so." Poetry becomes a long-term guest in the poorly soundproofed Parisian building. During his life in Paris, Malte Laurids Brigge never had a more agreeable house-mate than this Nikolai Kusmitsch.

2

The Midpoint of Life

How long does human life last? The Psalmist knows exactly—and a little inexactly: "The years of our life are threescore and ten, / Or even by reason of strength fourscore" (Psalm 90:10). From this it follows that the midpoint of life comes at thirty-five years of age, or perhaps somewhat later, up to a maximum of forty. Until the modern age many authors geared their lives in accord with this length of time and moreover used it as a literary theme.

If one follows the Psalmist in setting the normal length of human life at seventy years, then the lifetime of a man can be represented, borrowing an image from Theophrastus and in accord with the conception of many exegetes as well, as an archer's bow with a rising curve and a descending curve of thirty-five years each. The vertex of the bow thus represents the "midpoint of life." Dante represented metaphorically this rule regarding the length of life in his theoretical work the *Convivio*: "Our life follows the image of a bow. The highpoint of this bow comes at the thirty-fifth year" ("La nostra vita procede a imagine d'arco. . . . Lo punto sommo di questo arco è nel 35° anno"). This length of time also determines in an essential respect Dante's *Divina Commedia*.[1]

The *Divina Commedia*, in which Dante narrates in 14,233 verses his poetico-theological journey in the Beyond, through the three realms of Hell (*Inferno*), Purgatory (*Purgatorio*), and Paradise (*Paradiso*), begins with the verse: "Nel mezzo del cammin di nostra vita . . ." ("Midway in our life's journey"). For Dante, this famous line is saturated with theological and biographical significance.

We recall that the poet was born in Florence in 1265. Thus his thirty-fifth year of life fell in 1300. The year 1300 is an important one for Christianity, the first jubilee year in church history, declared by Pope Boniface VIII, following the Judaic-Old Testament model of the Holy Year (*annus sanctus*). Great numbers of pilgrims traveled to Rome from far and near in order to acquire there the "complete indulgence" the pope had promised those who made a pilgrimage to Rome on this occasion. The Florentine Dante Alighieri was one of these pilgrims. Christianity's holy year thus coincided with the midpoint of his own life.[2]

This symbolic temporal relationship also guided Dante in the creation of his *Divina Commedia* and allowed him to situate his journey through the Beyond, which lasts one week, during Easter time 1300, the time when he is midway in his life's journey. Over the two following decades he wrote his epic poem in such a way that all his imagined encounters in the Beyond are projected into this single week of the jubilee year.

Dante's life was long enough to allow him to complete his work. But the poet, who from 1301 on lived in exile far away from his native city, did not reach the biblical threescore years and ten. He died in Ravenna in 1321, fourteen years before "his" time, which according to the Psalmist should have come no earlier than 1335.

■ ■ ■

Unlike Dante's, the lifespan of Francesco Petrarca (Petrarch) corresponded precisely to the Psalmist's rule. He was born in 1304 and died in 1374, and thus lived exactly seventy years—long enough to allow him to leave behind him, as a humanist and poet, a considerable literary production that, in the form of "Petrarchism," put a decisive stamp on the age of the Renaissance and its heritage.[3]

At the midpoint of his life, we find Petrarch in Provence, where he is secretary to Cardinal Giovanni Colonna, who belongs to the pope's entourage in Avignon. He has lots of time to read, write, and travel, and is already known throughout Europe as a brilliant humanist. His fame as a young genius was already sufficient to have won him in 1339 the high honor of being offered the poet's laurel crown by both the Sorbonne in Paris and the Roman Senate. He accepted the Roman offer. And so on April 9, 1341 Petrarch was crowned as poet on the Capitoline hill, in a splendid ceremony sponsored by King Robert II of Anjou. He considered this Easter Monday, when Apollo's crown of laurels was laid upon his brow, as the highpoint of his life's arc. Only in old age did he write, in a letter looking back on this event, that for such a *laureatio* he was at that time really still somewhat "immature in age and spirit" (*immaturus aevo atque animo*), since he completed his most important works long after he received this honor.

But it was just these works that the Roman *laureatio* produced. It gave his literary creativity a strong impetus. At first, he pinned his highest hopes for the second half of his life on his epic *Africa*, a poem that he had begun some time earlier and that was to celebrate, in Latin hexameters, the Roman general Scipio Africanus's exploits and victory over the Carthaginians.[4] This *magnum opus* was to be dedicated to Robert of Anjou, and Petrarch tried to equate him with Scipio Africanus, with whose triumph after the victory over Carthage the epic ends. In the final lines of the epic, Petrarch makes his poetic point: at the Roman general's right hand as he makes his triumphal entry into Rome marches, also crowned with laurels, the Roman poet Ennius, with whom Petrarch identifies himself. Thus from beginning to end, the epic is related to the crowning of Petrarch as a poet, the triumphal midpoint of his life.

At that time Petrarch was already thinking about another work that was to follow the epic *Africa* and that was to have Robert of Anjou himself as hero. But the king and patron of the arts died unexpectedly in 1346. After this stroke of fate, Petrarch still completed his *Africa*—though with diminished enthusiasm, but his thoughts soon took another direction, turning from epic to lyric poetry: a momentous event for Italian literature, and indeed for Western literature as a whole.

After this "paradigm change" (Karlheinz Stierle), the literary fame that awaited the poet took new paths. For a steadily increasing readership, it was now connected almost exclusively with the poems of the *Canzoniere*, which are written in Italian and on whose composition Petrarch worked for the rest of his life—though without ever being able to imagine the literary success, indeed, the worldwide success, they were to enjoy. In the second half of his life, he carefully collected these poems—the majority are sonnets and songs, so that there are exactly 366 pieces, that is, one for every day of the year 1300,[5] but he never gave them a genuine Italian title. He put them together under the somewhat carelessly selected Latin title, *Rerum vulgarium fragmenta* ("Fragments in the vulgar tongue"). Only in the sixteenth century did posterity give them the title *Canzoniere*, under which they have subsequently been known and become famous in the literary world.[6]

The transition from epic to lyric, and from Latin to Italian poetry, was thus for Petrarch an important turning point in his poetic life. Therefore we find in Petrarch's writings in the second half of his life many statements regarding the rapid passing of time and lamenting the brevity of life. Here are only few examples, the last of which is particularly reminiscent of Hippocrates:

> life is short (*la vita è breve*)
> in this short and mortal life of mine (*in questa breve mia vita mortale*)
> so short is time, and so rapidly thoughts [pass away] (*sí breve è il tempo e 'l penser si veloce*)
> for the road is long and time is short (*perché 'l camin è lungo e 'l tempo è corto*)

As is well known, all these poems are love poems. They are addressed to a young woman named Laura, who seems to the poet as lovely (*dolce*) as she is hard (*dura*).[7] This is precisely the special mixture of feelings that is characteristic of Petrarch and all later Petrarchan lyric poetry. About the dates of Laura's life the poet tells us only that he encountered her for the first time on April 6, 1327, while attending church in the papal city of Avignon, and that she died in 1348, during the plague that swept over all Europe. Today, it is still unclear whether Laura—like Dante's Beatrice—ever really existed in flesh and blood or was, with all her attributes, including the dates in her life, imagined by the poet. As evidence for the latter view, one might point out that the name "Laura" is derived from the laurel tree (Italian *lauro*). This etymological relationship, which Petrarch develops as a motif in numerous poems in his *Canzoniere* and embellishes metaphorically, once again alludes to the Apollonian laurel branch of Petrarch's coronation as a poet in Rome and in general to the laurel as a symbol of poetic fame.

Here we will leave the question regarding Laura's historicity unanswered. It is in any case relatively unimportant for the poetic character of the *Canzoniere*. But there remains, concerning Laura's possible and Petrarch's certain lifetimes, one aspect to be considered, which Roberto Antonelli saw in his edition of the *Canzoniere* as very important: namely, the fact that according to all the authoritative manuscripts, Petrarch laid great value on the division of his collection of the *Rerum vulgarium fragmenta* into two parts. The first part contains the poems 1–263, which the author tells us were written during the lifetime of his beloved ("in vita di Madonna Laura"), whereas the second part contains poems 264–366, which he wrote after her death, in memory of her ("in morte di Madonna Laura"). In both parts the poet says that his love for Laura endured a long time, which, as a poetic proof of his unchanging reverence, can be checked against the calendar. In the first half of his life, time is still in league with love:

> Blessed be the day, and the month, and the year, and the season, and the time, and the hour, and the minute . . .

> Benedetto sia 'giorno, e 'l mese, et l'anno, et la stagione, e 'l tempo, et l'ora, e 'l punto . . .

Here Petrarch refers to the time in which, according to his vivid memory, the first meeting with the beloved took place. But soon, in other poems of the *Canzoniere*, many years have already passed since this meeting. And in the second part it is soon twenty-one years that have gone by since Laura's death, even though during this time every day has lasted "longer than a thousand years" ("ogni giorno mi par piú dí mill'anni").[8] With these short or long years the poet's time now also hastens towards impending death, and he sees his end as near: "vedendo ogni giorno il fin piú presso."[9]

Thus not only the individual poems but also the whole composition of the *Canzoniere* are related to the rising and falling arc of Francesco Petrarca's life, and this form and structure show how for this classic author life and art are significantly interconnected.

Intensive thinking about time also remains a fundamental theme in Petrarch's Latin works, which he did not forget during the second half of his life devoted to the *Canzoniere*. For example, his prose text

On the solitary life (*De vita solitaria*), on which he labored from 1346 to 1366, is largely inspired by Seneca's *De brevitate vitae* (see above, chap. 1, sect. 2) and continues its satire of the "very busy man" (*vir occupatus*). Even more sharply than Seneca, Petrarch here opposes the caricature of a city dweller rushing frantically about to the ideal image of a philosopher living in rural retirement (*vir solitarius*). This solitary man observes in peace and leisure the passing of time and lives his life without haste or rush.[10]

However, in this work that so clearly refers to Seneca, Petrarch, as a Christian, is already thinking beyond his own death, about the afterworld and eternity. At the same time, this shows that Petrarch, like his whole age, was also capable of calculation and market-economy thinking. If, according to Petrarch's deep conviction, man's life in this world is blessed with little happiness and really deserves to be called a life of misery (*miseria*), this short lifetime is always well employed, in a mercantile economic sense, if it allows men, by leading here on earth a life pleasing to God, to "negotiate" (*negotiari*) an eternal beatitude in Heaven. Thus for Petrarch in a more exact settlement with the Beyond, the happiness one may have missed in this life is not a "loss" (*iactura*) but rather a "profit" (*lucro*).[11] This is a far-reaching thought that already points ahead three centuries toward Pascal's "wager" (*pari*) (cf. below, chap. 7, sect. 2).

■ ■ ■

We have seen in Dante and Petrarch that the apex of life's arc at the same time designates the point in time at which it becomes clear how the first half of life differs qualitatively from the second. And poetry is the place that makes itself available for this reflection. In German literature, it is Friedrich Hölderlin who most succinctly conceived in poetic language the valences of this break between the two halves of life.[12] This is shown first of all by his much-admired poem, "The Midpoint of Life" ("Hälfte des Lebens"):

> With yellow pears
> And full of wild roses
> The land hangs in the sea,
> You graceful swans,

And drunk with kisses
You dip your heads
In the sacred sober water.

Alas! Where shall I find flowers
When winter comes,
And where earth's sunshine
And shadows?
The walls stand
Silent and cold, weathervanes
Clatter in the wind.

Mit gelben Birnen hänget
Und voll mit wilden Rosen
Das Land in den See,
Ihr holden Schwäne,
Und trunken von Küssen
Tunkt ihr das Haupt
Ins heilignüchterne Wasser.

Weh mir, wo nehm ich, wenn
Es Winter wird, die Blumen, und wo
Den Sonnenschein
Und Schatten der Erde?
Die Mauern stehn
Sprachlos und kalt, im Winde
Klirren die Fahnen.

The poem is short. The brevity of life is contained in its form. It consists of two stanzas of seven short lines each, unrhymed, but with a powerful rhythm. There is no express mention of the lifespan to which the title alludes. But it is metonymically represented through the two seasons, summer and winter. Spring and autumn are omitted, so that the two most prominent seasons are directly juxtaposed. The summer scene in the first stanza is vividly painted, with yellow pears, wild roses, graceful swans, and the reverently sanctified water. Only at the interface between the two stanzas does the author's speaking voice make itself heard in a lament: the season of flowers and fruit is over, and a hard winter lies before him. The time of losses is coming: the sunshine and its shadow play are already past. And then abruptly, in the middle of the stanza, winter is there. With the clatter of the icy weathervanes, the final verse also becomes winter-hard.

In conjunction with two other poems by this author, "Lebenslauf" ("The Course of Life") and "An die Parzen" ("To the Fates"), we can think of this poem as one panel of a triptych in which Hölderlin subjects his poetry to the law of life. The poem "The Course of Life" already indicates this theme in its title. Its four stanzas are expressly organized around the metaphor—inspired by Theophrastus and Seneca—of the arc of life (*unser Bogen*) that rises out of the "night" (*Nacht*) of the time before birth and at the end sinks into "Orcus" (*Orkus*). Life has led the poet "upwards or downwards" (*Aufwärts oder hinab*), but never along a level path (*ebenen Pfades*). For this, he thanks the heavenly powers:

> Man should try everything, say the heavenly powers,
>> so that, powerfully fed, he may learn to be grateful for everything
>>> And understand the freedom
>>>> To break out, to wherever he wants.

> Alles prüfe der Mensch, sagen die Himmlischen,
>> daß er, kräftig genährt, danken für Alles lern
>>> Und verstehe die Freiheit
>>>> Aufzubrechen, wohin er will.

But break out toward what? The poem "To the Fates" can be read as an answer to this question:

> Grant me just one summer, you mighty ones!
>> And one autumn to ripen my song,
>>> so that my heart, sated
>>>> with sweet playing, may more willingly die.

> The soul that in life has not received
>> its divine right has no rest, even down in Orcus.
>>> Yet if I ever achieve the holy thing
>>>> Dear to my heart, the poem,

> Then welcome, O stillness of the world of shades!
>> I shall be satisfied, even if the music of my strings
>>> Does not escort me down; once
>>>> I lived like the gods, no more is required.

Nur Einen Sommer gönnt, ihr Gewaltigen!
  Und einen Herbst zu reifem Gesange mir,
    daß williger mein Herz, vom süßen
      Spiele gesättigt, dann mir sterbe.

Die Seele, der im Leben ihr göttlich Recht
  Nicht ward, si ruht auch drunten im Orkus nicht;
    Doch ist mir einst das Heilge, das am
      Herzen mir liegt, das Gedicht, gelungen.

Wilkommen dann, o Stille der Schattenwelt!
  Zufrieden bin ich, wenn auch mein Saitenspiel
    Mich nicht hinab geleitet; Einmal
      Lebt ich, wie Götter, und mehr bedarfs nicht.

The metaphor of the arc of life is implicitly present in this poem as well. With grateful humility, the poet here begs the Fates, who control the course and duration of the arc of life, to grant him only so much— or rather, so little: only *one* summer, only *one* autumn—life-time as is necessary to reach the highpoint where he will be able to write "*the* poem." "No more is required."

REJUVENATION IN ROME—THROUGH ROME · Goethe

As a young man, Goethe was thought by everyone in Strasbourg and Wetzlar to be a genius. His early lyrics, especially the deeply felt poetry written when he was in Sesenheim, found sympathetic readers who willingly allowed themselves to be carried away by this poetic "Sturm und Drang." Goethe's *Sorrows of Young Werther* aroused emotional turmoil and poetic fever in the hearts of readers not only in Germany but also throughout Europe. And the hopes and expectations of the reading public that were unleashed by the first drafts of his *Faust*, today often called the "Urfaust," rose to extraordinary heights. The honor of being called to the princely court at Weimar meant for the young author an early coronation as a poet—but in Germany he had to forego the outward sign of the laurel wreath.

Had Goethe died at that point (for instance—like Werther—by his own hand, an idea that sometimes passed through his mind), posterity would have considered him a genius who died an untimely death. However, in Weimar Goethe began a new phase in his life that did not amount merely to a sinecure but rather increasingly involved political and administrative duties. The German reading public was obliged, with some difficulty, to get used to recognizing the admired poet of Strasbourg and Wetzlar in the Privy Councilor and later Minister of the duchy of Sachsen-Weimar-Eisenach. This and other tensions in Goethe's life at Weimar did not leave him unmarked, and he finally found himself forced to decide which direction he should give his life.

Near the midpoint of his life, that is, at the age of thirty-five according to the Psalmist, he began thinking more and more seriously about breaking out of his golden cage at Weimar and escaping to Rome. He may also have been driven to act on this plan, which he had at first kept to himself, by the memory of Seneca's reflections on the brevity of life (see above, chap. 1, sect. 2). In Goethe's private notes we find a maxim drawn from Seneca's work *De brevitate vitae*: "Life, if you know how to use it, is long" (*Vita, si uti scias, longa est*).[13] We recall that in this work Seneca, the Stoic philosopher and dutiful servant of the state, claimed for himself as well the right to have a certain amount of "leisure" (*tempus suum*). And in his mid-thirties Goethe took, with Duke Karl August's generous permission (a permission Nero denied his minister Seneca!), the leave he had been granted and traveled to Rome.[14]

Goethe carried out his plan in the autumn of 1786. Without telling his immediate entourage (Frau von Stein!), he left Karlsbad at 3 a.m. on September 3 and headed south. Traveling by mail-coach, he required several weeks to reach his destination. He crossed the Italian linguistic border at Rovereto. That was a day of joy for Goethe: "How happy I am, that from now on the beloved (*scil.* Italian) language will be truly the language of use!" A few days later, in Verona, he took off his German boots and henceforth wore light Italian shoes.[15]

Goethe continued his journey with a lighter step. He had planned the overall trip so that he would arrive in Rome on time for All Saints' Day. As a Protestant, at the outset of his stay in Rome he wanted to experience this eminently Catholic ceremony. But at the altar was an old, infirm pope, whose unintelligible mumbling of the Mass disappointed him.[16]

This remained, however, Goethe's only disappointment during his travels in Italy, which went on for a year and a half, until spring 1788. He was happy, his highest expectations were daily fulfilled, and becoming accustomed to life under the sunny Italian skies never diminished his happiness. His letters therefore always have the same tone: "I am very happy here." Or: "Share my joy that I am happy." Or again, right at the end of his stay: "I can say this much, that in Rome I have become more and more happy." Goethe liked to write, but the testimony of Roman works of art and also the Neapolitan "school of easy, fun-loving life" inspired him more to draw and to paint. Out of all these stimuli and exciting new experiences he derived a "constant pleasure and enduring profit."[17]

Thus a "youthful dream" of Goethe's was fulfilled, and in his letters and later in his *Italian Journey* (*Italienische Reise*) this happiness was often described using expressions that designate this time as a "second birthday, a genuine rebirth." This is to be understood this way: "In Rome, I first found myself, first became one with myself, happy and reasonable." Further, in another letter we read: "I have truly been born again and renewed and fulfilled." And in the following statement, also in a letter, we even find an almost verbatim echo of Seneca's idea of the "time for oneself" that should be demanded: "I am very well, I am increasingly finding the way back to myself, and I am learning to distinguish between what is proper to me and what is alien. I am working hard and taking things in from all sides and growing from the inside out."[18]

These happy reports from Rome were not always received with unmixed pleasure by Goethe's friends in Weimar. A little envy was sometimes combined with their joy for him, even in Schiller, who once calculated how long a Weimar day-laborer would have to work in order to earn enough to spend as much of his duke's money in Rome as the privileged privy councilor did. For that reason Goethe occasionally had to mention that his *Wilhelm Meister* was "really growing" in Rome, so that he could expect patience from his friends in Weimar: "Grant me my time, which I am spending here so wonderfully and strangely, grant me this with the approval of your love."[19]

Now let us examine still more closely how this journey to Italy is related to the economy of Goethe's life-time. According to the *Italian Journey*, on his very first day in Rome, All Saints' Day, Goethe wrote in his diary:

> So I have finally arrived in the capital of the world! Had I seen it fifteen years ago in good company and guided by some well-informed

person, I would consider myself lucky. But I have to see and visit it alone, with my own eyes; so it is good that this joy was granted me so late. . . . Now I am here, at peace and, it seems, at peace with my whole life. For it can truly be said that a new life is beginning.

In this passage Goethe has in view another model of life-time that contrasts with the course of his own life: the educational journey of the young nobleman or scion of the upper middle class who, accompanied and guided by a tutor, performs the pleasant task of making his "grand tour," just as in his youth Goethe's own father also traveled to Italy to consolidate his classical education. However, Goethe himself had missed this time of the youthful educational tour, since as a young man in his twenties he was studying and writing his brilliant early works, and began his court life at Weimar immediately afterward. So now he needs to make up, fifteen years later ("so late"), for this journey he missed taking in his youth. For this purpose, the midpoint in life is precisely the right and perhaps even the best time, because it has its own measure, so that Goethe can of his own accord "start to change his mind and begin over again from the beginning." In another passage in his notes, just ten days after his arrival in Rome, he puts the same point this way: "I am not here to enjoy myself in my fashion, I want to work hard on the great subjects, learn and educate myself, before I turn forty." Here, the reference to his age makes it clear that for Goethe his travels in Italy, even if they come a little late, fall precisely at the midpoint of his life, which for him is the phase between his thirty-fifth and fortieth years.[20]

Among the literary works on which Goethe labored intensively in Rome, I mention here only Wilhelm Meister's "Indenture" (*Lehrbrief*), in which Hippocrates' first aphorism is cited prominently. The text begins like this:

Art is long, life short, judgment difficult, opportunity fleeting. Action is easy, thinking difficult; acting in accord with thought awkward. Every beginning is serene, the threshold is a place of expectation.

The "Apprenticeship Indenture" continues in this vein a few sentences further, wholly in the Hippocratic aphoristic style of the "Tower Society," but is itself presented only in fragments.[21] In the Bildungsroman *Wilhelm Meisters Wanderjahre*, which appeared decades later, the temporal motif is continued in a modified form, and Odoard formulates a few of his society's maxims as follows:

> The greatest respect for time will be impressed upon everyone, as the loftiest gift of God and Nature and the most remarkable companion of our existence. . . . Our ethics, which is therefore entirely practical, insists chiefly on prudence, and this will be strongly fostered by planning time and paying attention to every hour. Something must be done in every moment, and how can that be achieved if work is not respected as is the hour?[22]

Seneca and Alberti would probably have endorsed this practical doctrine of time and ethics. In Weimar, where Goethe had somehow to throw himself back into the business of his government office without putting his literary and artistic existence into question, he was able to make good use of this doctrine.

THE PHYSICIAN'S ART OF PROLONGING LIFE · Hufeland

We have now returned with Goethe from Rome to Weimar. Before we follow his life path further, we meet in Goethe's immediate environment a man who made a lasting contribution to the incorporation of Hippocratic wisdom about life into German culture. This man is the important physician Christoph Wilhelm Hufeland (1762–1836), who by his attitude fits very well into Weimar classicism.

Hufeland had already spent his youth in the court-city of Weimar. He studied medicine and the natural sciences in Jena and Göttingen. His doctoral supervisor was no less a figure than the physicist and aphorist Georg Christoph Lichtenberg. At first, Hufeland practiced medicine in Weimar, where Goethe, Herder, and Schiller were his patients. Duke Karl August also soon took notice of Hufeland's medical skill and made him, while still young, his court physician and a professor in Jena. Hufeland's later career took him to Berlin, where he served as personal physician to the Prussian king and head physician at Berlin's Charité hospital. He also became the first dean of the faculty of medicine at the newly founded University of Berlin. During his whole career as "personal physician and educator of the people" (the title of his autobiography) he considered Hippocrates his "ancestor." With the latter's teaching in mind, he became one of the founders of gerontology and geriatrics. He himself lived to be seventy-four years old.

Hufeland's major work, which he published in 1797 and which immediately made him known to a broad readership, was also inspired by Hippocrates. The book is entitled *Macrobiotics, or the Art of Prolonging Human Life* (*Makrobiotik oder Die Kunst, das menschliche Leben zu verlängern*).[23] This title clearly alludes to Hippocrates' first aphorism, which had by then become a familiar saying in Germany. We recall that in the Greek, this aphorism reads "*Ho bios brachys, he de technē makrē.*" Hufeland took the word "life" (*bios*) from the first half of the saying and the word "long" (*makros*) from the second half, and harmoniously combined these two words, which are still in conflict in Hippocrates, into a concept. I refer to long-livedness (*Langlebigkeit*), which in another passage Hufeland also calls "longevity" (*Longävität*). And so the subtitle is expressly related to the Hippocratic "art" (*technē*) of prolonging human life. In Goethe's house in Weimar Hufeland's book was read with interest, not only by Goethe himself but also by his wife Christiane, who sent it on to Goethe's mother in Frankfurt.

Hufeland's book, which modern German physicians unfortunately neglect, can still be recommended to readers who want to attain longevity. It is written in a clear style that is accessible even to laymen and shows genuine literary talent. True, much of what one finds in the book is out of step with more recent medical knowledge. But many of the author's reflections and not a few of his practical suggestions regarding the medical art of prolonging life are still worth heeding. Anyone who follows his advice in everyday life will certainly thereby prolong his life. This favorable prognosis can be justified by the fact that among Hufeland's recommendations for attaining longevity are a moderate and preferably vegetarian diet, regularly "rinsing" one's teeth after eating, avoiding overworking (this is Seneca's oft-lamented *occupatio*) in one's profession, and above all giving up smoking ("one of the most incomprehensible indulgences"). On the other hand, he advises the obedient reader not to entirely give up wine, though "the best beverage is water." Here we will not give further details from the "practical part," but we must not omit the sentence in which he sums up his congenial dietetics: "The more a person remains true to nature and its laws, the longer he lives, the more he deviates from them, the shorter his life."

It would nonetheless be an error to consign without further ado Hufeland's book to the literature of medical advice. Hufeland also has a theory to offer in support of his macrobiotics, for which he draws mainly, not only on Hippocrates, but also on a book written by the English philosopher and essayist Francis Bacon, *Historia vitae et mortis* ("History of Life and Death," 1637). From Bacon he takes in particular the concept of "life force," which Hufeland describes as follows: "It fills, it moves everything, it is very probably the basic source from which all the other forces of the physical, mainly organic, world flow." However, as Hufeland says in another passage, in the course of life the flame of this "energy" is used up, through a natural process of "consumption," to which must be opposed an equally natural process of "regeneration" if the person concerned does not want carelessly to shorten his life. A certain "retardation" of the process of living, with the least possible indulgence in excesses and adequate sleep, is in any case beneficial for human longevity (and perhaps also for simplicity?).

Here we hardly need to explain in detail why Hufeland's theory of the life force did not itself become a long-lived theory. Modern medicine gets along very well without the assumption of such a mysterious force. However, Hufeland's attempt to gain a synoptic view of many individual aspects of health, even more than of illness, and to bring them under a comprehensive principle was accompanied by an effort to seek out the "means of prolonging life" not only in man's physical nature but also in the conditions of his mental life. Thus this "classical" physician does not doubt that nature and culture must work together to attain the goal of longevity, since "a certain degree of culture is also necessary for human beings and promotes a long life." As an educator, Hufeland also urged the establishment, on medical grounds, of many good schools, in which children were not, however, to be driven to learn too early.

When all these material and intellectual conditions have been met, then the most important aid for achieving longevity can finally come into play: a serene nature. In Hufeland's work serenity is invoked and praised as "the finest state of mind for longevity." Let us also note that according to Hufeland "a day in the country, in fine weather (*in heiterer Luft*, lit. "in serene air"), spent in the company of serene friends, is a more reliable positive means of prolonging life than all the elixirs in the world." Goethe, in whose vocabulary "serene" (*heiter*) is a favorite word, indeed even a key word for his whole literary activity, would have endorsed this medical advice, and in fact Hufeland was able to use a quotation from Goethe as a motto for his "macrobiotics": "Sweet life! Fair, friendly habit of existing and working!—how can I part from you?" ("Süßes Leben! Schöne freundliche Gewohnheit des Daseins and Wirkens!—von dir soll ich scheiden?")

A LONG LIFE WITH FAUST · Goethe

We now go back, for the sake of Faust, to Goethe, and turn first to his early years. In his long life—he lived to be eighty-two—the first phase of his life and work is clearly marked off, from the beginning through his initial legal studies in Leipzig (1765) and ending with his move to Weimar (1775). In this decade he found particularly stimulating the time he spent studying in Strasbourg (1770–71), where he met Herder, read Shakespeare, and wrote his Sesenheim poems. Regarding his legal studies at the University of Strasbourg there is little to be said, but he developed an interest in medicine, which can probably be explained by his having barely survived a life-threatening illness while in Leipzig. So in Strasbourg Goethe not only attended lectures on medicine but also took part—we have to imagine, dressed in a white gown—in the very respected Professor Ehrmann's clinical visits. In his autobiography, *Poetry and Truth* (*Dichtung und Wahrheit*), Goethe later recalls with pleasure these interdisciplinary (as we now say) studies and explains his inclinations at the time thusly: "Medicine attracted me because it showed me nature from every side, and allowed me to glimpse even what remained obscure." In this context he also mentions with respect "the fine Hippocratic method" which apparently underlay the Strasbourg curriculum. In still another passage in his autobiography he refers to Hippocrates, and calls him reverently "a star . . . that could serve as an example of everything desirable."[24]

Not long after the previously mentioned initiation into the mysteries of medicine in Strasbourg, Goethe first began thinking about a poem on Faust, and it is no surprise that, as we learn from his opening monologue, in addition to philosophy, law, and theology the hero of this drama has also studied medicine (in this case, he does not say, "unfortunately")—and in fact "all the way," that is, as far as the examination. Since the later Master and Doctor Faust employs an assistant who is well informed about medical matters, we can conclude that Faust is active chiefly as a physician, in the office inherited from his father—and this is explicitly confirmed in the later versions of the drama. Moreover, there is considerable evidence that in Faust's practice, just as in the clinic at the University of Strasbourg, the Hippocratic method is the assumed basis of the healing arts. This is also confirmed by Faust's assistant, Wagner: during his first conversation with Faust, who erupts in complaints about the limits of his knowledge and the weaknesses of his cognitive faculties, Wagner, full of sympathy, adopts his tone and echoes him, citing Hippocrates' first aphorism:

> Dear me! how long is art!
> And short is our life!

> Ach Gott die Kunst ist lang
> Und kurz ist unser Leben!

The sigh that accompanies Wagner's quotation of Hippocrates is an empathetic reflex to Faust's melancholy assessment, whose justice Wagner immediately relates to the Hippocratic problem, as he continues:

> And long before the halfway point is reached
> They bury a poor devil in the ground.

> Und eh man nur den halben Weg erreicht,
> Muß wohl ein armer Teufel sterben.[25]

These verses, with their reference to the "halfway point" (*halben Weg*), read like an intertextual allusion to the famous opening line of Dante's *Divine Comedy*, already cited above ("Nel mezzo del camin di nostra vita"), and they clearly refer to the Psalmist's limit of thirty-five years as "half of life" (see above, chap. 2, sect. 1). Dr. Faust is given about that age in Goethe's early drafts of *Faust*, which today we call the "Urfaust." In the concise sense of time, Wagner's quotation of Hippocrates to Faust is related to his reference to the precarious time-limit of the "halfway point" as a rather indiscreet warning to this "dry pedant" (*trockenen Schwärmer*) to see that he must now finally make full use of the remaining time span of the second half of his life, in order in any case to realize the goal of art. Wagner's warning can thus be understood as a small treatise *De brevitate vitae*. Faust's assistant is such an indispensable companion for him precisely because he confirms, by appealing to Hippocrates' authority, just how much Faust's self-doubts in the introductory monologue were justified.

In contrast to Faust, Wagner is not inclined to be put off by the Hippocratic warning. As a scholar, he will follow steadily and sedulously the path of long art and knowledge, and let nothing stop him from "conscientiously and punctually practicing / the art that has been taught him," remaining always true to his maxim: "It's true that I know a great deal / Yet I'd like to know everything." But even this industrious scholar cannot pack all the available wisdom into his head, though he can be and remain a useful person who knows many things. In this way he will earn his doctoral degree, gain the respect of other scholars, and ultimately be, or seem to be, "the most learned man in the world."[26]

Faust is entirely different. Having arrived at the critical turning point in his life, he draws up a balance sheet of his previous activities and—unlike his self-satisfied assistant Wagner—comes to the depressing realization how *little* he has accomplished during his scholarly existence. Thus immediately after his introductory complaint about the hopeless unattainability of the goal of his striving for knowledge, he bitterly discards his whole scholarly baggage, in order "go native" and gain a different kind of experience. So far as his later life is concerned, he declares himself "cured of the thirst for knowledge."[27]

We see that when he was in his twenties and a rising star of German literature at the Weimar ducal court, Goethe had already made, in a succinct way, a place for the Hippocratic problem in his "Urfaust." However—and this is constitutive for the whole Faust drama—at the midpoint in his life, the professor breaks out of this threateningly asymmetrical time-shear and abandons the hopeless race between life and art or science. With Mephistopheles' help he tries the alternative path of a short-circuited art of living in which Hippocrates' "long" art disappears far beyond the temporal horizon.[28]

Part of Faust's new life without Hippocrates' art, but with the Devil's ruses, is his stormy love for Gretchen, who is only fourteen and thus just barely an adult, according to contemporary law. The story ends in tragedy for the young woman. For Faust, in contrast, it remains only a "short" episode that requires continuation in other registers. None of this, however, is in the fragment that Goethe took with him to Weimar and read before a fascinated audience at the ducal court.

. . .

However, when a decade later Goethe broke away to travel or "escape" to Italy, he took this "Urfaust"—still in the form of a fragment—with him in his luggage. The drama was supposed to be completed in Rome. Nothing came of this intention. In Rome, only one scene was added to the manuscript—the scene in the "Witches' Kitchen." Why did Goethe write, under sunny Italian skies, this very Teutonic witches' scene? The answer is obvious if we recall that Goethe saw his time in Italy as a great rejuvenation cure, as a genuine fountain of youth. The Goethe who returned from Italy to Weimar was, as if by magic, a young man again, and in accord with his subjective sense of youthfulness, he soon entered into a relationship with the very young Christiane.[29]

This was precisely what he had intended in Italy for the hero of his drama, Doctor Faust, who had to wait so long for his story to continue and thus grew older at about the same rate as did his author. In Goethe's later work on *Faust*, and especially in the edition of the first part of *Faust* (*Faust: Der Tragödie erster Teil*) published in 1808, we must assume that Doctor Faust is, as Thomas Mann wrote, "about sixty" years old.[30] This reference to Faust's age significantly accentuates, of course, the personal and professional crisis and doubts expressed in his introductory monologue. In view of the evident shortness of his remaining life, he can expect far less than he could when he was in his mid-thirties to still achieve the art and knowledge that now seem longer than ever.

This hopelessness surfaces with particular starkness in the scene in which Mephistopheles proposes his own magical and now clearly no longer Hippocratic "arts" (*Künste*) as an alternative to "art" (*Kunst*), and, explicitly, to Faust's own pastime. Regarding this dealing in lifetime values, it is also remarkable that being a devil, Mephistopheles is already "several thousand years old." However, he appears to Faust in the guise of an "itinerant scholar" or "freshman," so that he must be imagined as a very young student no older than twenty. In his later appearance as a "young nobleman" (*Junker*), he is not much older and clearly belongs to the *jeunesse dorée*. And even in the garden scene with Frau Marthe, who presses him to marry, Mephistopheles wants to view his years as a bachelor only "from afar." This provocative young devil cites our Hippocratic aphorism a second time in a conversation with Faust:

I fear just one thing, for my part:
Short is time, and long is art.
In this, I trust, you will be guided.

Doch nur vor Einem is mir bang':
Die Zeit ist kurz, die Kunst ist lang.
Ich dächt', ihr ließet euch belehren.[31]

Faust allows himself to be guided. For scarcely has he accepted Mephistopheles' wager before he is confronted by the witches' kitchen, which offers the aging professor a drastic kind of rejuvenation. Our reflections are confirmed by the fact that in the scene in the witches' kitchen Goethe calculates the rejuvenation effect at precisely thirty years:

Will this absurd swill-cookery
Charm thirty winters off my back?

Und schafft die Sudelköcherei
Wohl dreißig Jahre mir vom Leibe?

That's easy for the witches. At first, however, Faust shows little interest in the rejuvenation drug prepared by the witch, and asks Mephistopheles whether some other "balm" might not also be helpful. Yes, there is an alternative cure for age. Mephistopheles replies:

The know-it-all, as always! Look—
True, nature's way to youth is apter.

Mein Freund, nun sprichst du wieder klug!
Dich zu verjüngen gibt's auch ein natürlich Mittel.

Mephistopheles goes on to refer ironically to the "curious chapter" in another book, in which the following method of rejuvenation is recommended:

Go out into the fields, today,
Fall to a-hoeing, digging,
Contain yourself, your mind and mood,

> Within the narrowest of spheres,
> Subsist on uncommingled food . . .

> Begib dich gleich hinaus auf's Feld,
> Fang' an zu hacken und zu graben,
> Erhalte dich und deinen Sinn
> In einem ganz beschränkten Kreise,
> Ernähre dich mit ungemischter Speise . . .

Astonishing: these verses offer right in the middle of the Faust drama a regular advertisement (more precisely, an anticipatory advertisement) for Hufeland's "macrobiotics" of rejuvenation and life-prolongation. Yet Faust cannot achieve this healthful way of life, and so he must "go back to witching after all." By means of magical fluids from the witches' kitchen, which following the text we must imagine as time cooked down and condensed through a long process, the aging scholar becomes precisely thirty years old again, that is, younger by a generation. And he immediately feels the bodily stirrings of a young rake, so that no difference in age now inhibits his pursuit of the fourteen-year old Gretchen.[32]

· · ·

From now on Mephistopheles sets a tempo that is entirely determined by speed ("the rush of time") and novelty ("only new things draw us on"). In his wager with the Devil Faust assumes these conditions in the bold hope of being able, with Mephistopheles' help, of someday catching that unheard-of moment that makes up for all the other times in a man's life:

> And beat for beat!
> If the swift moment I entreat:
> Tarry a while! you are so fair!
> Then forge the shackles to my feet,
> Then I will gladly perish there!
> Then let them toll the passing-bell,
> Then of your servitude be free,
> The clock may stop, its hands fall still,
> And time be over then for me!

Und Schlag auf Schlag!
Werd' ich zum Augenblick sagen:
Verweile doch! du bist so schön!
Dann magst du mich in Fesseln schlagen,
Dann will ich gern zu Grunde gehen!
Dann mag die Totenglocken schallen,
Dann bist du deines Dienstes frei,
Die Uhr mag stehn, der Zeiger fallen,
Es sei die Zeit für mich vorbei![33]

The shortness or length of time according to the Hippocratic calculation no longer counts for Faust. The moment, which is what is at stake
in the wager with the Devil, is time of a quite different kind, a qualitative time (Greek *kairos*) that is not to be measured by its duration, and
is a paradoxical time-span of the most extreme brevity, into which an
extremely long and full experience of life and the world is compressed;
at the limit, eternity in a fleeting second. Is it even humanly possible to
hold on to this unique moment, as the wager with the Devil prescribes?
And if it isn't, has then Faust perhaps lost the wager but nonetheless
experienced the fulfilled moment for the non-duration of an instant?
That is a question that Goethe does not answer with a clear yes or no.
But in the drama's final verses it is at least implied that for Faust, at the
end of his life when the rejuvenation-bonus provided by the witches'
kitchen has been used up, this "greatest age" of precisely one hundred
years has not been too limited a time for him to experience the striven-
for "highest moment," whether on earth or in that realm toward which
the angels bear his soul.[34]

NEW ART AND ANOTHER LIFE · Vittorio Alfieri, Schiller

At the beginning of 1789, the Piedmontese author Vittorio Alfieri
(1749–1803) traveled to Paris. In his baggage he carried the tragedies
he had thus far written, in order to publish them in French translation
in six volumes. Among them were also his two dramas about Brutus
(*Bruto primo, Bruto secondo*), whose titles already show that they are
about freedom and, like many of this author's other plays, were written
"*in tyrannos.*" That is also the political impulse behind his prose work
On Tyranny (*Della tirannide,* 1777–89). Thus in both his preference for

tragedy and his bourgeois hatred of tyrants, Alfieri is close to the German poet and dramatist Friedrich Schiller.[35]

Soon after he arrived in Paris in February 1789—that is, at a time at which perceptive contemporaries were already able to sense that some great upheaval was at hand—Alfieri wrote, as an *écrivain engagé avant la lettre*, the following sonnet:

> Sublime art is long, short is life,
> Venture difficult; and high art
> Always meets with obstacles to its daring:
> That is why a distinguished style is lacking.
> And the more he drinks from the Hippocrene spring,
> The more he is able to provide himself with wings,
> The less will such a man be able
> To write strongly, truly, and frankly.
> Ah, tyranny, how you sadden the world!
> How you spoil, denature, and kill everything;
> The darker it grows, the more radiant you become;
> You laugh at suffocated, lofty spirits;
> But the day is coming when your tears will mix
> With the triumph in which you foolishly trust.

> Lunga è arte sublime, il viver breve,
> Ardua l'impresa; e l'alto artefice anco
> Ostacol sempre al bello ardir riceve:
> Ecco perché lo egregio stil vien manco.
> E qual più in copia ad Ippocrene beve
> Quanto ei potria dell'ali armar più il fianco
> Tanto vie meno ad un tal uom fia lieve
> Lo scriver forte, veritiero, e franco.
> Ahi tirannia, che il mondo empia contristi!
> Che tutto guasti, e disnaturi, e uccidi;
> E più si abbuja, maggior luce acquisti;
> De' soffocati ingegni altera ridi;
> Ma, verrà il dí, che i pianti pur fien misti
> A' rei trionfi in cui stolta ti affidi.

The sonnet begins in the Hippocratic tone but nonetheless deviates in a crucial aspect from the wording and meaning of the first Hippocratic aphorism. The art here called long is not a *techné* or *ars* to be learned through protracted effort. In Alfieri, it is the "sublime" art that the (Romantic) poet receives from higher powers in the form of inspiration and enthusiasm. But what good is all that, if the poet is otherwise prevented from developing a high style? In any case, it is no longer the brevity of life that stands in the way of poetry, but rather—as the two tercets make clear—a dark political power that prevents the poet from being able to write his verse openly and frankly: tyranny, which suffocates everything good in men. Will the tyrannical power of kings continue to torment the people? That is not Alfieri's political belief. He is convinced that the day of freedom will come. That this day was to come so soon, scarcely five months later, he probably had no inkling when he was writing this sonnet.

■ ■ ■

From Paris we now return to Weimar and Jena. The time is only a decade later. The French Revolution has taken place, and Napoleon Bonaparte is already preparing to complete it in an imperial mode. Neither Vittorio Alfieri nor Friedrich Schiller had imagined the new freedom in this way. They are similarly disappointed by the tragedy staged by history. But they are not disappointed by the new art, which demands the temperament of a genius.

This new poetic art is the main subject of the great essays on aesthetics that Schiller wrote in the 1790s.[36] In his view, the art produced by geniuses in the new age is infinitely distant from the teachable and learnable art of the ancients (technē, ars), since in the former, as he writes in one of his essays, "everything mortal is redeemed." For Schiller, the new art is therefore outside any calculation of life-time. While it is true that in choosing his subject matter the poet remains, as Schiller also says, "a son of his time," he selects the form—the only decisive form in the artistic sense—"of a time that is nobler, indeed outside of all time, of the absolute immutable unity of his essence." From all this it follows that for a conception of art constructed in this way the "length" of art can no longer represent a meaningful criterion. This temporally defined conception of art is replaced by an idealist, atemporal idea of art.

Schiller's idealist aesthetics was revealed to the public on the evening of October 12, 1798 in the Weimar theater, whose director was Goethe. Schiller's tragedy *Wallenstein* received its first performance as part of the festive dedication of the new theater building. On this occasion, however, only the first part of the trilogy was performed: *Wallenstein's Camp* (*Wallensteins Lager*), provided for this celebration with a prologue specially written by the author. In this prologue, Schiller explains why, as a poet and historian, he chose to write this historical drama about the terrible period of the Thirty Years' War. With this play, which he elsewhere calls a "beautiful tragedy," he seeks to show on the Weimar stage how a dramatist, in this case himself, "transfers the gloomy image of truth into the serene realm of art." Schiller's prologue ends with a verse that almost immediately became a standard quotation: "Life is serious, art is serene."[37]

Regarding form, we should not overlook the fact that here the first sentence of the first Hippocratic aphorism has been transformed into Schillerian blank verse. The physician Schiller is correcting his ancestor Hippocrates. But in this new form as well, the aphorism, like its "intertextual" predecessor, is sharply pointed and consists of two hemistiches whose strict formal symmetry express an asymmetry of content between life and art. But Schiller is now referring to an entirely different art than the one Hippocrates and his followers had in mind. To call an idea "long" is meaningless, and thus on grounds of the formal symmetry it is also meaningless to go on calling life "short." For this reason, in his aphorism Schiller replaces the temporal-quantitative predicates "short" and "long" with the modal-qualitative predicates "serious" and "serene."

In the context of Schillerian aesthetics that is a natural choice of words. So far as the first hemistich is concerned, Schiller basically limits himself to interpreting Hippocrates anthropologically, since if life is incurably short, then humans must inevitably take it seriously. Schiller's intervention is more radical in the second hemistich of the Hippocratic aphorism, for in Hippocrates there was no mention of serenity. But by nature serenity is quite well suited to the "length" of art. In contrast to the strenuous seriousness of life, serenity can take its time. Just a year before the event at the Weimar theater, this was also confirmed by Hufeland's "macrobiotics," which appeared in 1797, and in which serenity is repeatedly praised as the royal road to longevity (see above, chap. 2. sect. 3).

For Schiller himself, however, the Weimar theater event on October 12, 1798 turned out to be an irritating and certainly not serene evening, because Goethe, as director of the theater, had on his own authority altered several passages in the text of the prologue. The most important change concerned the final verse, where in the second hemistich Goethe, without asking Schiller's permission, substituted for the indicative "ist" the subjunctive (or more precisely, optative) "sei." Thus the actor Heinrich Vohs recited on the Weimar stage the line "Life is serious, let art be serene" ("Ernst ist das Leben, heiter sei die Kunst"). Behind this change (which Schiller naturally reversed before the play was published) stands a deep difference between Schiller's and Goethe's conceptions of art, which leads to the question whether in art serenity represents an ideal quality or a real one. Which of the two princely Weimar poets has the right answer to this question is not for the present writer to judge. Ultimately, it may be that so far as the serenity of art is concerned, if one only strongly enough *wishes it to be* an elixir of longevity, it soon really *will be* such an elixir.

MAGIC AND STYLE IN LIFE-TIME · Balzac

In 1831, the same year that Goethe completed in Weimar the second part of his *Faust* and put his seal on the manuscript, there appeared in France the novel *The Wild Ass's Skin* (*La peau de chagrin*), with which Honoré de Balzac (1799–1850) established his reputation as an author.[38] Goethe read this "philosophical novel"—as Balzac called it in his subtitle—shortly before his death and greatly admired it.[39] He was so interested in it chiefly because in this work Balzac had written a sort of Faust novel with an explicit relationship to Goethe. Of course, at that time Balzac knew the text only in Gérard de Nerval's translation of the first part of *Faust* (1827). In addition, he was able to draw on Germaine de Staël's detailed discussion of the drama in her book *De l'Allemagne* (1813). But it is not only Balzac, the novel's author, who has read *Faust*; according to the text, Raphaël de Valentin, the novel's hero, has also read it, and since then his greatest fear has been that he might encounter a fate similar to that of Doctor Faust in Goethe's drama.

In Balzac's novel, Raphaël de Valentin is a young man of twenty-five who has, despite his aristocratic status (he is a marquis), pursued advanced studies, and more specifically oriental studies. He is a writer and a journalist by trade. Alongside all these activities he retains ample time for love and gambling, with fatal results in both domains. Betrayed by a heartless beloved and ruined at the gaming table, Raphaël decides to put an end to his young life. He allows himself only a few more hours of life-time so that he can throw himself into the Seine under cover of darkness.

During this short span of time he wanders by chance into the jumbled shop of an old antique dealer. Stumbling around in the dimly lit shop, his eye falls on a piece of leather. The dealer, a wizened old man a hundred and two years old, tells him that it is a shagreen (*peau de chagrin*) made from the hide of a wild ass (*onager*).[40] But out of all this Raphaël, in his world-weariness, hears only the word *chagrin* (grief), which exactly corresponds to his state. Nonetheless, as an orientalist, he notices an explanatory note that is written on the hide in Arabic and indicates that this piece of wild ass's skin—here we are smack in the middle of Romanticism—possesses the magical power to fulfill every wish its owner may express, but with the unpleasant side-effect that every time it fulfills a wish, the shagreen shrinks, and at the same time the owner's remaining life-time is reduced by a corresponding amount.

Raphaël de Valentin, who in his world-weary state has nothing to lose, takes the shagreen and thereby enters into a "pact" (*pacte*) with a mysterious power whose Mephistophelean nature is not unfamiliar to him, since he has read *Faust*.[41] Because he now possesses this piece of junk, his planned suicide can be postponed (*retardé*) for a time. But not only that: at the same time, the mysterious wild ass's skin is, as the antique dealer put it, a "talisman" that brings good fortune. With its help the novel's hero can henceforth enjoy life to the full in accord with his boldest wishes and "live excessively" (*vivre avec excès*).[42]

And so it happens. A carefree life begins in which no wish remains unfulfilled. Raphaël is immensely wealthy, beloved of everyone, and successful in his profession as a journalist. With his many friends he enjoys life to the full, those who envy him or are his enemies cannot touch him. He even engages without danger in a life-threatening duel: he has only to wish for victory. Yet he is not unaware that with each wish that is fulfilled, the wild ass's skin shrinks, and he now measures more closely this shrinkage from wish to wish. Shuddering with fear, he realizes how small the skin has already become, and accordingly how short a time he has left to live if he continues to wish as carelessly as he has thus far.

From this moment of panic on, Balzac's novel, which up to that point could be read as a Romantic phantasmagoria, develops into a magnificent character study. Raphaël's triumphant awareness that he can determine at will the length of the life that remains to him suddenly turns into fear and worry focused solely on managing the shortness of his life. With this plunge into awareness, Balzac has entirely transformed his hero's character. The man who is used to enjoying the happiness of a life unfolding completely in accord with his desires becomes an anxious loner who mistrustfully shuts himself off from the world, so as to avoid being seduced into wishing for something: "he could do everything and no longer wanted anything" ("il pouvait tout et ne voulait plus rien"). Thus we now see before us a time-miser who hates life, who with regard to his life-time combines in himself the characteristics of both Molière's *Misanthrope* and *Avare*, for he subordinates all action, or rather inaction, to a single goal: if his life cannot be lengthened, he seeks at all costs to avoid shortening it through further wishes. This obsession is also reflected, in the Balzacian manner, in Raphaël's physiognomy: "An observer would have thought he recognized in the marquis the eyes of a young man behind the mask of an old man" ("Un observateur aurait cru reconnaître dans le marquis les yeux d'un jeune homme sous le masque d'un vieillard"). Here the hero's shortage of life-time has definitively passed over into a shortage in quality of life.[43]

While Raphaël is animated by a single concern, never again to wish for anything, love now comes back into play. This time it promises the lonely hero the purest happiness of soul—a happiness that, as Balzac's kind retarding moment will have it, he does not even need to wish for, since the good-hearted Pauline already bears him, in accord with her own wishes, a boundless love. So it seems that this happiness is to endure for a long time. But there arrives a critical moment at which for Raphaël love rises ecstatically into a desire for absolute possession, so that with the fulfillment of this highest and last wish the shagreen and its owner's life-time are simultaneously exhausted. Thus Balzac's novel ends, like Goethe's drama, with the experience (or the illusion) of a culminating moment whose happiness coincides with the hero's death.

Up to this point, my discussion of the novel has omitted one aspect of the action whose importance is also emphasized by the fact that Balzac dedicated his novel to a scientist, the mathematician and astronomer Félix Savary, "Membre de l'Académie des Sciences." When the hero of the novel, on seeing the shrinking shagreen, fully understands for the first time how short the life allotted him has become, he turns, in his helplessness, to the Academy of Sciences in Paris, asking it to use all scientific methods to investigate the skin's mysterious power. And so the skin moves through the Academy's various institutes and laboratories, where it is measured and weighed, pressed and stretched with machines, and treated with acids—all without any discernible result. Finally, the Academy is forced to acknowledge that even it cannot explain all natural phenomena, because—as one of its most renowned professors puts it—"Science is vast, and human life is very short" ("La science est vaste, la vie humaine bien courte").[44]

In concluding this section, let us return once more to the antique shop where the novel's hero found his wild ass's skin. From the conversations about the skin there, it emerges that the aged antique dealer is a philosopher of life. In the course of his long life he has seen the world and observed human strivings. The quintessence of his art of observation is the insight that human nature is governed by two forces, which have a consuming effect on human life and thereby shorten it. These two forces are will (*Vouloir*) and power (*Pouvoir*). Both forces consume life-energy: "The will burns us and power destroys us" ("Vouloir nous brûle et Pouvoir nous détruit").[45]

These statements, which also reflect the author's own views, must be taken literally. Like Hufeland, Balzac is convinced that part of the bodily and mental equipment of human beings is an individually limited quantity of life-energy, which is used up in the course of a life through the chemical process of burning or "combustion." An individual's character determines whether this process is accelerated by the consumption-intensive forces of *Vouloir* and *Pouvoir*, which by nature lead to a shortening of life-time such as can be observed, for example, in the case of Raphaël de Valentin. The example of the sprightly old antique dealer, on the other hand, shows that in life there is also a way to manage our energy budget more sparingly. One needs only to make room for the protective life-force *Savoir* ("knowledge") instead of squandering one's life-force through *Vouloir* and *Pouvoir*. Then longevity sets in by itself, as we can see from the lively one-hundred-and-two-year-old antique handler—*quod erat demonstrandum*.

. . .

From another of Balzac's novels we may gain an entirely different perspective on life and life-time. It is entitled *The Thirty-Year-Old Woman*

(*La femme de trente ans*).[46] If it were the most pressing task of literary criticism to distribute praise and blame to authors and their works, then a suitable portion of blame would have to be assigned to this novel. For according to all the rules of poetics, it is very poorly constructed and also rather carelessly written. And yet it is one of the works that established Balzac's worldwide reputation as a novelist. There are reasons for this, negative ones that we will discuss quite briefly, and positive ones that we will examine in detail.

The novel has won little applause for its artistic form largely because it was cobbled together, in a series of stages, from several thematically related short stories (one of which was titled "La femme de trente ans," 1832). The final version, published under this title in 1842, is held together less by unified structures than by a central idea (Balzac: *pensée*). However, this idea was so revolutionary for its time that one critic, Pierre Barbéris, has said that Balzac discovered the type of the thirty-year-old woman just as Marx discovered the proletariat.[47] And in fact in this novel we find the finest compliment that can be paid a thirty-year-old woman: "this lovely age of thirty years, the poetic highpoint of women's lives" ("ce bel âge de trente ans, sommité poétique de la vie des femmes"). Balzac the novelist should be praised for having with this work lengthened the previously short life of a whole generation of women by at least a full decade.

How this should be understood more precisely can be seen from another text that was written with more theoretical pretensions and that Balzac published in 1831—that is, before writing the novel—under the title *The Physiology of Marriage* (*Physiologie du mariage*). This is the somewhat overly ambitious book of a young man who at the ripe old age of thirty-one wants to see himself as a connoisseur of women and who tries to impress, on the slippery terrain of this "science," not only by his knowledge of the natural science of physiology but also by the witty aphorisms of a moralist (*historien des moeurs*). One of these aphorisms goes like this: "A respectable woman is less than forty years old" ("Une femme honnête a moins de quarante ans"). We will leave this remark uncommented for the moment and work out more precisely, at Balzac's instigation, the age in life of a woman suitable to appear in a novel.

One thing is clear to Balzac the physiologist: youth is the "fleeting span of time in which a woman remains in bloom" ("la rapide saison où la femme reste en fleur"). That is, no matter how it is calculated, a very short span of time. Balzac probably does not think it begins with the end of puberty, that is—in the nineteenth century—at fourteen, like Faust's Gretchen. But a woman must realize as early as possible in her life that "the charms of youth are love's only baggage" ("les charmes de la jeunesse sont l'unique baggage de l'amour"). The time in question is thus very limited, if she first becomes acquainted with the man of her life at the age of nineteen, as does the heroine of our novel, and wants to marry him at twenty. For only after marriage is a girl freed from the tutelage of her parents and as a "young woman" is henceforth able, within the bounds set by mores and her husband, to lead a social existence at her own discretion. She then has about ten years, in which, however, children must be brought into the world and cared for. This must all happen, in the general view of society up to Balzac, before the threshold age of thirty, because the life of a woman who has reached and passed that threshold is henceforth supposed to be devoted primarily to virtue—and little else that might interest a novelist.

In the case of men, the calculation is very different. For them, the borderline age of thirty is not valid, and they have significantly more time for everything related to love and marriage in their lives, significantly more time available to them than is available to women. In Balzac's *Physiology of Marriage*, this is recorded in almost bookkeeping terms: "Relating to marriage, the difference in duration between a man's romantic life and that of a woman therefore amounts to fifteen years" ("Relativement au mariage, la différence de durée entre la vie amoureuse de l'homme et celle de la femme est donc de quinze ans"). Balzac reformulates this as an aphorism: "Physically, a man is man longer than a woman is a woman" ("Physiquement, un homme est plus longtemps un homme que la femme n'est femme"). But this conflicts with Balzac's sense of justice and fairness, and so when his heroine soon thereafter reaches the threshold age of thirty, he summarily dismantles the barrier and grants her a ten-year reprieve—that is (see above), until she is forty. However, a decade later, old age is already knocking at the door. When the novel's heroine turns fifty, Balzac does not fail to mention that she is a little hard of hearing, which love finds it hard to accept and can certainly be seen as a first sign of approaching old age.

How does Balzac's heroine make use of the extra decade granted her, calculated according to the old or the new standards? In accord with the old standards, Balzac's Miss Julie marries Colonel Victor d'Aiglemont of the Guards when she is twenty and brings her first child into the world when she is twenty-two. A few years later, the couple drifts apart, and Victor takes a mistress. This is not an unbearable misfortune for Julie, however, because the young Lord Grenville, called Arthur for short, conceives a romantic, passionate love for the beautiful twenty-seven-year-old. Before long, Julie yields to him just as romantically. But during a secret rendezvous the lovers are surprised by the husband, and the young lord, as a gentleman concerned about the lady's honor, conceals himself under such acrobatic circumstances that he ends up dead. He has sacrificed his life for love. Julie reaches her thirtieth year full of melancholy and mourning for her dead lover.

For a novel of Balzac's period, that was enough subject matter, and for an earlier heroine of a novel, enough life-time. But not for Balzac or his heroine. In Balzac's novel, Julie turns "only" thirty after this unhappy love affair and thus is at this age already a "experienced woman" (*une femme expérimentée*). There is therefore no reason for her to withdraw—in fidelity to her husband, who continues to be unfaithful to her, or in memory of her *one true* love—into a boring life of virtue. Only now has she become a genuinely interesting person in a novel. This is already shown by her physiognomy (Balzac's favorite object of study!), for "A woman's physiognomy begins only at the age of thirty" ("La physionomie de la femme ne commence qu'à trente ans"). For Balzac, up to that point the features of a woman's face are as inconspicuously regular as the surface of a lake. However, if a woman's life has already been marked, as in Julie's case, by having been beloved, spouse, and mother (in that order in the text!), then her face takes on an expression that can be read like a book—at least for the novelist Balzac. And thus only starting at the age of thirty (*à trente ans seulement*), after she has lived a good part of her life-time, can she exercise an "irresistible attraction" on a lover, especially if the latter is himself scarcely thirty years old—like the diplomat Charles de Vandenesse. But at this age he is still a young man, whereas she is already "an abyss with a pretty face" ("cet abyme dans une jolie tête"). He loves her—she is his first real love—with the guileless passion of youth, but in his intimate relations with her he often remains "mute and small before this great and noble woman" ("silencieux et petit devant cette grande et noble femme"), who is ahead of him by one love—that is, she is almost infinitely far ahead of him.[48]

EVERY DAY IS A SONNET · Oscar Wilde

In his novel *The Picture of Dorian Gray* (1891), Oscar Wilde, deliberately deviating from the puritanical mores of the Victorian Age and anticipating the end-of-the-world mood of the *Fin de siècle*, celebrates the lifestyle of a London dandy who has freed himself from all the inhibitions of narrow morality, and whose highest and perhaps only law is aesthetics. This novel, not entirely unlike the one by Balzac discussed above, is a second- or third-degree Faust-book, in which Faust's bold pact-making with time is carried further in a new perspective.[49]

At the beginning of the story, the eponymous hero is—like Faust, like Raphaël de Valentin—a young man, who has to face growing old like everyone else. But nature has given the young Dorian Gray all the perfections of body and soul, so that no one can escape his charismatic attraction. Thus he also quickly finds his Mephistopheles, in the person of his older friend Lord Henry Wotton, who becomes his elegant mentor in the aesthetics and way of life of a London dandy. Lord Henry's artistically polished maxims and aphorisms strengthen the young man's certain awareness of his radiant youth and irresistible beauty: "Your days are your sonnets." But this seducer plants a thorn in his young friend's soul: How long can such a wonder of nature stand fast against the erosive power of time, against whose attack nothing is less secure than beauty?

According to Lord Henry's calculations, Dorian Gray has little time left, and his advice is harsh: "You have only a few years in which to live really, perfectly, fully." The first maxim of the hedonistic art of life must therefore be to avoid anything that might get in the way of artistically experienced beauty, and above all morality. Therewith is Dorian Gray's "egotism" begun, the seed of corruption planted in his heart. The well-educated young man suddenly becomes a Narcissus more in love with himself than the one in Ovid's Metamorphoses.

Apart from his seductive rhetoric, Lord Henry has no power over Dorian Gray. The society painter Basil Hallward comes to his aid by offering to capture in a picture the now very vain young man's radiant beauty, so that it will never fall victim to the passing years. Soon Dorian Gray is able to admire his own perfection in the completed picture, which we must imagine to be as deceptively life-like as the trompe-l'oeil pictures of the Greek painter Zeuxis. However, for this overwhelming moment Lord Henry has already planted another doubt in his young friend's heart. It may now happen that the ideal beauty fixed in the artist's likeness will last longer than the real beauty that the young man has been granted in his limited lifetime. Dorian Gray wishes it were the other way around: "I would give my soul for that!"

This "mad wish" is magically fulfilled. The young man is granted, like a god, permanent youth and unchanging beauty. But over the years the picture shows, in his place, the destructive marks of time, just as its living image is spared them. And so it happens that Dorian Gray remains young and handsome, while his picture changes for him, revealing ever more clearly "the hideousness of age." Youth and beauty, age and hideousness are now divided between Dorian Gray and his image in such a way that the latter takes on, like a kind of scapegoat, all the adversities of life and conceals them behind a curtain.

At this point, a few comments on the novel's form are called for. The novel consists of two clearly distinguishable parts (chapters 1–10 and 11–20). Each part is characterized by a rapid narrative tempo that remains close to the events and also gives much space to dialogue. Between the two parts is chapter 11, which has an entirely different narrative structure. In an accelerated style, it summarizes eighteen years of the hero's life. This chapter also divides the two parts of the novel from the point of view of content. In the first part the thematics of morality is in the foreground. Only in the second part is the thematics of time fully developed.

For the moral (or amoral) thematics of the first part, Oscar Wilde leans heavily on Goethe's *Faust*. Dorian Gray is (the young!) Faust, and Lord Henry is his Devil. The Gretchen of this novel is the beautiful dancer Sibyl Vane; Dorian conceives a brief passion for her, but as soon as he feels certain of her love and devotion to him, he pushes her away. She commits suicide. Undisturbed, the corrupter registers his guilt only as a small "stain" on the canvas of his portrait. Many other stains later appear as records of an increasingly unrestrained way of life. However, these ugly marks on the canvas become visible to Dorian himself only when he happens to notice with horror, while secretly contemplating his portrait, how strongly and rapidly his features have been twisted into those of a devil. However, the painter Basil Hallward is still more horrified when Dorian finally shows him the portrait. Hallward's first thought is to destroy the spoiled picture, but Dorian prevents him from doing so stabbing the painter as he stands in front of his work: One more death—what difference does that make? It means nothing more than another trace of blood on the picture.

Now two kinds of disfigurements are piling up on the picture, and Dorian doesn't know which is worse, the "signs of sin," or the "signs of age." But neither of them worries him much, since he can cling to the maxim of careless oblivion he has learned from Lord Henry: "What is past, is past." This oblivion clears the way for an amoral aesthetics that equates art and life; as Lord Henry is pleased to tell his obedient pupil, "Life has been your art."

One character is still missing from the Faustian cast in this novel: James Vane, the brother of the dancer whom Dorian Gray drove to suicide. He plays the role played by Gretchen's brother Valentin in Goethe's drama. Eighteen years later—that is probably why so many years have to pass in chapter 11—Vane is still on the trail of his sister's "murderer." When James finally has the monster in his power, Dorian uses his youthful features to convince him that so young a man could not be guilty of a crime committed so long ago. Instead of Dorian, it is the disappointed avenger who dies, another victim on the former's list of murders.

Now the full measure of evil deeds has been accomplished, and the picture completely disfigured. Suddenly realizing what has happened, Dorian attacks the painting with the same knife that he has already used to kill the painter, seeking to destroy it. The next morning his servant finds him lying dead before the canvas, stabbed by his own hand. He is so withered and ugly as to be unrecognizable, but over his body his picture shines with youthful beauty, just as the artist painted it so many years before.[50]

· · ·

In 1895, four years after the triumphant success of this novel (and many other triumphs on the stage and in society), disaster overtook Oscar Wilde. He was put on trial in London for homosexual offenses and ultimately sentenced to two years' imprisonment. This was a moral and social fall from which Wilde was never able to recover in the time remaining to him. However, while he was in Reading Gaol he wrote two works that show us a man broken in body and soul who deserves our pity. These are his autobiographical *De profundis* and the famous "Ballad of Reading Gaol" (1898). We will briefly examine the latter here, because it also affords us a view of the inhuman world of the prison.[51]

The ballad is first of all a testimony to the way the monotony of imprisonment makes time unbearably long:

> And that each day is like a year,
> A year whose days are long.

However, one of these days has been chosen by the authorities for the hanging of a fellow prisoner on the jail's gallows. He is a murderer, but his crime may not be more iniquitous than those of many other people who will be able to go on living unpunished:

> The man had killed the thing he loved,
> And so he had to die.
> Yet each man kills the thing he loves,
> By each let this be heard.

For the imprisoned Oscar Wilde, who experiences with all his empathy, as if with his own body, every phase in the fate of his fellow prisoner, the latter is a terrifying image of himself, on which his own sins and failings have been unloaded and made visible. Thus he has not only lived the wretched man's life along with him but also suffered his death with him, as the memorable closing lines of the ballad suggest:

> For he who lives more lives than one,
> More deaths than one must die.

UNTIMELY DEATH OR VENERABLE OLD AGE
Chatterton, Keats, Benn, Thomas Mann

Earlier, we spoke of the midpoint in life, the highpoint from which poets (Dante, Petrarch, Hölderlin, Goethe, . . .) moved on with renewed energy or even haste through their remaining years. But what are we to say about those who did not reach this age, or only barely surpassed it? Perhaps they were aided by their genius, since the latter, according to the firm conviction of eighteenth-century "genius aesthetics," is not subject to the rules of time. For example, in his youth in Strasbourg, Wetzlar, and Weimar, up to his journey to Italy, Goethe was the ideal model of original genius, and later, as his life continued on into old age, he had considerable difficulty reconciling his poetic genius with the mature art of his classical years.[52]

A genius is really not supposed to grow old. What is the point of so much surplus life-time, if in youth everything has already been said, painted, and composed? The true genius seems destined to die young and through his tragic death to certify that he is a genius. Art "consumes," and so no energy remains to carry on a long life "on a low flame." This is shown by the biographies of many young authors and artists who died an early death and lived as if from childhood on they had sensed that they would die young and therefore lived more rapidly, intensely, and completely than other people.

Here is a short list (with age at death in parentheses), limited— after a brief reminder of Schubert (31), Mozart (35), Raphael (37), and van Gogh (37)—to writers, not excluding those whose early deaths were the result of violence, accident, or suicide: Thomas Chatterton (18), Raymond Radiguet (20), Georg Büchner (24), Lautréamont (24), Georg Heym (25), Wilhelm Hauff (25), Mário de Sá-Carneiro (25), John Keats (26), Sándor Petőfi (26), Georg Trakl (27), Mikhail Lermontov (27), Rupert Brooke (28), José de Larra (28), Novalis (29), Percy Bysshe Shelley (30), Heinrich von Kleist (34), Lord Byron (36), Vladimir Mayakovski (37), Alexander Pushkin (38), Guillaume Apollinaire (38), Federico Garcia Lorca (38). The German historian Reinhart Koselleck comments: "A life can be short or long. If it is short, like that of Schiller, Kleist, or Büchner, biography is overlaid by mourning, because it cannot be written out of the life."[53]

The first and youngest writer on this list is the English poet Thomas Chatterton (1752–70), who took his own life while he was still almost a child. He doubted his genius and left us only a few poems. He would probably have been entirely forgotten by posterity had not another author, the French poet, novelist, and playwright Alfred de Vigny, made his fate, which many people had found moving, into the subject of a Romantic drama (*Chatterton*).[54]

The play had its premiere in 1835 and was a great success. It is still performed on the stage of the Comédie Française. Its popularity was in part due to the moving story of Chatterton's love affair with the young

Kitty Bell, which is interwoven with the main action and doubles the catastrophe in this Romantic tragedy. The play's cast of characters also includes an eighty-year-old Quaker, a man of empathy and wisdom who tries to dissuade the poet from committing suicide. The leitmotif of the whole dramatic action is the shortness of life. In particular, the latter is the theme of Chatterton's melancholy monologues, of which there are many in this play. "I am losing quite a lot of time," the young poet complains. Every minute he does not spend working on his poems he sees as a "theft" of time, which is slipping away from him: "nothing is written!" (*rien n'est écrit!*). In particular, his great historical poem "Harold" remains unfinished, and he finds the verses he has written completely unsatisfactory. They were written far too quickly because he needed to earn money, and under such conditions they cannot be as good as his lofty ambitions require. Tortured by doubts, Chatterton tears up his manuscript: "I believed I was a poet" ("J'ai cru être un poète"). Finally, when a newspaper accuses him of plagiarism, he resorts to the poison he has long had at hand. His beloved Kitty follows him into death. It falls to the Quaker to utter the closing line: "Lord, receive these two martyrs!" ("Seigneur, reçois ces deux martyrs!").

. . .

John Keats (1795–1821), who himself died of tuberculosis while in the bloom of youth, also wrote a poem "To Chatterton," in which he proclaimed his predecessor a "Genius": "Thou art among the stars / Of Highest Heaven."[55] At the time, Keats saw his own death approaching, and in Rome he wrote the following sonnet:

> When I have fears that I may cease to be
>   Before my pen has glean'd my teeming brain,
> Before high-piled books, in charactery,
>   Hold like rich garners the full ripen'd grain;
> When I behold, upon the night's starred face,
>   Huge cloudy symbols of a high romance,
> And think that I may never live to trace
>   Their shadows, with the magic hand of chance;
> And when I feel, fair creature of an hour,
>   That I shall never look upon thee more,

> Never have relish in the faery power
>> Of unreflecting love;—then on the shore
> Of the wide world I stand alone, and think
> Till love and fame to nothingness do sink.

When he wrote this poem, Keats had only a short time left to live. He lies buried in Rome, the "eternal" city.

. . .

An alternative to this group portrait of artists who died an early death is provided by Gottfried Benn's sensitive survey of long-lived artists. Benn (1886–1956) wrote his essay "Aging as a Problem for Artists" in 1954, when he was himself already sixty-eight.[56] Among the writers who reached an advanced and "venerable" (*gesegnet*) age, he names first of all Goethe (83), and then, among many others, Leo Tolstoy (82), André Gide (82), Victor Hugo (83), Gerhart Hauptmann (84), Voltaire (84), Paul von Heyse (84), Knut Hamsun (93), George Bernard Shaw (94). What could the literary public still expect from these elderly authors if they had already done their best work in their youth? For Benn, their biographies fall into two groups, depending on whether their old age is characterized by classical maturity and serenity or by weariness and decline of intellectual powers. According to Benn, there are grounds for complaining about "the evenings of life, these evenings of life!" On the other hand, it is astonishing "how many old and very old people there are among the most famous writers." This aspect is also part of the "Methuselah conspiracy" (Schirrmacher)[57] that increasingly threatens our society.

Benn, a physician, draws on a recent medical theory to explain his thinking on this point. According to this theory, in many cases life benefits from the fact that it can be associated with art, which, as a "cathartic phenomenon," emerges as a mode of liberation and relaxation. Thus it may be that the prolongation of the lives of these aging artists is precisely the result of art. However, in this context we should also note August Graf Platen's skeptical verdict, cited by Benn, in one of his finest poems:[58]

> Who has ever been able rightly to grasp life,
> Who has not squandered half of it

On dreams, fevers, conversations with fools,
On torments of love, empty time-wasting?

Even a person calm and relaxed,
And born knowing what he should do,
Who early on chose his life path,
Must blanch before life's contradiction.

Everyone hopes happiness will smile on him,
Only bearing happiness, if it really comes,
Is not for men, but for God alone.

But it never comes, we merely wish and wager:
It never falls on the slumberer's head,
Nor is it caught by him who runs after it.

Wer wußte je das Leben recht zu fassen,
Wer hat die Hälfte nicht davon verloren
Im Traum, im Fieber, im Gespräch mit Toren,
In Liebesqual, im leeren Zeitverprassen?

Ja, der sogar, der ruhig und gelassen,
Mit dem Bewußtsein, was er soll, geboren,
Frühzeitig einen Lebensgang erkoren,
Muß vor des Lebens Widerspruch erblassen.

Denn jeder hofft doch, daß das Glück ihm lache,
Allein das Glück, wenn´s wirklich kommt, ertragen,
Ist keines Menschen, wäre Gottes Sache.

Auch kommt es nie, wir wünschen bloß und wagen:
Dem Schläfer fällt es nimmermehr vom Dache,
Und auch der Läufer wird es nicht erjagen.

When Benn wrote his essay on the problem of the aging of the artist, Thomas Mann was still alive and ought to have been included in
Benn's canon. Mann himself composed no comparable theoretical reflections on this subject, but his novella *Death in Venice* (1913) can be
read as his contribution to the "problem" of long-lived authors who
seem to have escaped the ravages of time.[59] Gustav von Aschenbach

is in fact, as the text states, such an "aging artist," who is in danger of "outliving" himself because his long life as a writer has not been long enough for him to complete the work for which he has lived. He has "used up" his life in a long, laborious effort to knot many threads into a "carpet-novel." Has he thus paid the appropriate "fee" for his art (as Mann put it in economic terms in the novella *Tonio Kröger*), has he paid, in the currency of life-time, for its success? In any event, the work has not been completed. And now, in Venice, it is "too late."

Then Tadzio appears before Aschenbach's eyes. Tadzio, the beautiful boy from Poland, the very image not merely of youth but of life itself. Aschenbach's last days, before he is carried off by cholera epidemic in Venice, are devoted to the visual pleasure that this image of radiant, youthful life—life such as he himself once enjoyed—evokes in his artist's soul. And the Eros that resides in the vigor of life as a whole, and not only in the seductive power of the other or the same sex, now dominates the last and most precious days of his life.

Aschenbach's "carpet-novel" will never be completely knotted. On the beach in Venice, the fragment of this work on the shortness of life is brought into the final reckoning carried out by Time in the guise of Death.

REVOCABLE AND IRREVOCABLE TIME · Ingeborg Bachmann

In 1953, one year after giving a reading before the "Gruppe 47," Ingeborg Bachmann (1926–73) was introduced to the general public by her volume of poetry entitled *Revocable Time* (*Die gestundete Zeit*), and it was not long before she was considered Austria's greatest poet.[60] At the same time, she also became, with her first volume of poetry, a commentator on time and the limited nature of time. Let us first consider briefly this volume's title poem:

> Harder days are coming.
> Time by the hour until payment is due
> Looms on the horizon.
> Soon you'll have to tighten your belt.
> And drive the dogs into the marshes.
> For the fish's entrails
> Have grown cold in the wind.

The lupine's light burns with a meager flame.
Your eyes peer into the fog:
Time extended until payment is due
Is becoming visible on the horizon.

Over there your beloved sinks into the sand,
It piles up around her flowing hair,
Interrupts her,
Commands her to be silent,
Finds her to be mortal
And willing to part
After each embrace.

Don't look back.
Just tighten your belt.
Drive the dogs into the marshes.
Throw the fish into the sea.
Put out the lupines!

Harder days are coming.

Es kommen härtere Tage.
Die auf Widerruf gestundete Zeit
Wird sichtbar am Horizont.
Bald mußt du den Schuh schnüren
Und die Hunde zurückjagen in die Marschhöfe.
Denn die Eingeweide der Fische
Sind kalt geworden im Wind.
Ärmlich brennt das Licht der Lupinen.
Dein Blick spurt im Nebel:
Die auf Widerruf gestundete Zeit
Wird sichtbar am Horizont.

Drüben versinkt dir die Geliebte im Sand,
Er steigt um ihr wehendes Haar,
Er fällt ihr ins Wort,
Er befielt ihr zu schweigen,
Er findet sie sterblich
Und willig dem Abschied
Nach jeder Umarmung.

Sieh dich nicht um.
Schnür deinen Schuh.
Jag die Hunde zurück.
Wirf die Fische ins Meer.
Lösch die Lupinen!

Es kommen härtere Tage.

In this poem fog, darkness, and cold evoke a repellent landscape that is located on a northern sea, perhaps the North Sea. The only source of light remaining in this barren marsh-landscape is the dimly glowing flower-candles of the lupine, which may however only show that the temporal setting is the last days of autumn.[61]

With this scene, which must have been almost a no-man's-land for the poet from the Austrian Alps who later lived in Rome, the text represents a time-poem dealing with finitude and mortality. Up to the "willing" sinking into the sand, every line alludes only to a provisionally extended (*gestundet*) time, a debt that can be simply called in, and must soon be paid off once and for all. Elementary clocks are also made from water and sand, and in the second stanza they indicate, through enigmatic images, the remaining hours. For "harder days" will "soon" be here, and then there will no longer be any lupines to remind us of better times. However, in this poem we find no trace of rebellion against this silting up of a time that is so stingily doled out. The extinction of the lupines is also accepted with resignation, and even deliberately accelerated. Nonetheless, it remains uncertain whether in this poem, contrary to the warning to Lot's wife not to look back one more time toward the sinking Sodom, Orpheus looks back toward the lagging Eurydice.

In "Fall Maneuver" ("Herbstmanöver"), a poem that immediately precedes "Revocable Time" in the volume mentioned above, time is the theme, and it is burdened with a vague guilt. In this poem we read:

Time works miracles. But if it comes at the wrong time,
with the knocking of guilt: we are not at home.

Die Zeit tut Wunder. Kommt sie uns aber unrecht,
mit dem Pochen der Schuld: wir sind nicht zu Hause.

These two verses characterize, with an economy possible only in a poem by Bachmann, a thawing of memory that is surely not only private but also public and political, and indeed above all the one that took place in German and Austrian society during the first years following World War II. In rhythm with the pulse of time, the consciousness of a repressed guilt knocks within us, and thus it is not impossible that this guilt may come forward at some inappropriate ("wrong") time and demand atonement. Yet the same time also performs miracles and heals. And so we allow ourselves only too willingly to be carried away and are meanwhile ("until called in") not available for unpleasant memories.

. . .

A few years later, Ingeborg Bachmann returned to the theme of revocable time again, this time in her story "The Thirtieth Year" (1953).[62] The latter deals with a young man who sees the day he turns thirty as a time boundary sharply distinguishing his youth from his old age. We recognize the subject, that of the "midpoint in life," moved up a few years with respect to the one designated by the Psalmist. The Baccalaureus in Goethe's drama may be responsible for this abrupt shortening of the first half of life, since he tells Mephistopheles, dressed as an "elderly gentleman," that "One who is thirty years or over already is as good as dead."

We are never told the name of Bachmann's young man. But in a few places the author has made the striking shift in the gender of her narration clear. Thus, for example, the story takes place over precisely twelve months, from June to June, so that one can recall that the author was also born in June, or more exactly on June 25, 1926, and hence the thirtieth year of her life corresponds more or less to the year narrated in her story.

What does this "time-threshold" mean for the young man—now a few years older—when seen from the point of view of a young woman? The former, who will soon no longer be young, wants to find out, and so he takes exactly one year of time to learn, through changed circumstances and many new encounters, "how to show himself in his true character." But what is his true character?

Here we may first ask: Is Bachmann's character-seeker a young lord on his "grand tour?" A young man on an educational journey, carrying his Baedeker and his Dehio in his luggage? A youthful scholar on a sabbatical? A Flaubertian Frédéric, whose "éducation sentimentale" gets bogged down in triviality? A bachelor on his *Wanderjahr*? Or, finally, a Prodigal Son who has wasted his patrimony on the attractions of vice and is now ruefully returning home? All conceivable questions of this kind are to remain unanswered here, along with the central question: whether the protagonist of this little *Bildungsroman* (or a counterfeit of one), once he has crossed the aforementioned time-threshold, with a first gray hair on his head, will be a different person.

Only time, of which he will have little, will concern us here. For up to this time-threshold Bachmann's male character has been careless with time. After all, a young man "still has so much time" before him. Countless possibilities are open to him. And the ideas about the world he has formed for himself are also revocable, easily and without consequences, as if they were only rented or leased. "On every occasion he had spoken to a circle of friends, on request, and all of it always as it were on probation, revocable. The word seems to him revocable, he himself seems revocable."

All that must cease if he doesn't want to fall into the trap of time. He has to "change the rules." So he has to pack his bags and not merely travel but leave, not merely change places but people as well. He goes to Rome. Does he find in Rome his true character and personal style? Obviously not. Even in Rome the network of the past is already waiting for him, forces upon him the character he earlier had and no longer wants. And the same happens to our traveler in Genoa, Brindisi, and above all in Vienna, that "city subject to change." Everywhere time, which he wants to escape, seizes the large or small events of his *Wanderjahr* and incorporates them into itself, so that at the end of his year away, our adventurer does not know whether, as a "drop-out" (*Aussteiger*), he has gone with time or has stood up against it. However, the storyteller hopes that he has "survived with great difficulty" his thirtieth year, day by day.

In this story, Ingeborg Bachmann set herself a difficult task. In the short narrative time of her story she had to represent the relatively long time of a year of life in such a way that the impression of a short probationary and testing time emerges—as she herself puts it, a "year of atonement" (*abgebüßtes Jahr*). The storyteller, who was new to prose and had not yet acquired the mastery evident in her later stories, only partly succeeded in carrying out this task. Her narrative prose is still a little clumsy and wavers abruptly between reportorial discourse and interior monologue, between foreshortened time and time stretched out under a microscope. With these properties, the story "The Thirtieth Year" is itself a time-threshold—and this is what many readers have prized in it—by means of which Bachmann has tested, through writing, what for her has proven revocable and what has proven irrevocable in the course of a year.

3

Limited Time in This World
and in the Next

The Jewish Bible, which Christians call the Old Testament, is well aware that time is precious. "All our days," the Psalmist tells us, "pass by speedily, and we fly away."[1] It is therefore a sign of wisdom to manage time sensibly and to allocate it correctly in one's life, for—as we read in Koheleth (Ecclesiastes), "A season is set for everything, a time for every experience under heaven." What follows from this? First of all, that it is a sign of foolishness to waste precious life-time on vain things. Vanity and foolishness consist above all in using many words where a few would suffice. "Keep your mouth from being rash, and let not your throat be quick to bring forth speech. . . . Your words should be few . . . so does foolish utterance come with much speech." In many passages, the Bible itself is as concise as possible, for example when Daniel recounts his dream "briefly" (Vulgate: *brevi sermone*), or 2 Maccabees, where the five books of the first version were condensed into a single book so that the story of Judas Maccabeus might be more pleasant to read and more easily retained by the memory.[2]

Jesus of Nazareth, who was granted only a short life of thirty-three years on Earth, knew the value of brevity—after all, he preferred to teach in parables. The parable is a short genre that even in oral form cannot have been much longer than it is in the Gospels. Bible theologians assume that before the Gospels took on their canonical form, they first existed as a collection of "master words" (*kyrioi logoi*) whose structure allows us to conceive them almost as aphorisms. In their textual embedding, their memorable nature also makes them resemble "proverbs"; for example, "Except ye be converted and become as little children, ye shall not enter into the kingdom of heaven."[3]

However, Jesus's explicit recommendation that prayers be short is of special theological importance. When his disciples ask him how they should pray, he warns them against emulating the pagans' long-winded prayers (Vulgate: *multiloquium*), as if many words were more likely to be heard than few. And immediately after giving this clear answer, he teaches his disciples the Our Father: "After this manner pray thee . . ." This is the model of a short prayer.

In another passage in Matthew, Jesus makes the point still more explicit when speaking to a group of Pharisees: "I say unto you, that every idle word (Vulgate: *omne verbum otiosum*) that men shall speak, they shall give account thereof in the day of judgment. For by thy words thou shalt be justified, and by thy words thou shalt be condemned."[4]

When at the age of about thirty, Jesus begins teaching as a rabbi, from the outset he places his message under the imperative of a temporality that demands a prompt decision: "The time is fulfilled (Vulgate: *Impletum est tempus*), and the kingdom of God is at hand; repent ye, and believe the gospel." This had already been taught by John the Baptist, who nonetheless sought only to be Jesus's precursor. When Jesus makes this message his own, the kingdom of God is "nigh" (Vulgate: *appropinquavit*), "the hour is come" (Vulgate: *venit hora*) Now the time is short for everyone who follows the master's teaching and wants to enter the kingdom of God with him. They have only "a little while" (Vulgate: *modicum tempus*) to make their decision.[5]

Time is so short that Jesus does not allow his twelve apostles even the slightest delay in taking up their vocations. They must follow him immediately, abandoning other duties. Thus his first apostles, the brothers Peter and Andrew, immediately leave "the ship and their father" on the Sea of Galilee in order to follow him. When the brothers James and John are called, they do the same. Mark writes: "They left their father Zebedee in the ship with the hired servants, and went after him." Another disciple is said to have asked Jesus whether he should first bury his father, who had just died. Jesus does not allow him this time and demands that he come along without delay: "Follow me, and let the dead bury their dead." The severity of this demand must have caused a sensation, and perhaps also resistance, on the Sea of Galilee, for Jesus comes back to it and reaffirms it: "He that loveth father or mother more than me is not worthy of me."

The haste shown by Jesus in calling his apostles to him is astonishing and at first hard to understand. Does the Fourth Commandment—which explicitly demands that one honor one's father and mother, and thus also that one care for one's parents and not simply leave them in the lurch—no longer hold on the Sea of Galilee? The suggestion that one should fulfill this commandment so that "your days may be long in the land" is surely to be understood in connection with this temporal care and concern. On another occasion Jesus himself incorporates the Fourth Commandment into his teaching and emphasizes its validity. So why does he not obey this commandment himself?[6]

The answer is brief: because time is short. No time is to be lost on Earth, not even in caring for others, which according to divine command is otherwise one of the primary duties. And this clearly does not entail poverty and harm for parents, because the imminent transformation of the world makes long-term care and precautions superfluous anyway. With Jesus an exceptional time has begun, in which men are to obey short-term norms as they are proclaimed by him with the authority of the Son of Man. During this short time all other care and concerns can be left to the heavenly Father. In the other world whose appearance (*parousia*) is soon to occur, one will in any case be able to live—though only after passing through days of apocalyptic terror—"in splendor" if the path thereto is opened up by faith and repentance.

In many of his parables Jesus also teaches that time is short and must be used in the right way. One of these parables has to do with workers in a vineyard. At the center of the biblical text stands the head the of the family (Vulgate: *paterfamilias*). In ancient contexts—we learn this from Aristotle, for instance—the head of the family is responsible for the family's "economics," for the family is conceived as an economic unit.

The head of the family in this parable owns a vineyard. There is a great deal of work, including temporary work. It is probably just at harvest time, and the head of the family hires additional workers—day-laborers, as people used to say. They stand in the marketplace and wait to be "taken on" for a limited time. Here a twelve-hour workday has to be assumed. The head of the family hires workers on five occasions, at varying times of day: in the morning, then again at the third, seventh, ninth, and eleventh hours. All workers are offered the same pay: a penny a day.

When at day's end the agreed amount is paid out, the workers in the five groups notice that they have all received the same pay. No account has been taken of the fact that they have worked differing lengths of time, from a maximum of twelve hours to a minimum of one. They grumble about this injustice. I can easily imagine that many present-day listeners or readers of this parable have also sided with the workers and in solidarity with them demanded that head of the family give equal pay for equal work.

The head of the family refuses to be persuaded. He considers it his right to pay his workers in accord with the (paternalistic) principle of the freedom to distribute his goods as he pleases, without disclosing the calculation of the time worked. The kingdom of heaven, Jesus says, is like this head of a family. True, today one could not make the moral of this parable the basis of a politically viable economic and social policy. Was this once possible? I can't very well imagine even in earlier times a society that would manage labor relations the way this head of family does. The general grumbling would probably still be heard down through history.

So why does Jesus tell his disciples this parable? What does he want to teach? It seems to me that in this parable we are not in a money economy but rather in a temporal economy. In this parable, Jesus teaches, as he does in many other passages in the Gospels, that time is short. The reference here is once again to the fact that men have only a "little longer" to live before the great transformation of the world brought about by the Son of Man. This span of time is growing shorter from day to day, just as in our parable the time worked as measured in hours is dramatically shortened. For the "last called," as they are known in the language of theology, there is only a single hour before time is up.[7]

In the context of the eschatological temporality taught by Jesus, in which the time allotted for the salvation of the faithful has run out, the tiny difference of a few hours (in the parable) or a few days, weeks, or months (of life) is no longer important. A theologically and morally exceptional situation is in force that invalidates the normal economy. In the eschatological economy it is no longer "worth it" to haggle over a few pennies, because soon—in only "a little while"—there will be a higher justice which for the faithful who are saved can be called simply "charity."

Anyone who finds this parable (and the reading of it given it here) too economic or anti-economic is advised to re-read, as a compensation (also an economic concept!), the parable of the "birds of the air" and the "lilies of the field" (also known as "day-lilies" because their blooms are short-lived). What these uncared-for creatures do or fail to do (they neither preen, nor sow, nor reap) likewise runs counter to all economic rationality and can be regarded as sensible only if time has already become so short that all longer-term care and precautions are meaningless. Plants and animals are about to be transformed into another life as well, but they have the advantage of not needing to know so precisely when this transformation will occur.[8]

Jesus's path continues on toward Golgotha. He has only three years left to proclaim the kingdom of God. In this short life-time the time of salvation has not yet been fulfilled. Did Jesus know this from the start? Or did he first learn it in the course of his life? Before we answer this question, we must not overlook the fact that when Jesus is on the cross and has only a very short time to live, he is still concerned about his mother and entrusts her to the care of his favorite disciple, John, just as the Fourth Commandment requires. Does this imply a return of human time, to which care and precautions also belong? However that may be, as a "true man" Jesus can claim that he is also subject to time and might have underestimated its unruliness. But the apostles' trust was not shaken by this discovery, and after Jesus's death on the cross they believed in a *parousia* that was delayed, to be sure, but not ultimately forfeited, and they soon expressed the hope that not only the survivors but also—on the model of the resurrected Christ—those who died in the faith would share in the Resurrection.

For St. Paul, to be sure, the end of time always remained imminent, and he was certain that he would still be alive to experience it himself. Thus in 1 Corinthians he writes concisely: "Time is short" (Vulgate: *tempus breve est*).[9] However, in St. Paul this statement occurs in a context in which the question is whether, if time is so short, pious Christians ought still to marry. Paul's answer allows us to see that he is thinking of a longer period of time, but still not in terms of generations: "So then he that giveth her in marriage doeth well; but he that giveth her not in marriage doeth better."[10]

The Second Epistle of Peter expressly addresses the delay in the *parousia* and thereby heralds the true turning point in the consciousness of early Christians. As Peter puts it, "scoffers" will appear, asking "Where is the promise of his coming?" Peter answers with a quotation from Psalms, given here as "one day is with the Lord as a thousand years, and a thousand years as one day." In the perspective of the delayed *parousia*, human life is lived against the background of this-worldly time, and time is once again as long or as short as it always was.[11]

IN PURGATORY, TIME IS PRECIOUS · Dante

In the fourteenth century, a period of obsession with time began in the economically most advanced regions of Europe (northern Italy, northern France, southern Germany, England . . .) and has endured down to the present day. Ever since, human life, and in particular human economic life, has been increasingly regulated in accord with temporal measures that are not so much provided by nature (life spans, seasons, lunar cycles, hours of the day) as constructed by human beings. In this way a society shaped primarily by time has emerged, with worldwide consequences. This society has eagerly adopted and increasingly internalized the goal of subjecting all human life and activity to clocks and calendars.

In recent decades, many historians of time have produced striking documentation and analyses of this situation. Among them, we should mention in particular the French historian Jacques Le Goff, who discerned the emergence, at the beginning of this period, of two different forms of time he called "clerk's time" and "merchant's time." In his view, the merchants increasingly wrested from the "clerks" (clerics and intellectuals) domination and control over time and reorganized it in accord with the principle of utility.[12]

We will want to keep this thesis in mind, but first let us turn to another of Le Goff's books, *La naissance du Purgatoire* (*The Birth of Purgatory*").[13] Here Le Goff uses the term "purgatory" to refer as well to the "Purgatorium" in Dante's *Divina Commedia*, and he sees Dante as one of the medieval theologians who shaped or even invented the conception of a realm of the Beyond intermediate between Paradise and Hell. The theology of purgatory thus marks a significant step forward in the history of European thinking about time, since in the *Purgatorio*, the second part of his *Commedia*, Dante brings human time into the Beyond, thereby inserting an intermediate realm conceived in terms of human life-time between the twofold eternity of Hell (the first part of the *Commedia*) and Paradise (the third part).

In Dante's *Purgatorio* we read that "time is precious in this realm" ("Il tempo è caro in questo regno").[14] Therefore time must be diligently calculated not only by merchants for this world but also by clerics for the next, and in the most precious currency of all, the currency of time. All Christians, and first of all clerics, must be familiar with this currency in order to be able to calculate or at least estimate, in relation to life-time, the corresponding time of penance required for the salvation of the soul after death. This in turn presupposes that God himself not only knows the day and hour of our death in this world but is also concerned, as the Judge of the World, with the computation (*computus*) of human destiny in the Beyond. Thus in the late Middle Ages *homo mercator*—whose earthly calculating and haggling were not pleasing to the heavenly powers, according to the teaching of earlier theology—created in his own image a *Deus mercator* with whom he could deal and perhaps even haggle on the market of salvation—an innovation in human and divine matters that was for a certain time very problematic and extremely durable.

All the same, the invention of Purgatory in the world of the late Middle Ages made possible for the first time a fairly elegant and to some extent dialectical solution to a serious theological problem: How can God as the Lord of time and eternity make, without damaging the idea of his perfect justice, an unalterable, definite judgment of every individual human being immediately after his death and for all eternity—a judgment that assigns the individual to either a good eternity (Heaven) or a bad eternity (Hell), even though it seems to us that most people are neither very good nor very bad, and in a typically human way waver between right and wrong throughout their lives? Is this kind of severity and moral selectivity even conceivable in a God who the Bible tells us is not only just but also generous and merciful and who provided the sacraments for this purpose? To some extent, in this question lies concealed a moral-theological proto-theodicy that in analogy with the later metaphysical theodicy (Leibniz: How can God be defended against the accusation that as creator of the world he is also the source of the evil in the world?) raises the question: How can God be protected from the conceivable reproach that with his boundless mercy for weak and sinning human beings he cannot simultaneously be an unmerciful, severe judge of the dead who draws a razor-sharp distinction between those who are good and those who are evil? That is the hard question to which the intermediate realm of Purgatory is the soft answer.

Let us now examine the time-theology contained in Dante's Purgatory and accompany the poet, along with his "guide," Vergil, on one segment of his journey through the Beyond. The descent into the deep funnel of Hell (*Inferno*) already lies behind him. Now he is about to follow his path through the second realm of the Beyond, Purgatory. On this path Dante meets a large number of "poor souls" who have been promised eternal salvation but who will achieve it only after a more or less difficult climb to the pinnacle of the conical mountain of purification. This ascent involves great trials and sufferings that serve to atone for sins. Thus, to borrow Le Goff's apt phrase, Purgatory is "a temporary Hell" (*un enfer à temps*).[15]

Like Hell, with its eternal atonement for sin, Purgatory is governed by the ancient principle of retribution or "payback" (*lex talionis*)—in Dante's language, *contrappasso* (lit., counter-step). Retribution involves the repayment of the same (or of the exact opposite), so that one of the sinners in Hell can say: "What I was living, that am I dead" ("Qual io fui vivo, tal son morto"). Retribution is carried out according to the rule of *qualis-talis*; the term *lex talionis* is derived from the Latin word *talis*. The peculiarity of the temporally determined realm of Purgatory is that here retribution is not only qualitative but also quantitative, roughly in accord with a temporally measured "*lex quantionis*" (*quantum-tantum*). In Purgatory, God's justice is expressed above all in the form of temporal justice.[16]

As Dante's readers and companions, we cast a very sympathetic glance on an especially charming figure among the sinners in Purgatory: a man who was a friend of Dante's in his youth, Forese Donati.[17] Dante does not immediately recognize his old friend, since he is a "thin," fleshless shadow, whereas in life Forese, at whose deathbed Dante wept, always looked especially well-fed. But in fact it was precisely by following his appetite to excess ("per seguitar la gola oltra misura") that he committed the sin that resulted in his temporary suffering in Purgatory. He has now to atone for his vice by enduring an equal amount of hunger and thirst (*qualis-talis*) for the same length of time that he squandered on the pleasures of the palate while he was alive (*quantum-tantum*). Thus Dante the theologian tells us here that in Purgatory "time is repaid with time" ("dove tempo con tempo si ristora").

Dante is astonished to discover that Forese has already moved up to the sixth of Mount Purgatory's nine rounds. It seems to him that up to this point Forese has completed his atonement with unexpected speed. Dante knows that Forese died in 1296. Not even five years have passed since his death ("cinqu'anni non sono vólti infino a qui"). That is a short length of time in comparison with the expected eternal bliss. How can this "speed" be explained? Forese offers an explanation in a few verses that reveal a certain cheerfulness in the midst of his willingness to do penance. It was his dear Nella, the "sweet little widow" (*vedovella*) he loved so much, whose urgent prayers in this world brought about a certain acceleration and shortening of the time of his atonement in the next.

Yet not all sinning souls move forward so quickly in Purgatory: many of them have to first get through an especially lengthy and painful period of waiting in "Antepurgatory" (*Anti-Purgatorio*), placed like a sort of waiting room before the true path of purification. There Dante has already met another boyhood friend named Belacqua.[18] Among the other souls waiting there, he is especially tired and drags himself about "as if sloth were his sister."

Belacqua is making no preparations for the difficult ascent of Mount Purgatory. But Dante knows him—that's how he was in life as well! Now he must do penance in Purgatory for his lifelong lethargy, enduring a punishment that is both qualitative and quantitative, in accord with the principle of retribution. Thus slowness in life is paid back with slowness in atonement, in accord with a strict justice conceived quantitatively in terms of length of time. In general, the rule is that a person who has been lethargic in his life must now wait just as many years in the Beyond as he wasted on this sin while he was alive. This is deducted year by year from his atonement balance, keeping a sharp eye on the starry heavens above.

The lethargy with which Belacqua wasted his precious time in life endangers his salvation for another reason. He had additional sins on his conscience, for which in his earthly life it was already high time to repent and to return to God's grace. In his life, Belacqua repeatedly postponed this Christian duty. Only when he had reached old age and saw death approaching did he repent of his sinful life, just in time to avoid going to Hell. From this, Dante's reader can see what a danger to one's eternal life wasting earthly time can be. This lesson is taught in Purgatory even by the "pagan" Vergil: "Time lost irks him most who knows most" ("ché perder tempo a chi più sa più spiace"). That is also why Vergil constantly urges Dante to get on with his journey when he lingers too long with someone he meets along the way.

Therefore we can say that in the *Divine Comedy* Antepurgatory constitutes, by virtue of its structure, a theological treatise on the value of time. At this place in the Beyond all the wasters of time are gathered together—those who have stolen time from themselves, their fellow men, and ultimately from God, and now, especially far removed from the goal of their reformation, they must provide restitution in the currency of time. This means that in accord with the principle of temporal justice the time wasted in this world must be earned back in the next.

Wasting time weighs particularly heavily in the balance when it involves the mighty of the earthly world; it was their special princely duty to use time to do good things for their subordinates. Thus in Antepurgatory Dante also encounters a royal sinner: Manfred, king of Apulia and Sicily.[19] Manfred died in 1266 at the battle of Benevento, during the war with Charles I of Anjou, who was allied with the pope. In 1265 King Manfred had been excommunicated by Pope Clement IV, in the first year of the latter's pontificate, and he remained excommunicate until his death. When Dante meets the king in Antepurgatory, the latter acknowledges that he is a terrible sinner: "Horrible were my sins" ("Orribil furon li peccati miei"). He is surely referring as well to the political sins of his life as a ruler. In Dante's age, how could a Christian excommunicated and burdened with grave sins avoid going to Hell?

Nothing is impossible for divine grace. King Manfred found time shortly before his death to beg God's mercy, obviously in a "quick prayer" (*oratio iaculatoria*). As he tells the travelers Vergil and Dante, he was pierced by two mortal stabs on the battlefield of Benevento, but these left him just this short time to pray. That is enough to gain divine mercy:

> ma la bontà infinita ha sì gran braccia,
> che prende ciò che si rivolge a lei.

> but the Infinite Goodness has such wide arms
> that It receives all who turn to it.

In King Manfred's case, however, the reckoning in the Beyond is still incomplete; his excommunication has not yet been taken into account. For the excommunicate, there is a special system of calculating time, based not on addition but rather on multiplication. Multiplication is calculation for rulers. Manfred himself explains it: "True it is that whoso dies in contumacy of Holy Church, even though he repent at the last, must stay outside upon this bank thirty-fold for all the time that he has lived in his presumption" ("per ognun tempo stato, trenta").

Now we can make the calculation as well. King Manfred lived one year under this pope's anathema. This number is to be multiplied by thirty to calculate the time of atonement after death. Manfred died in 1266. We are now in 1300. Thus he has already done penance for thirty-four years, of which thirty are assigned to the "special account" for excommunication and only four to his other "horrible sins." Thus Manfred still has a long way to go in his atonement, and that is why he is still in Antepurgatory and has not yet even begun the ascent toward the pinnacle of Mount Purgatory. Excommunication clearly plays a role in calculating the required time of atonement: in 1300 Manfred has already spent as many years in Purgatory as he spent on Earth (1232–66). These are two half-lives that correspond more or less to those that, according to the Psalmist's reckoning, a human being can expect to live on Earth.

MORE TIME FOR A NEW WORLD · Benjamin Franklin

In the eighteenth century, the North American subcontinent seemed an immense realm whose occupation and settlement in accord with European standards would require hard labor by several generations. So there was also an immense amount of work for the settlers who sought in this new land lives better than those they and their ancestors had been able to live in the Old World. They were confronted by an enormous task that far surpassed what could be achieved in a single lifetime.

Thus within the immense spatial problem of the new continent lay concealed an equally immense temporal problem. The man who brought this problem to the attention of not only the American public but also the European public of the Enlightenment was Benjamin Franklin (1706–90), whom Carlyle called "the father of all the Yankees," and whom a recent biographer, H. W. Brand, has called "the first American."[20] As a respected businessman, journalist, politician, and diplomat, Franklin was one of the founding fathers of the United States. As the inventor of the lightning rod, he was also recognized in both the Old and New Worlds as a scientist. He was generally regarded as an exceptionally sociable man whom even his political opponents liked, and who had very few enemies. This was largely the result of his way with words in both speech and writing, which helped him to reduce the precipitousness and sharpness of many personal and social conflicts and to make agreement and compromise attractive to early American democracy.[21]

The son of a candlemaker, Franklin was born in Boston, the youngest of seventeen children. In the course of his long life he developed rather strong convictions regarding the kind of life that was pleasing to God and to men. These convictions are based on a morality that is both Christian-Puritanical and Deistic-Enlightened, and they take as their starting point God-given time, which must be economically managed, just like money, for "time is money." This equation is already hinted at in a work Franklin printed in 1736, when he was thirty years old, under the eye-catching and rather utilitarian title "Necessary Hints to Those that Would Be Rich." In Franklin's own *Advice to a Young Tradesman Written by an Old One* (1748) we read: "Remember that time is money!"[22]

In detail, Franklin's reckoning goes like this: Someone who could expect to earn by his labor a salary of ten shillings, and instead spends half the day idling about, must take into account not only the sixpence he spends on his pleasures but also the sum of money he has not earned during the time he has wasted. Here we see that Franklin's advice, which he takes eclectically from various sources, equates time with money and thereby expresses a maxim that long defined the path taken by the social consciousness of Anglo-American Puritanism. Thus it is only right that Benjamin Franklin's portrait appears on the hundred-dollar bill.[23]

The same idea that Franklin on several occasions expressed as an admonitory maxim is presented many years later by the elderly politician in a "bagatelle" he published in 1778 in Paris (where in addition to his diplomatic duties he also established, for his own pleasure, a small publishing house) under the title "L'Ephémère" ("Ephemera" or "Mayfly").[24] This is a little fable written in French and addressed to a woman friend belonging to Parisian society. In a fable ephemeras can of course speak in human language, despite the shortness of their lives, and so we listen to an old, gray-headed ephemera who from his point of view assumes that the whole world will last only eighteen hours. He has already used up seven hours of this time: a considerable time of 420 minutes of lifespan. "How few of us continue so long!" But the old ephemera also knows that he now has at most seven or eight minutes of life-time left. Hence his complaint: "Alas! Art is long and life is short!" ("Hélas, l'art est long et la vie est brève!"). Human beings are also ephemeras—that is the simple moral of this story.[25]

In order to examine Franklin's thought more closely, we now leave the Parisian salons of the 1770s and accompany Franklin back to America, and specifically to his publishing house in Philadelphia. There, between 1733 and 1758 he published a popular calendar known as *Poor Richard's Almanac*. In this title we discern a humorous self-deprecation that probably seemed to Franklin appropriate in a humble calendar-maker. "Poor Richard," or "Poor Dick," here stand for the fictitious or half-fictitious name Richard Saunders, behind whose worldly-wise authority the calendar-maker Benjamin Franklin concealed himself. Over the many years this almanac was published we find in it numerous "adages," "good advices," and "wise sentences" attributed to this "poor Richard." Here again time plays a major role, and we gain the impression that on this subject the author or his wise informant has used Seneca's writings as his main source.[26]

It is quite plausible that the morality of short time, as we know it from the ancients' writings on time, and the literary art of calendar-making were destined to meet and combine in the course of history. The calendar or almanac is itself the most temporal of all literary genres, and since a page of the calendar is irretrievably turned on every day of the year, it reminds us of the shortness of life. No wonder, then, that calendar-makers have so assiduously collected all the aphorisms and other memorable sayings that deal with the shortness of time. Thus over the years a comprehensive collection of old and new aphorisms piled up on Franklin's desk and were included, more or less randomly, in the various annual issues of the almanac.

In 1757, right at the end of his successful career as a calendar-maker, Franklin brought together a number of these maxims in a short preface to the last volume of his almanac, putting them in the mouth of an experienced old man called "Father Abraham"—who himself draws on *Poor Richard* as his source. In front of an auction booth at the annual fair, many eager buyers have crowded together. While waiting for the auction to begin, they are listening to Father Abraham, who speaks to people's consciences in a sententious manner. His speech, which covers about nine printed pages, became widely known under the suggestive if misleading title *The Way to Wealth* (1758) and made Franklin almost as famous in the Old and New Worlds as had his invention of the lightning rod. The reader should not be surprised by the brevity of this text; it had been characteristic of the genre ever since Hippocrates. Thus Father Abraham begins his harangue as follows: "If you'd have my advice, I'll give it you in short, for 'A word to the wise is enough,' and 'Many words won't fill a bushel,' as Poor Richard says." This is followed first—as a *captatio benevolentiae*—by a glance at taxes, which are naturally too high. But for men, taxes are far less injurious—and here Father Abraham arrives at his true subject—than "idleness" and "sloth." These are the vices that "absolutely" shorten life. What conclusion can we draw from this fact?

> "But doest thou love life? Then do not squander time; for that's the stuff life is made of," as Poor Richard says. . . . "If time be of all things the most precious, wasting time must be," as Poor Richard says, "the greatest prodigality"; since, as he elsewhere tells us, "Lost time is never found again"; and "What we call time enough always proves little enough."

We now skip a few further maxims that could be read as further elaborations on the theme of saving time and turn with Father Abraham to money, with which we must also deal (but only secondarily!) sparingly. "Away then with your expensive follies!"—for instance, costly tea for ladies and tempting punch for gentlemen. The worst of all pecuniary vices, however, is contracting debts: "The second vice is lying, the first is running into debt." In debts, Father Abraham goes on, time and money converge once again, but in this case to the certain disadvantage of the debtor. Father Abraham knows from reading Poor Richard that lenders remember repayment deadlines better than do borrowers. They are like astronomers, who have developed a sharper eye for fateful days and hours. The deadline for repayment, which at first seemed so far off, inevitably approaches: "Time will seem to have added wings to his heels as well as shoulders. 'Those have a short Lent,' saith Poor Richard, 'who owe money to be paid for Easter.'"

What success does Father Abraham's sermon have with the people at the fair? None, like all other sermons: "The people heard it and approved the doctrine, and immediately practiced the contrary."[27] When the auction begins, they buy with abandon and contract new debts. Only the narrator turns away from the auction and wears his old coat a little longer. Should we praise him for this? No, not necessarily, since—as a modern Poor Richard would have to point out—if everyone behaved as Father Abraham does things would go badly in commercial and social life and indeed in the economy as a whole.

A final leg of our journey with Benjamin Franklin takes us to London, where he lived for many years. Just as in the cities of the New World, in many parts of London the streets were often still unpaved and dirty. Wherever he dwelt, Franklin was an acute observer of such unhealthy conditions, and he was always looking for sponsors whom he could get to invest in order and cleanliness, even if the latter seemed at first glance to be matters of little importance for trade. In London, he found such a man in Dr. Fothergill, whom Franklin praised in his autobiography as "a great promoter of useful projects." He once told Fothergill about an accident that occurred in front of his house in Craven Street. One day, Franklin saw a poor woman who had obviously barely survived a serious illness, slowly sweeping the street with a birch broom. When asked who employed her to do this work, she replied that she swept the pavement in front of the doors of wealthy people in the vague hope that they would give her something. Franklin asked her to sweep the whole street and promised her a shilling in payment. This agreement was made at 9 a.m.

At noon the woman had already finished her work, and the whole street was swept clean. She received the promised payment. Franklin says no more about her. However, he did think about how much time this work required. It occurred to him that so long as the woman had no clear prospect of being paid, she swept the street very slowly. But afterward, with payment in view, she worked twice as fast. Franklin saw in this a lesson in the economy of time: "I then judged that if that feeble woman could sweep such a street in three hours, a strong, active man might have done it in half the time." This inspired in Franklin what was, to be sure, an extremely useful proposal to set up, with the help of Dr. Fothergill, a permanent street-cleaning service overseen by "several watchmen."[28] One can only wonder, however, whether the old woman would have been hired as part of this cleaning service, even though she was its true inventor. More "efficient" work would naturally be provided by young, healthy men; this is a matter of simple arithmetic that seeks to reduce the labor force required through optimal organization of work time. It seems to me that the old woman on Craven Street has taught something not only to the American Benjamin Franklin and the Englishman Dr. Fothergill but also to present-day readers (almost wholly at her own expense, however)—a lesson in the capitalistic economics of time such as would be found only in the greatest creators of economic theory.

A PURGATORY IN THIS WORLD · Max Weber

In Europe, one of Benjamin Franklin's most perspicacious readers was the German economist and sociologist Max Weber (1864–1920), who cites him extensively as the most reliable witness for his bold thesis regarding the rise of modern capitalism out of the spirit of Calvinistic and Puritanical Protestantism.[29] Weber's theory of society based on prototypes was warmly received in the new human and social sciences, especially since it tended to correct Karl Marx by showing that being does not always determine consciousness; often consciousness—in this case, the religious convictions of Protestantism—also determines being.

The Calvinist-Protestant "superstructure" that in Weber's view determines the economic "base" is first of all a time-consciousness. Hence the teaching of Benjamin Franklin on which Weber draws most extensively for his own theory is the morality expressed in *Poor Richard*, with its central maxim according to which time is money and consequently must be managed as a commodity that is in short supply.[30]

For Max Weber's capitalism, time has a monetary value primarily insofar as the accumulation of resources, which sets modern capitalism on an increasingly rapid path of expansion, is based at its historical beginning on a strict saving of time. Life-time is the fundamental individual capital that is converted, through rigorous exploitation of oneself and others, into working capital that can in turn be invested—without being eroded by spending on the pleasures of life—in ever-new economic ventures, and to that extent it produces constantly increasing yields that are likewise never really enjoyed. That is in fact approximately the way capitalism has worked. And has ultimately made the "Western World" rich. Happy as well?

What is unique in Max Weber's theory is the surprising corollary claim that the wealth necessarily produced by the advantageous effects of this strict asceticism—during the lifetimes of the first capitalists, or at the latest in the second or third generation—is at the same time supposed to be seen as a reliable sign of a divine "election" that otherwise remains imperceptible. For this wealth must already appear on Earth, despite the asceticism. Here it seems to me we find a "missing link" in Max Weber's generally brilliant analysis.

I hypothesize that the missing link in Weber's chain of argumentation is the Catholic Purgatory, which with its official theological name *Purgatorium* is, if not in substance, at least etymologically close to Puritanism (from Lat. *purus*, "pure"). As we have seen in Dante (sect. 2 above), in Purgatory as conceived by Catholics a longer or shorter time of atonement is required before entrance into Paradise, the length perhaps depending on how much time still remains on the sinner's salvation account.

From the point of view of Christian moral theology, this is a quite convenient if not entirely risk-free doctrine, since a sinner who is cutting it close might be able to be somewhat careless about his behavior on earth at the lower and middle levels of morality. If a sudden death does not draw a line across his balance sheet, Purgatory remains as a last corrective. There, with the support of pious prayers, the final and probably still merciful reckoning will take place. For exactly these reasons the very strict moralist (and rather un-Latin) reformer Jean Calvin fundamentally objected, in his *Institutio Christianae religionis* (1536), to the Catholic doctrine of Purgatory and dismissed it as presumptuous prattle: "This Purgatory is constructed out of many blasphemies."[31]

If a Christian adhering to Calvin's reformed doctrines cannot count on a helpful Purgatory where the failings of a sinful life can if necessary be reckoned up in a final court of mercy, then a pious or not so pious prudence commands this sinner to seek, already in his earthly existence, to atone, through an asceticism not unlike that of Purgatory, for as many of the sins on his account as he can. This may indeed diminish to some extent the quality of his life-time on Earth, but in any event it protects him—assuming that his reckoning is correct—from the dreadful prospect of a possible damnation at the Last Judgment. If this ascetic way of life also happens to produce, as an unintended but nonetheless welcome side effect, so much profit that it provides the basis for economic prosperity in this world, this can be taken as a sure sign that the individual's account in the register of atonement time is developing favorably, which is crucial for his salvation. Anyone who has foregone physical enjoyment of time here on Earth and practices self-denial with pious intentions has already anticipated his individual Purgatory in this world and after his death can consequently count on participating without delay in eternal bliss.

REVOLUTIONARY HISTORICAL TIMES, IN RAPID FIRE
Heine, Marx

Revolutions are historical events that result, in a short (sometimes extremely short) time, in the overthrow of power relationships, with far-reaching consequences for the political and social order. The French Revolution was first conceived, not by historians but rather by contemporaries, as an event whose practical consequences history would develop with increasing speed. Thus in 1830 the July Revolution that put the "bourgeois king" Louis-Philippe on the throne was still seen by more than one contemporary observer as the end and culmination of the historical epoch that had begun in 1789. For some time, France seemed to be a country in which freedom had finally won out.

The good news spread quickly from Paris over all over the world. In Germany, it reached even the island of Helgoland, where Heinrich Heine was living at that time. He was fascinated by the message of freedom emanating from Paris and immediately decided to go live there, far from the hindrances and threats of Metternich's restoration government. Soon after he arrived in Paris, he undertook the "pacific mission" (*pazifike Mission*) of opening the intellectual world of the Germans to the French and that of the French to the Germans. In this mission he was guided by a view of history according to which the French Revolution in 1789 inaugurated a historical cycle in France that lasted about forty years, until the "second" French revolution of 1830. In these few decades Heine distinguished four historical phases: first, the Revolution and Robespierre's reign of terror; second, the reign of Napoleon, first as Consul and later as Emperor; third, the Bourbon Restoration; and fourth, the rule of the bourgeois king Louis-Philippe, which he regarded as liberal within certain limits. Within this short historical period of a little more than one generation France changed more than it previously had in many centuries. This was for France an era of "action."[32]

What happened at this same time on the other side of the Rhine? According to Heine's cyclical conception of history Germany also underwent fundamental change, primarily through its four great thinkers, Kant, Fichte, Schelling, and Hegel. They represent on the German side a thought-cycle that is just as important for history as the French revolutionary action-cycle, and that also passed through four phases more or less simultaneous with those on the French side. This is Heine's "thought-action" model, inspired by Madame de Staël and Hegel. With the aid of this philosophical model he constructs a historical parallel between France and Germany whose captivating elegance is typical of his way of thinking.[33]

In this form, however, the thought-action model still lacks the historical dynamics that Hegel's philosophy of history implanted in Hegelians. Actions such as those that so powerfully transformed French history do not arise out of nothing. They presuppose a phase of powerfully transformed thoughts. In France, this was the period of the Enlightenment, which with its thinkers also constituted a historical thought-cycle. As history has shown, in France there were two time-cycles of about forty years each, the first characterized by enlightened thought and the second by revolutionary acts. The regularities of the philosophy of history require that these correspond to two cycles on the German side, but these cycles are out of phase with each other, so that up to the time of Hegel's death (1831), Germany, as the "belated nation" (Plessner, *verspätete Nation*), had passed through only the historical thought-cycle. From this it can also be concluded, however, that in accord with the French model an action-cycle is to be expected in Germany, immediately following the thought-cycle.

This is the historical background against which Heine, from the point of view of his Parisian present, can predict a great revolution in Germany within a single generation's time (given the "slow" Germans, perhaps a few years longer). This revolution will turn society upside down, just as a generation earlier the French Revolution had turned it upside down, for good and for ill. This German revolution will seem even greater and more powerful than its French predecessor because in their thought-cycle German philosophers produced even more powerful ideas than had the *philosophes* of the Enlightenment in France. The expected revolution in Germany will therefore be the definitive revolution, and indeed a "world revolution"—an expression coined and put it into circulation by Heine in 1842.[34]

However, we find this same expression in Heine's work as early as 1835, in the famous final section of *On the History of Religion and Philosophy in Germany* (*Zur Geschichte der Religion und Philosophie in Deutschland*), a book whose German edition (though not the French one) was immediately prohibited by the censor. In it, Heine gives prophetic and apocalyptic expression to the expectation that within a short time a revolution will begin in Germany and spread to the whole world:

> German philosophy is an important matter that concerns the whole of mankind, and only our descendants will be able to decide whether we should be blamed or praised for having first developed our philosophy and then our revolution. . . . Do not laugh at the dreamer who awaits the same revolution in the phenomenal realm that has taken place in the intellectual realm. Thought precedes action the way lightning precedes thunder. However, German thunder is like a German man who is not very agile and comes along rather slowly—but he will come, and when you hear a crashing such as has never before been heard in the history of the world, you will know that German thunder has attained its goal. At this sound aristocrats will fall dead out of the air and lions in the farthest deserts of Africa will tuck in their tails and retreat into their royal dens. A play will be staged in Germany in comparison with which the French Revolution might seem only a harmless idyll.[35]

. . .

Only a year later, in his verse satire "Germany, A Winter's Tale" ("Deutschland, Ein Wintermärchen," 1844), Heine returns to this prophetic vision and gives it the form of a nocturnal apparition. On a quiet, moonlit night in Cologne, the narrator is followed by a "masked guest" who, when asked to explain himself, finally reveals his emblematic nature:

> I am no ghost of the past,
> No bundle of straw rising from the grave,
> And I am no friend of rhetoric,
> Nor am I very philosophical.

I am practical in nature,
Always quiet and peaceful.
But know this: what you devise,
I carry out, I do it.

And though the years pass by,
I will not rest until I transform
Into reality what you have thought;
You think, and I—I act.

You are the judge, and I the bailiff,
And with a servant's obedience
I execute the judgment you have made,
Even if it is unjust.

In Rome, in olden days,
An axe was carried before the consul,
And you also have your lictor, but
The axe is carried behind you.

I am your lictor, and constantly
follow you with the shining
Axe of judgment—I am
The act of your thought.

Ich bin kein Gespenst der Vergangenheit,
Kein grabenstiegener Strohwisch,
Und von Rhetorik bin ich kein Freund,
Bin auch nicht sehr philosophisch.

Ich bin von praktischer Natur,
Und immer schweigsam und ruhig.
Doch wisse: was du ersonnen im Geist,
Das führ ich aus, das tu ich.

Und gehn auch Jahre drüber hin,
Ich raste nicht, bis ich verwandle
In Wirklichkeit, was du gedacht;
Du denkst, und ich, ich handle.

Du bist der Richter, der Büttel bin ich,
Und mit dem Gehorsam des Knechtes
Vollstreck ich das Urteil, das du gefällt,
Und sei es ein ungerechtes.

Dem Konsul trug man ein Beil voran,
Zu Rom, in alten Tagen,
Auch du hast deinen Liktor, doch wird
Das Beil dir nachgetragen.

Ich bin dein Liktor, und ich geh
Beständig mit dem blanken
Richtbeile hinter dir—ich bin
Die Tat von deinem Gedanken.

These lines clearly reflect the motifs and topoi of the French-German parallel described above, and at the same time they suggest that the underlying thought-action model is to be realized within a short time. Here Heine, traveling from France to Germany heavily laden with ideas, encounters an alter ego who follows him as a politically active self. The thinker is at the same time the judge, and in this role is also called a consul; the actor is an executioner who in Roman dress is called a lictor. However, the fact that, contrary to the usual Roman custom, the lictor carries his axe not before but after the consul is at the same time the metaphorical expression of the historical sequence in which action follows thought and not the other way around.[36]

· · ·

When Heine wrote his "Germany, A Winter's Tale," he was a close friend of Karl Marx, who had also emigrated to Paris a short time before.[37] Heine was a frequent guest in Marx's home, where his writings were not only read with pleasure but also subjected to critical commentary. However, it is likely that the young Marx—at that time, he had just turned twenty-five—was at least as much stimulated and influenced by Heine, who was more than two decades older, very experienced, and highly respected in both Germany and France. To put it another way, in 1843–44 Marx was at least as much a "Heinean" as

Heine was a Marxian or even a Marxist *avant la lettre*. This is especially clear in a crucial essay Marx published in Paris in 1843–44—that is, at the time Heine wrote "Germany, A Winter's Tale"—under the title *On the Critique of the Hegelian Philosophy of Right (Zur Kritik der Hegelschen Rechtsphilosophie)*.[38] This essay has a special place in the early history of Marxism because in it the proletariat first emerges in Marx's thought as a politically active force in history, and it thus marks a decisive revolutionary turning point in his thinking.

Closer examination of this important text and the conditions under which it was produced shows that it can only be understood against the background of Heine's German-French parallel and its short-term temporal phases. It seems that Heine, who at first allowed himself to be lent and soon willingly assumed the authority and aura of a student of Hegel, was intensely queried about him by Marx. In this exchange, the Hegelians' thought-action model, with which Heine was very familiar, along with its application to the relationship between France and Germany and the corollary idea of Germany's historical belatedness, must have played an important role. Support for this view can be found first of all in the fact that Marx published the previously mentioned essay in the *Deutsch-französische Jahrbücher*. This journal, to which Heine also contributed, was founded in Paris by Karl Marx and Arnold Ruge with the express purpose of making the philosophical idea of a historically necessary parallel between France and Germany more widely known to readers in both countries, in order to establish mutual hospitality between the two nations.[39]

If we now compare Heine's "literary" text with Marx's "political" one, we can easily see that they agree on numerous points. These concern above all the thought-action model, which both Heine and Marx regarded as fundamental, and which Marx formulated as follows with respect to France: "In politics, the Germans have *thought* what other peoples have *done*." Furthermore, we find in Marx the same historical periodization of this model that we have already encountered in Heine. Thus in Marx we read that the French had had their great period of action immediately following their Enlightenment, and that this period lasted from 1789 to 1830, whereas the same time in Germany was *still* one of deep thought. If, as Marx thinks, there is a necessary and rapidly emerging transition between the metaphysical principles of thought and action, then in Germany a great phase of action is imminent, and the resulting change in all social relationships will be as deep as the thought of German philosophers was.

Thus the young Marx echoes an idea Heine had expressed long before when he concluded his essay in the *Deutsch-Französische Jahrbücher* with a moving peroration that announces, in a quasi-prophetic way, the great revolution in Germany: "When all the internal conditions are met, the *German day of resurrection* will be foreshadowed by *the crowing of the French cock*."

However, at this point Heine and Marx part ways. Heine's rather light-hearted nature led him to be so sure of his elegant historical model that he saw the short-term passage from thought to action as a kind of natural law as inevitable and as prompt as that connecting lightning and thunder.[40] This is the political metaphor that guides Heine in all his writings, and with its help he orchestrated numerous literary incarnations of the German-French parallel and of the thought-action model associated with it. Yet we also find in Marx, and even in the essay on Hegel, the same thunder-and-lightning metaphor; in his work this metaphor is bound up, as it is in Heine, with the expectation of an imminent revolution. But Marx does not believe as firmly and absolutely in the natural-law character of this sequence, for "It is not enough that thought impel toward action, reality must impel itself toward thought." This should be understood as follows: According to Marx's political convictions, revolutionary action rapidly follows philosophic thought only when a historical force is present that brings about by violence the transition from thought to action, from philosophy to revolution. This historical force is the proletariat. Marx writes:

> Just as philosophy finds its *material weapons* in the proletariat, so the proletariat finds its *intellectual weapons* in philosophy, and as soon as the lightning bolt of thought has deeply struck this naive popular ground, the emancipation of *Germans* into *men* will take place.[41]

In this connection we must nonetheless mention not only that with his doctrine of the revolutionary potential of the proletariat Marx deviated from Heine, but also that the latter, with his notion that a world revolution would take place by itself in his own lifetime, moved further and further away from Marx. For this there is much evidence in Heine's writings, and especially (though not exclusively) in the work of his last years. For example, in 1855, a year before his death, he foresees an imminent time of revolution in which the people, that "clumsy sovereign," will have necessarily seized power: "They cut down my laurel forests and plant potatoes instead."[42]

In fact, however, this dreadful vision was to be realized in a very different way and far later in history than Heine expected; on both sides of the Rhine the passage from thought to action took much longer than Heine and Marx had assumed. And so these realizations were recorded on another page of world history.

Short and Shortest Times

The Greeks had two concepts for expressing time: *chronos* and *kairos*. Both were personified and allegorized in human form: Chronos as an old man, Kairos as a young one. Given this difference in age, they followed very divergent paths in mythology, art, and science, as Erwin Panofsky in particular has described.[1]

As far as Chronos is concerned, we note first that because of the similarity of their names, from the earliest times he was confused and equated with the venerable god Kronos, the father of Zeus. The Romans called Kronos Saturn, and he was highly respected as a god of agriculture. Identified with Chronos, Kronos/Saturn was worshiped in both Greek and Roman culture as a god of time (Isidore of Seville: "Chronos, id est tempus"), and his attributes, as Tiepolo's (1696–1770) painting *Il Tempo* shows, are the scythe or sickle and the hourglass. But this god was feared because he devoured his children, the years, as is vividly shown in Goya's famous painting *Saturn Devouring his Children* (1819–23).[2]

The conceptions of time associated with Kronos/Saturn are based on long periods and biological rhythms. This god takes his time; he *is* time. Thus Isidore of Seville (560–636) proposes two alternative etymologies for the name Saturn: the latter comes either from the word "to sow" (*a satu*) or alludes to "length of time, since he sated himself on the years" (*a temporis longitudine, quo saturetur annis*).[3]

Cultural history long remembered Kronos/Saturn. As an example, we may mention Goethe's early poem "An Schwager Kronos" ("To the Mail-coach Driver Kronos," 1774), whose theme is the journey of life, made—appropriately enough for the period—in a mail-coach. Here, Kronos is the driver (*Schwager*). In the opening verse, his passenger, who is still young, urges him to hurry (*Spute dich, Kronos!*). Uphill and down goes the wild ride, "swiftly into life" (*rasch ins Leben hinein*). And just as the passenger, "striving and hoping," had imagined when setting out on his journey, much happiness—perhaps including a girl's "healthy glance" (*Gesundheitsblick*)—awaits him. Even if in old age the journey leads to Orcus, the host at Hell's gate will say respectfully, "A prince is coming!" Goethe, who had not yet settled in Weimar, ends his time-poem in jaunty *Sturm und Drang* manner with a trumpet call. Years later, as he traveled by mail-coach across the Alps on his way to Italy, Goethe was to complain about the vehicle's "terrible speed." In Italy, he encountered a new, still faster vehicle that the Italians called a *velocifera* (from Latin *velox*, "fast," and *fero*, "I carry"). The *velocifera* must have impressed Goethe, for he derived from it, as Manfred Osten reports, a neologism that he used to criticize European society's terrible addiction to speed: "Everything velociferous!" (*Alles veloziferisch!*).[4]

.   .   .

We have an entirely different picture of the god Kairos, who represents the "right" time. This young god has wings on his shoulders and feet, and maintains his equilibrium even when dancing on a knife-edge. His attribute is the scale, but his most striking characteristic is that his head is nearly shaved; only his forelock remains. If a mortal wants to seize and hold this nimble god, he must approach the latter head-on and try to grasp his forelock. If he fails, his hand finds no purchase on the smooth skull, and the right time has already passed and escaped him.[5]

Among the Romans kairos is usually called *occasio* and interpreted as "auspicious opportunity." Yet the word *occasio*, which is feminine in gender, does not offer a meaningful allegory in comparison with Kairos's masculine allegory. To some extent, this gap was later filled by the feminine allegory of the (capricious) goddess Fortuna.[6]

Nonetheless, in archaic Greece *kairos* played a role in science, and once again in the work of Hippocrates.[7] We recall the first part of his first aphorism, which goes: "Life is short, art is long." Immediately afterward we read "(for) opportunity is fleeting." Hippocrates' Greek is *ho de kairos oxys*. Thus hardly has Hippocrates noted the chronological asymmetry of life (*bios*) and art (*technē*) than he refers, in the same medical context, to the other Greek conception of time: *kairos*, which we have already examined in its mythological and iconographic form. Hippocrates clearly emphasizes the temporal character of *kairos* by using the predicate "fleeting" (Greek *oxys*, Latin *praeceps*). As he sees it, this is a circumstance that further sharpens the asymmetry between art and life already noted in the first part of the aphorism. The fleeting nature of time as Kairos makes the brevity of time as Chronos/Kronos still shorter than it already inherently is.

In Galen's detailed commentary on the Hippocratic aphorisms, the clause regarding kairos is examined as closely as the preceding clause regarding Chronos. In particular, Galen asks why the "right time" for successfully treating a patient is so easily missed in medical practice. The main reason is that the bodily conditions that are influenced by medical art are in constant flux (*rheon aei*). Hence the favorable opportunity for treatment also changes very quickly. As Galen puts it, kairos is not only "fleeting" (*oxys*) but also "extremely fleeting" (*oxytatos*). Therefore the physician's activity is limited to a very narrow, short span of time (*oligochroniotatos*).[8]

This last remark of Galen's is not without importance for understanding the concept of kairos. The "right time" that the physician has to recognize and use to heal his patient is not a "point" but rather a span of time, even if it is short. There is no need to seize Kairos's forelock in a sudden reflex action. There is always time to wait and weigh—as is suggested by the scale the allegorical youth carries in his hand. Yet the time for acting always remains very limited, and kairos-time offers no opportunity for hesitation or delay. It is just this fact that constitutes the incomparable value of kairos-time in the art of medicine.

The idea of kairos was already detached from the art and science of medicine in antiquity. This is best shown by Cicero, who discusses kairos-time (*occasio*) in one of his writings on rhetoric. He defines "opportunity" as a span of time (*pars temporis*) that in some respect shows a particular suitability (*idoneam opportunitatem*) for acting or not acting. Consequently, kairos is a conception of time in which a quantitative characteristic (shortness) is semantically connected with a qualitative one (the advantage of the opportunity).[9]

．　．　．

In the later age that was, as a result of the Enlightenment, no longer protected from the provocations of modernity, that is, in the age of pre- and early Romanticism, kairos dropped out of view. We can say that in this period the short span of time in which one could nimbly seize opportunity's forelock is reduced to a single kairos-point that must be instantly grasped. This reduction to a point deprives kairos of temporal duration but increases its intensity, so that the dramatic "instant" is distinguished from all other conceptions of time by its powerful intensification and sublimation.

The result of the process of sublimation is called the "fulfilled moment" (*gefüllter Augenblick*). Even so self-possessed person as Goethe was unable, during his *Sturm und Drang* period, to escape the fascination of this tremendous moment, and he wrote unforgettable lines describing the poetic feelings it evoked. Thus many of his Sesenheim poems are immediate expressions of experiences of kairos, in which greeting and bidding farewell are blended into *a single* poetic moment. Later on, his "Alexis and Dora" (1797) is a particularly clear example of a kairos-poem, and it has been interpreted as such by several of his interpreters, even if they disagree over details.[10] Let us listen to the young Alexis, who must say farewell to his beloved and is now looking back on the moment when they confessed their love to each other:

> I was alive only for a moment, but it outweighs
> All days, which now seem to me tiny and cold.

> Nur Ein Augenblick war's in dem ich lebte der wieget
> Alle Tage, die sonst kalt mir verschwindenden, auf.

In these lines we see that chronos-time is the reservoir from which this memorable moment is filled. In the poetically sublime limiting case, it is the full length of a lifetime that is concisely summed up in this kairos-time and that constitutes its fullness and even excess. Dora, we later learn, calls it "eternal" (*ewig*).

We have already seen (chap. 3, sect. 4) how Goethe embodied the motif of time in the figure of Dr. Faust. In Faust's boundless striving Goethe sublimates time into the "highest moment" that in the exhilaration of its suddenness not only outweighs a long human life with its joys and suffering, but also—regardless—promises or foreshadows a view of eternity in a moment that overpowers everything temporal.[11] Whether nonetheless this temporal drug that Mephistopheles administers to the ever-striving Faust is truly guaranteed to work right up to the latter's final breath, or will instead lose its tonic or toxic effect when a higher power intervenes, still remains a debated question among readers and admirers of this mighty chronos and kairos drama.

STARS AND HOURS · Schiller, *Wallenstein*; Stefan Zweig

As a historian and dramatist, Friedrich Schiller (1759–1805) reflected at length on the propitiousness and unpropitiousness of great moments in human action and about the "kairos myth" (Hillebrand)—skepticism clearly dominating his thinking.[12] The theme plays a particularly large role in his historical dramas, but always with rational reservations regarding "quiet madness," as Mary Stuart calls this idea and temptation. In Schiller's play bearing her name, it is her impetuous supporter Mortimer who wants to calculate life solely by the dimensions of the moment: "Life is/ Only a moment, and Death is only one too!"

Thus it is no surprise that in doubtful situations as well Mortimer calls for bold action at the favorable moment. But even as he speaks, his political downfall in the battle for power between the Queen Elizabeth and Mary Stuart is already imminent, and he knows it:

> Seize the moment! Anticipate it!
> . . . .
> And at the last instant my heart
> Will freely open, my tongue will be unleashed.[13]

The stage direction immediately following this passage reads: "He stabs himself with the dagger."

Similarly, in Schiller's historical drama *Don Carlos* the Marquis of Posa sees his great dialogue with the king ("Give them freedom of thought!") as a kairos-situation: "One must take advantage of a moment like this, which comes but *once*" ("Nützen / Muß man den Augenblick, der *einmal* nur / Sich bietet"). But he misgauges the weight of his words. In all that Posa says, the king hears only the stammering of a "strange dreamer." And so for the Marquis of Posa the play ends as a tragedy, which he experiences, however, as kairos: "O Carl, how sweet, how great is this moment!" ("O Karl, wie suß, / Wie groß ist dieser Augenblick!").[14]

As might be expected given its subject matter, Schiller's Wallenstein trilogy is ultimately about missing the moment of kairos. At the center of this great historical drama set during the Thirty Years' War stands Wallenstein, who is the Holy Roman Emperor's military commander but is already toying with the idea of leading his army to Sweden and switching from the Catholic to the Protestant side. His influence at the court in Vienna is waning, and he no longer trusts his good fortune. So he has decided to rely on astrology and expects the stars to tell him when the right time for action has arrived.

Wallenstein's good fortune, as he and his entourage understand it, is the "old luck" that—like his model, Caesar—he has always been able to "captivate" (*bannen*) up to this point in his life as a warrior. But now at this turning point in a long, cruel conflict it must finally be seen whether his luck in war is right in leading him to seize the "opportunity" (*Gelegenheit*—the term Schiller repeatedly uses in referring to the *occasio* of kairos) by decisive action, since "the moment has come"— with these words he urges even a woman, the countess, to act.

Has the moment really come? Wallenstein hesitates. He sees that his "fateful hour" (*Sternstunde*) has not yet arrived. Jupiter, "his" star, is still not in the right constellation. However, Wallenstein's general, Illo, sees this as a mere excuse made by a man who prefers to "temporize" (*temporisieren*) rather than act. Thus Wallenstein has to listen to Illo lecture him on the laws of kairos:

> Oh! Take advantage of the hour before it slips away.
> In life so seldom comes the moment
> That is truly important and great. Where a
> Decision has to be made, many things
> Must by luck intersect and come together—
> And only a few scattered ones prove to be
> The lucky threads, the opportunities

That constitute, but only when compressed
Into a *single* point in life, the heavy, fruitful knots.

Oh! nimm der Stunde wahr, eh' sie entschlüpft.
So selten kommt der Augenblick im Leben,
Der wahrhaft wichtig ist und groß. Wo eine
Entscheidung soll geschehen, da muß vieles
Sich glücklich treffen und zusammenfinden—
Und einzeln nur, zerstreuet zeigen sich
Des Glückes Fäden, die Gelegenheiten,
Die nur in *einem* Lebenspunkt zusammen-
Gedrängt, den schweren Früchteknoten bilden.

Wallenstein's answer is curt: "The time has not yet come." [15]

Finally—but this comes in the third part of the trilogy, entitled *Wallenstein's Death*—the moment designated by the stars does arrive. Wallenstein says, "Now we must act, quickly . . ." But it is already too late. While he was hesitating, others—the imperial authorities, the Swedes, and the defectors supposedly under his command—have been acting. They now all know what Buttler knows: "His [Wallenstein's] lucky star has fallen." Wallenstein has not seized his kairos, if indeed there ever was one for him, and now his time is inexorably running out. As Bruno Hillebrand has noted, "It is the pressing, compressed moment that makes Schiller's plays so dramatic."

In the fortified city of Eger, in Bohemia, where Wallenstein is waiting for the Swedish army to arrive, the conspirators are already planning to kill him. Their leader is Buttler, who is blunt about luck in war:

It is a great moment in time,
Favorable to the bold and resolute.

Es ist ein großer Augenblick der Zeit,
Dem Tapfern, dem Enschloßnen ist sie günstig.

Wallenstein will be murdered in his sleep. He will not even have time to repent or atone. When Gordon asks the fortress commander to allow Wallenstein at least this short reprieve, the conspirator Buttler contemptuously rejects the request:

Gordon (*holds him*): Only one hour!
Buttler: Let me go. What good
    Can a short reprieve do him?
Gordon: Time is
    A wonder-working god. In one hour run
    Many thousand grains of sand, as quickly
    As thoughts move in the minds of men.
    Only one hour! . . .
    What can an hour not do!
Buttler: You remind me
    How precious minutes are.

Gordon (*hält ihn*): Nur eine Stunde!
Buttler: Laß mich los. Was kann
    Die kurze Frist ihm helfen?
Gordon: O die Zeit ist
    Ein wundertätger Gott. In einer Stunde rinnen
    Viel tausend Körner Sandes, schnell wie sie
    Bewegen sich im Menschen die Gedanken.
    Nur eine Stunde!
Buttler: Ihr erinnert mich,
    Wie kostbar die Minuten sind.

Thus Wallenstein's murderer will shorten still more the moment of his death.

However, in a certain sense the fortress commander at Eger has the last word in this play. Adopting the historian's point of view, he concludes that "On this moment the world depends." Is it also a kairos? If so, is it for good or for evil? Later historians can say no more than the commander could.[16]

. . .

With Gordon's last words still ringing in our ears, let us now turn to another military leader: Napoleon. The year is 1815. The army led by Napoleon, who has just returned from Elba, and the troops allied against him are seeking a decisive battle. The fate of Europe is to be determined near the Flemish village of Waterloo. Will this battle some day be counted among "humanity's fateful hours" (*Sternstünden der Menschheit*)? That is how Stefan Zweig saw it. In the widely read collection of stories he published under this title (1927), one of the stories—probably the best—is devoted to the Battle of Waterloo. It is titled "The World-minute of Waterloo" ("Die Weltminute von Waterloo"), and subtitled "Napoleon, 18 June 1815").[17]

In this story, Zweig's hero is not Napoleon but rather Marshal Grouchy, whom Napoleon has assigned to attack Marshal Blücher's army and prevent it from joining up with Wellington's. But unfortunately for Napoleon, Grouchy proves to be a "mediocre man" (*mittlerer Mann*) who cannot find the Prussian army in the pouring rain and does not dare to override Napoleon's order. So Grouchy goes on vainly looking for his opponent while Napoleon has long since been engaged in heavy fighting against Allied forces on the battlefield. Without reinforcement from his marshal, Napoleon has to resist the enemy's attacks alone and is forced to pull back. The retreat becomes a rout. Napoleon's fate is finally sealed. The next chapter in European history will be called the Restoration.

Why then should this battle be called a "fateful hour" (*Sternstünde*)? Fateful for whom? Perhaps for the victors, Blücher and Wellington? A painting by Adolf von Menzel (1858) depicts the meeting of the two victorious commanders on the battlefield at Waterloo. But the Prussian and the Englishman sit quite peacefully on their horses and greet each other politely. That is not how a fateful hour looks. It is more likely that the opportunity to reinforce Napoleon that was prevented by fate and by Grouchy's stupidity constituted once again a "favorable opportunity" neglected for only a short time ("die entscheidende Sekunde"), but nonetheless irretrievably. Thus it can be called a fateful hour *ex negativo*, since in it Napoleon's star finally sinks and Europe's star does not rise.

BETWEEN AUSTERLITZ AND WATERLOO · Émile Zola

In Émile Zola's novel *Money* (*L'Argent*, 1892), historical time plays a role. But the book is less a historical novel than a novel that makes use of historical material. Zola cuts up this material like a jigsaw puzzle and rearranges the most striking pieces, along with many fictional elements, into a new and imaginative whole. In *Money*, Zola draws not only on the recent past (the 1870s and 1880s) but also on the history of the Napoleonic period, from which he borrows in particular the symbolic names of Austerlitz (victory) and Waterloo (defeat). [18]

So far as the recent past is concerned, it is the bizarre story of the dazzling rise and disgraceful fall of a speculative banking and investment firm, the Union Générale (1878–82), that especially fascinates Zola and provides him with crucial elements of his novel's action. But in this story of a Parisian scandal there is also an allusion to intrigues of the great financial manager John Law, who a century and a half earlier had already induced the French to make extremely risky speculations by investing in the dubious shares of his Compagnie des Indes. This earlier financial adventure also ended in a frenzied crash (1720).

The first hero of Zola's "naturalistic" novel about the stock market is a man with the significant name of Saccard (sacker, thief). As a businessman, he is a gambler and an adventurer. The stock market is the most tempting arena for such a person. But at the end of the nineteenth century, the dealings of a man like Saccard are no longer limited to France and Europe; money is to rule the whole world. And so Saccard founds the *Banque Universelle* as the instrument of his quasi-Napoleonic will to power, with the goal of controlling the flow of money all over the globe. This early global player needs only four or five hundred million more before he can say: "The world belongs to me!" ("Le monde est à moi").

The leap made here into (still rudimentary) globalization was made possible, at the period in which Zola's novel is set, by an invention that revolutionized the communication of news. This invention was the telegraph, which allowed investors to follow developments on the stock market almost as they were occurring. Depending on rapid changes in market news, the price of shares could be driven frantically up or down. This made those who invested in stocks all the more aware that on the stock market, time, and indeed short time, is the true medium of wealth, and that this time in the form of speed has to play a role if one wants to make money through speculative investments.

So Saccard also lives a "turbulent" life (*une vie tumultueuse*) that is determined in every phase of its being by the shortness of time. His sanguine temperament, which incessantly drives him to act with great haste, here stands him in good stead. He runs his bank in a constant state of stress, as if "galloping." All his decisions are based on the inspirations of the moment, sometimes as he wakes up in the morning.

During the day, he keeps a nervous eye on the clock, never has a minute to spare, and fears nothing more than visitors that steal his time by talking too slowly: "Say what you have to say, quickly, I'm in a terrible hurry!" ("Dites, vite, car je suis horriblement pressé"). Naturally, in such a life there is no time for love, not even for the Baroness Sandorff, who as a businesswoman has a precise idea of the "price of time" (le prix du temps).

This chronic lack of time connects Saccard with his bitter enemy, the Jewish banker Gundermann. The latter also has not a minute to lose. He gets up at five in the morning and runs his business, as Saccard does, "at a gallop." As a result, this rich man has developed a stomach problem that obliges him to follow a strict diet. But his temperament is entirely different from Saccard's: he is phlegmatic. The passions to which Saccard is prey are alien to him. He runs his investment firm with constancy and cold precision. He also strives never to show any exterior sign of haste. And one more thing differentiates him from Saccard: he has a wife and children, and as a pious Jew, he always has time for his family.

In the sixth chapter of the novel action on the stock market is dramatically centered on the duel between Saccard and Gundermann. Saccard is the aggressor. He has assembled all he needs for the great "coup" by which he hopes to finally bring his old opponent to his knees. Everything takes place in a single day, between the opening bell of the stock market at one o'clock and the closing bell at six o'clock. One must almost hold a watch in one's hand while reading the description of these five hours, so closely does money now obey time. On this day, Saccard wagers all his money on a rise in the market. He buys whatever is for sale. He has good reasons for speculating on the premise that the armed conflict over Venetia in which the French emperor and Austria are involved will be peacefully settled. And this is what happens. Shortly after the opening bell, at exactly a quarter past two, the news Saccard is expecting hits the market like a "thunderclap": Austria will cede Venetia to France (in history, 1866). Peace has arrived, stock prices quickly rise, and Saccard has had his "fateful hour," his victory and triumph, his Austerlitz. Now he is the master of the economic world, and Gundermann's empire has been—almost—destroyed.

But that is not the author's last word in this magnificent novel. In chapter 10, the sun of Austerlitz suddenly ceases to shine on Saccard's affairs. Carefully and with mathematical precision Gundermann has prepared his revenge. His "coup"—he also uses this stock-market term for kairos—is to be the precise opposite of Saccard's great triumph. Gundermann speculates on a fall in prices. Once again, in the course of a single market session, a few minutes or even seconds will decide whether in the frenzy of buying and selling one of the two competing investment strategies will win or lose. Once again the two adversaries are opposed like generals on a battlefield the coordinates of which lie, however, in time, in the limited time that dominates the stock market. And the one who has reckoned on the shortest time will be victorious.

The victor is Gundermann. This day at the stock market is his fateful hour. For Saccard, on the other hand, it is a day of defeat, of catastrophe, his "Waterloo." An irony of fate or perhaps *nemesis divina* ("easy come, easy go") has caused a man who has founded his financial empire on speculating on rising prices to be brought down by his opponent's speculation on falling prices. Now the game is up. Justice is on the march. But even in his prison cell this Napoleon fantasizes about globalizing his Austerlitz and his Waterloo.

5

The Economy of Limited Time

When the shipwrecked Odysseus is washed up on an island unknown to him, he is concerned about the kind of people who might live in these alien regions. "What *are* they here—violent, savage, lawless? / or friendly to strangers, god-fearing men?" His concern is unfounded. He is on the island of Scheria, among the Phaeacians, who peacefully carry travelers from island to island and are known for their hospitable nature. They immediately show Odysseus the warmest hospitality that can be imagined in the Greek world.

Homer reports all this in detail in the course of several books of his *Odyssey*. In these books we find a paean to hospitality, and even, if we read the text didactically, a handbook of good behavior for the host and for the guest. In this case, the host is the Phaeacian king, Alcinous, and the guest is a shipwrecked man who only the reader knows is Odysseus. His identity is unknown to the king and his people, and the rules of hospitality leave it up to the guest to decide whether he wants to reveal his name and his ancestry. It suffices that he is *ho xenos*, which means both "stranger" and "guest." The guarantor of this kind of hospitality is Zeus, who as the supreme god is the highest host of all strangers (*Zeus xenios*). Thus the stranger is treated "like a god."

However, this fortunate situation does not go on indefinitely. There is a three-day limit on hospitality, which is to be observed by both host and guest. How strictly is this limit determined? Not very. There is a certain temporal flexibility, depending on how the arrival and departure are calculated. In the shortest version, the day of arrival and the day of departure are counted, so that they are separated by a single day. But a generous host can extend his guest's stay one or two days by not counting the day of arrival and/or the day of departure. Then, however, the limit of hospitality has been reached, and the guest becomes a stranger again and has to take care of himself.

The hospitality Odysseus experiences is in accord with these rules. While he is still on the beach where he was washed up, Princess Nausicaa and her servants come to meet him and offer him her people's hospitality, as she has been taught to do. She knows that "Every stranger and beggar / comes from Zeus." When they arrive in the city, Alcinous confers on the stranger the status of guest and invites him to take his rightful place at the royal table—the place of honor, which the eldest son must cede to him.

The Phaeacians honor their guest as if he were himself of royal rank. The most comfortable couch and the most delicious foods, music and dancing, poetic and athletic contests: the guest is given the best of everything, and not only in adequate but in extravagant quantity. Just as no one asks his name, no one asks when he plans to leave. But gifts are already being secretly prepared for presentation on his departure.

Modestly, since Odysseus is behaving as a guest, he asks no more than the minimum three-day stay. But his hosts won't hear of such a short visit and urge him to be so generous as to extend it. As modern Westerners, we can't help being surprised that the Phaeacians seem not to take their own interests into account. Have they, out of sheer delight in giving, abandoned calculative reason? Do the laws of economics no longer hold under the noble rules of hospitality? No, they hold here as well. When Odysseus in fact gives in to his host's urging, the latter is happy, but at the same time he thinks the expenses of hospitality are going to be too great for him to bear alone. He must get his people to share the costs. If we project his behavior onto a larger scale and into modernity, we can say that he creates a supplementary budget to deal with unplanned expenses.[1]

This kind of thing can happen with any guest. However, Odysseus proves to be a special kind of guest in that in return for the gifts he has been given he offers his hosts a gift in return—a gesture highly prized in ancient laws regarding hospitality. As a man who has traveled widely and has seen a great deal of the world, Odysseus is a wonderful storyteller. He "repays" his hosts' hospitality by telling stories about a world of which, even though they are themselves travelers, they know nothing until Odysseus, drawing on his long experience, reveals it to them. In Homer's epic, these stories constitute no less than four full books. They deal with a long span of time stretching from the fall of Troy to Odysseus's arrival in Phaeacia. In this lengthy tale, the astonished hosts not only learn what is happening in the wider world but also hear about the Underworld, into which Odysseus has descended in the course of his adventures. He is not merely a reporter but also a poet, comparable to Dante, whose inspired verses also tell about the Afterworld. As a guest of the Phaeacians, Odysseus repays their splendid generosity with a kind of literary gift. This is not a matter of trade and exchange in accord with the rules of economics, but rather an exchange of gifts of the kind described by the French anthropologist Marcel Mauss, through which, it seems to me, an original and prototypical relationship between hospitality and literature is established that will have a continuing influence on subsequent history.

One of the stories Odysseus tells during his long narrative is worth special attention in relation to hospitality, as the latter's hostile counterpart.[2] I refer to the episode about Odysseus's perilous encounter with Polyphemus, the one-eyed Cyclops who hates all strangers, and for whom neither divine nor human law is holy. He scorns the law of hospitality as well, as Odysseus and his twelve companions learn as soon as they enter his cave in search of help and protection. When Polyphemus returns, he at once seizes and tortures them. They have to spend three anguished days and nights—again, the three-day period!—in the power of the terrible Cyclops, and during this time they see what the inverted image of Greek hospitality can look like. No appeal to hospitable Zeus can prevent the embittered Cyclops from killing and devouring two of his prisoners on each of the three nights. The only favor he shows Odysseus himself is to guarantee him that he will be the last to meet this cruel death. That is supposed to be the monster's peculiar gift to his guest.

But a further violation of the law of hospitality proves to be the undoing of the Cyclops himself. Against all the norms of hospitable behavior, he immediately asks Odysseus his name. The wily Odysseus replies: "No-one." Under the protection of this non-name the Greeks finally succeed in blinding the Cyclops and escaping from the cave. Instead of the refused guest-gifts, they carry off rich booty. Thus does Zeus himself punish Polyphemus for his disregard of hospitality.

. . .

Between Homer and the present lies a long stretch of history. Sometime during this almost immeasurable period of time something decisive must have happened to hospitality, so that today it is no longer considered as unquestionably valid as law and ethics but rather, if valid at all, then only as a poetic image, almost a mirage. Chronologically, this change can be said to have taken place in Europe in the second half of the eighteenth century, though it had distant precursors and its exact date cannot be fixed. This is quite clear in the *Encyclopédie* published by Diderot, D'Alembert, and their collaborators, in which the historical knowledge and political will of the Enlightenment are summed up with lexicographical precision. In this work we find a concise farewell to the old hospitality:

> Hospitality has thus naturally been lost in all Europe, because all Europe has taken to traveling and trading. The flow of money through bills of exchange, the security of the roads, the ease with which one can go anywhere in safety, comfortable ships, mail coaches, and other vehicles, and also the inns that offer travelers lodging in all towns and cities and on all highways—these have replaced the generous assistance associated with the hospitality of the ancients.

> L'hospitalité s'est donc perdue naturellement dans toute l'Europe, parce que toute l'Europe est devenue voyageante et commerçante. La circulation des espèces par les lettres de change, la sûreté des chemins, la facilité de se transporter en tous lieux sans danger, la commodité des vaisseaux, des postes, et d'autres voitures; les hôtelleries établies dans toutes les villes et sur toutes les routes, pour héberger les voyageurs, ont suppléé au secours généreux de l'hospitalité des anciens.[3]

To put it briefly, it is the ongoing victory of time over space that has fundamentally changed the economic conditions of hospitality and may also have caused it gradually to disappear. However, in German lands Adolf Franz Friedrich Freiherr von Knigge (1751–96) does not go so far in the famous theory of hospitality he published in 1788, on the eve of the French Revolution, under the title *On Dealing With People (Über den Umgang mit Menschen)*.[4] This still very readable handbook was written by a worldly-wise commentator on the morals and customs of his time, and it contains a chapter on hospitality that still states that "Hospitality toward strangers is highly recommended." But Knigge's warm recommendations of this ancient virtue nonetheless now turn out to be quite reserved, since in modern times "foolish curiosity, presumption, and restless activity" drive people in great numbers ("haufenweise") to travel. Thus the host is advised to be careful: "It is surely forgivable if in view of the steadily increasing extravagance and the abuses of people's good-heartedness seen in our time, a man consults his purse before he opens his house, kitchen, and cellar to every idler and sponger."

Thus even with the best will in the world, one can no longer offer the many guests for whom travel has been made so easy the abundance and superabundance of hospitality that originally characterized the exercise of this virtue. This makes it all the more important in practicing this abridged hospitality to abide by the old three-day limit, formulated somewhat crudely in an Italian proverb: "A guest, like a fish, stinks on the third day" ("L'ospite, como il pesce, puzza il terzo giorno"). Knigge tones down this proverb somewhat: "Both a fish and a guest remain good in the house for no more than three days " ("Ein Fisch und ein Gast halten sich beide nicht gut länger als drei Tage im Hause").

CLASSICISM AS ECONOMY OF TIME · From Plutarch to André Gide

When money was invented in Greece in the sixth century BC, it was at first used not simply as a convenient medium of exchange but rather as "holy money"—according to Bernhard Laum's hypothesis in a highly regarded book with this title. During ceremonial sacrifices in the temple, sacred coins struck by the state were intended to function as symbolic representations of the sacrificial animal, usually a calf or bull, and to placate the gods by sacrificing "only" a valid symbol rather than slaughtering an animal. Hence early coins often bore the image of a sacrificial ox and in this way unmistakably indicated their sacred function. The Latin word *pecunia* (money), which is derived from the word *pecus* (animal, esp. cattle) provides a semantic reference to this cultural context. In Greece and Rome, it was only later on that this pious sacrificial economy was considered a more convenient, time- and money-saving substitute for the natural economy.[5]

The Greek language confirms this view, since the word *nomisma* (coin), derives from the noun *nomos*, which means "convention," "agreement," "law." Aristotle was the first to draw attention to this connection, writing in his *Nicomachean Ethics*:

> Money was introduced among humans on the basis of an agreement or convention (*nomisma*). For that reason it is called money (*nomisma*), because its exchange value derives not from nature but from human law and custom (*nomos*). That is why we can modify the value of money or even make it worthless.[6]

Thus Aristotle is already defending what historians and numismatists call a nominalistic rather than a metallistic theory of money. This view is closely related to a theory of language widespread in ancient times that maintains that human language is not natural but rather based "only" on human convention.

In the works of the Roman rhetorician Quintilian (first century AD) we find a comparison that became standard during many centuries of European cultural history: "One must deal with language the way one deals with money, which is minted with the public stamp" (*utendumque sermone ut nummo cui publica forma est*). This suggests that one must be just as sparing with words as with money.[7]

How much this "set its stamp" upon later periods can be shown here by means of three witnesses. Francis Bacon writes: "Words are the tokens current and accepted for conceits, as moneys are for values."[8] Similarly, Leibniz, who already expressly takes into account the existence of paper money and coins, writes in his "Unanticipated Thoughts Regarding the German Language" (one of the few works he wrote in German):

> In using language we must note especially that words are signs not only of ideas, but also of things, and that we need signs, not only in order to convey our meaning to others, but also to help our ideas

themselves. For just as in great trading cities, and in gambling and other matters, people do not always pay in money, but instead bills or markers are given pending final payment or reckoning, so the understanding uses images of things, especially when it has many of them to think about, since without signs it would have to consider a thing anew every time it came up.[9]

We see that here Leibniz repeats the historical transition from a natural economy to monetary economic forms with explicit reference to language and understands this transition as a progressive rationalization of the use of signs. When there is "too much to think about," the simplest possible signs and the shortest possible paths of thought are required. The use of signs saves time.

Goethe is also fond of the comparison between coins and ideas. He cites with approbation the Latin tag *Verba valent sicut nummi* ("Words have value, as much as money") but immediately offers the following gloss: "But there are different kinds of money: there are gold, silver, and copper coins, and there is also paper money. The former are more or less real, the latter is based only on convention." The introduction of paper money fascinated him, as the corresponding scene in the second part of *Faust* shows, but at the same time the audacity of this invention disturbed him, since he accords paper money, in contrast with coins, "only" a conventional validity.[10]

In this four-stage development we see a historical process leading from the sacrifice of animals to coins bearing their image, then to coins with conventional stampings, and finally the verbal signs of language, which for their part open the way to the introduction of paper money. Each of these stages can be understood as a semantic "substitution" that reduces costs and achieves the same or a similar goal with a smaller expense of time.

. . .

We return again for a moment to the ancient world, in which so much of what still occupies the modern world was already a concern and experienced and reflected upon. I am referring to the Greek writer Plutarch (c. 46–c. 120 AD), who served as a priest of Apollo in Delphi. His most important work is the *Parallel Lives*, where he recounts the lives, for example, of the military commanders Alexander and Caesar and of the orators Demosthenes and Cicero. Less celebrated is his double portrait of the Greek politician Phocion (397–18 BC) and the Roman Cato the Elder (234–149 BC), who was known and feared among Roman politicians for his proverbially strict morals. In rhetoric, Cato was guided by the curt maxim: "Stick to the subject, the words will follow!" (*Rem tene, verba sequentur!*) Time is too short for superfluous words.

Plutarch reports that the Greek Phocion was a kind and friendly man, so that people even nicknamed him "the good." Only one characteristic marred his popularity. He always wore a dark and gloomy face, so that people found it difficult to believe that he was kind and friendly. And his discourse was just like his face. It was curt, severe, and unornamented. Once, as he sat in a popular assembly sunk in thought and looking morose, as usual, he was asked the cause of his apparent displeasure. He replied, "I'm thinking about what else I can cut out of the speech I want to give." With such character traits, Phocion had not only friends but also enemies who soon found a reason to condemn him to death. Like Socrates, he emptied the cup of hemlock.

The writer Plutarch, however, admired Phocion without reservations. What pleased him most in Phocion was the latter's concise way of speaking. He praises it in these terms: "His oratory, like small coin of great value, was to be estimated, not by its bulk, but its intrinsic worth."[11] Here Plutarch offers splendid praise of linguistic brevity that met with great response in history. In our further reflections we will keep in view his aphorism as a classical formula, and we will encounter it many forms and characteristic metamorphoses.

This holds for no period of European literary history more than for the classical period of French literature, the seventeenth century. In its ideas about style, this classicism is expressly opposed to the European Baroque and replaces the latter's "more" by "less." Therefore its poetic "rule" is that a classical author does not need to shine by the abundance and wealth of his verbal expression; on the contrary, his work is characterized by strict discipline and economy of expression. Thus French classicism scornfully disapproves of the waste of time that marked the preceding Baroque age and conceives itself in accord with Plutarch's classical formula of economy as an age in which literary quality is based first of all on conciseness and brevity of expression.

These were the characteristics that won a reputation for French classical authors in their nation's literary history: Corneille, Racine, and Molière in drama, La Rochefoucauld and La Bruyère in commentary on morals, Pascal in philosophical/theological prose, Madame de Sévigné in epistolary literature, and La Fontaine in the art of the fable. Along with Boileau, the main theoretician of this classicism, all these authors saw in any kind of "excess" (*abondance*) a defect and a violation of the "rules" of literature. Two critics of language in the seventeenth century, Bouhours and Vaugelas, explicitly called this a poetics of temporal economy.[12]

Should we therefore consider the classical principle, at least so far as France is concerned, only another word for an economy of time? That is a question that can best be answered by the Duke de la Rochefoucauld. His *Maxims and Reflections* (*Maximes et Réflexions*) is a masterpiece of aphoristic remarks on behavior in society. Writing in this genre, La Rochefoucauld employs a disciplined rhetoric in which brevity of expression occupies the highest stylistic rank. He defines this rhetoric as follows: "True eloquence consists in saying everything that is necessary, and only what is necessary" ("La vrai éloquence consiste à dire tout ce qu'il faut, et à ne dire que ce qu'il faut"). The literary historian Louis Van Delft called this the author's "soldierly style." But it is at the same time his classical style. This is seen even more clearly in what is probably his most famous aphorism: "It is the mark of great minds to communicate many things in few words" ("C'est le caractère des grands esprits de faire entendre en peu de paroles beaucoup de choses"). This apparent paradox sums up the very elegant economy characteristic of French classicism.[13]

This economical conception of classicism spread from France to many other European countries. I give here only three examples taken from Germany: Lichtenberg, Schopenhauer, and Nietzsche. In his *Waste Books* (*Sudelbücher*) Lichtenberg, a great natural scientist and essayist, notes that in his writings he wants to "convey in the smallest possible number of words that one has thought a great deal." Schopenhauer, in his essay "On Writing and Style" ("Über Schriftstellerei und Stil"), makes the same point in similar words: "Using many words to convey a few thoughts is in general an unmistakable sign of mediocrity, while putting many thoughts into few words is the sign of eminent minds." Finally, Nietzsche—who in questions of language and style learned most from Schopenhauer—returns with similar thoughts to the Romans, writing on the occasion of a text by Horace that fully satisfied his idea of classical style: "This minimum in the range and number of signs, this maximum sought in the signs' energy—all this is Roman, and in my view, sublime *par excellence.*"[14]

To conclude these reflections, let us turn our attention once again toward France, where classicism remained very much alive well into the twentieth century, as we can see in a particularly striking way in the works of the novelist André Gide. The occasion for Gide's confession of enduring classicism was trivial: an interview with a reporter for the literary review *Renaissance* who asked what classicism meant for him. In his answer, Gide appealed to the great authors of the seventeenth century and gave a concise definition of his own idea of classicism: "Classicism is the art of expressing the most by saying the least" ("Le classicisme, c'est l'art d'exprimer le plus en disant le moins"). We have nothing time-consuming to add.[15]

LIVING FASTER, TALKING LESS · Jean Paul, Madame de Staël

The works of the German writer Jean Paul Richter (1763–1825) have not won him a reputation as a paragon of speed, acuity, and laconic conciseness. Yet in his three-volume (!) *Propaedeutic to Aesthetics* (*Vorschule der Ästhetik*, 1804–13) there is a section on "Brevity of Speech" (*Sprachkürze*) in which brevity is prized above all because it opens the way into the reader's mind for wit—which in Jean Paul means genius conceived as an "abbreviator of understanding." "Brevity is the body and soul of wit," he writes, and he finds this "lex minimi" most clearly exemplified in Greece among the Spartans, in Rome by Cato, Tacitus, and Seneca, in England by Bacon and Gibbon, and in Germany by Lessing. Is the love for brevity fairly equally distributed over all nations, then? In his view, this is not the case, for at least in the philosophical prose that had recently become so important nothing seems to him to surpass "French abbreviation." And he adds: "For the understanding, which desires (like the imagination, for example) only relationships, not living figures, no brevity is too brief, for brevity is clarity." On the other hand, German philosophy, especially Kant and the Kantians, had better be translated into French, for they "make themselves obscure" in their books, not through their brevity (Horace!), but rather through their uneconomic repetitions (or as Jean Paul puts it, "through their doubling," *durch ihr Verdoppeln*).[16]

That things are objectively as different in Germany and in France as he describes them here results, according to Jean Paul, from the difference in the ways in which the two languages are constructed. For him, French is a naturally brief language. "In contrast, German makes everything long and accordingly broad, long in words and vague in ideas." Thus it is not surprising that the spice of wit is unequally distributed on the two sides of the Rhine.

．　．　．

Let us turn now to the French point of view, and look at Germany through Madame de Staël's eyes in her book *On Germany* (*De l'Allemagne*, 1813).[17] The precondition for the influence exerted all over Europe by this book was the fact that throughout the eighteenth century German intellectual life had remained virtually unknown in France. However, at the beginning of the nineteenth century, two decades after the French Revolution, the time for a revolution in literature as well had come in France. This literary revolution drew support from English Romanticism and also elicited an almost sensational interest in German Romanticism (which for the French included the whole of Weimar classicism). In the van of this movement stood Madame de Staël, who had become interested in Germany by reading August Wilhelm von Schlegel. She made two long journeys through the enigmatic land on the other side of the Rhine. The highpoint of her trips was her visit to Weimar, where she spoke with Goethe and Schiller—in French, naturally, for she spoke not a word of German.

Madame de Staël traveled to Germany with the firm intention of perceiving with enthusiasm a country of poets and thinkers that had remained up to that point hidden from French eyes, and she admired it almost without reservation. But in her comparison of the two countries she does not even attempt to discover any similarities between the Germans and the French. Her picture of Germany is based on a complete contrast (*le contraste le plus parfait*) with France, more or less as it had already been observed by Jean Paul, whom she knew and cited.

The most immediate impression Madame de Staël had on her journeys in Germany was that of a very much slower pace of life. In contrast to France, and especially to the world capital Paris, where people knew how to live quickly (*vivre vite*), life in Germany strolled along peacefully and dreamily (*une rêverie calme*), since this people "never hurried" (*il ne se presse jamais*). In the first chapter of her book we read: "It seems to me that time moves more slowly there than elsewhere" (*Il semble que le temps marche là plus lentement qu'ailleurs*). But even the characteristics of German slowness (*lenteur*) and inertia (*inertie*)—this is her perception, and she is inclined to be positive about everything in Germany—advances German literature and thought more than it inhibits it, since in Germany everything can be felt more "deeply" than in France.

Only in one respect does the dreamland on the other side of the Rhine remain naturally alien to her. Already as a young girl her entertaining talk pleased the guests in her mother's salon, and in Germany, even in Weimar, she missed terribly her Parisian elixir of life, the art of brilliant conversation. From the point of view of Paris—the "capital of conversation"—linguistic intercourse among Germans, and especially their intercourse with foreigners, seemed strangely clumsy and ponderous. Above all, in conversation the Germans lacked any "talent for abridgement" (*le talent d'abréger*). In making this judgment, she may have been recalling her countryman, the moralist Joseph Joubert, who had written in one of his aphorisms that "the homeland of brevity" (*la patrie de la brièveté*) was to be sought only in France.

Thus Madame de Staël devoted an entire chapter of her book to "The Spirit of Conversation." As a Frenchwoman, it is clear to her that without a quick wit (*rapidité d'esprit*) no conversation can possibly meet Paris standards. In conversation all *longueurs* are banned, since a slow speaker is immediately interrupted. Germans, however, do not like this, and after such interruptions they stubbornly return to what they were saying.

How do the Germans acquire this annoying characteristic, when they are otherwise so likeable? Madame de Staël is convinced that it has to do with a property of the German language, which because of its grammatical structure (placement of the verb at the end of a subordinate clause!) tends to produce long, endlessly long sentence structures. A witty conversation involving an exchange of brief remarks cannot consist of such sentences.

Is Madame de Staël right about this? Perhaps, or perhaps not, but one wonders from what sources she derived her knowledge of the language, since she did not know any German. She always spoke with

Germans in French, so that Schiller once complained that when conversing with Germans whose knowledge of French was less than perfect she spoke so breathlessly fast that a listener "had to transform himself completely into an organ of hearing in order to be able to follow her." Under these unequal circumstances it was not easy for the people in Weimar to show the Frenchwoman the natural tempo of the German way of thinking and speaking. We are nonetheless quite willing to acknowledge that on the whole this acute observer from France judged more or less correctly the differing relationships to time in life, speech, and writing on the two sides of the Rhine (which may or may not remain much the same today).

6

The Drama of Time in Short Supply

EPIC IS LONG, DRAMA IS SHORT · Aristotle

The theory regarding epic and drama that Aristotle develops in his *Poetics* can be summed up in a quasi-Hippocratic formula: "Epic is long, drama is short."[1] Aristotle did not invent *ex nihilo* the rule implicit in this formula; instead, he gleaned it from an examination of the great models of Greek literature available to him and carefully generalized it. For models of epic, he looked above all to Homer's *Iliad* and *Odyssey*. He considered the tragedies of Aeschylus, Sophocles, and Euripides to be exemplary dramas. We do not know precisely how comedies fit into this picture, since the part of Aristotle's *Poetics* devoted to comedy was lost, to the great regret of posterity (of which Umberto Eco made himself a spokesman in his bestselling novel *The Name of the Rose*).

Homer's epics are long; each of them consists of twenty-four books. Depending on the situation, it takes a certain number of days to listen to them as oral performances or even to read them (out loud). Consequently, audiences cannot listen to the whole poem at one sitting; its oral performance or reading must be interrupted by temporal hiatuses. During this time, there are other things to do, for example, eating and drinking, working and sleeping. After such "disturbances," however, the audience must be able easily to pick up the thread of the story again.

In his *Poetics*, Aristotle made a plausible case that the epic poet must take these temporal conditions into account, as Homer had already done in an exemplary way. Despite the poem's length and "epic breadth," the listener must be able to keep the overall story in view. This is best achieved if the action narrated, notwithstanding its possible complexity, is a unified whole. An epic's proper length, Aristotle says, can be recognized by the fact that "the action from beginning to end can be surveyed in a single glance." Later periods turned this recommendation into an unbreakable rule requiring "unity of action."[2]

Even more than for epic, the right length is a primary quality of drama. A play, during whose performance the audience gathers under relatively uncomfortable conditions in the theater, should be viewed in a *single* sitting (during which spectators also often stood), and must therefore necessarily be much shorter than an epic. We know, for example, that during poetic competitions three plays were performed on each day. Under these temporal limitations, a play's action could not cover a time as long as the ten-year periods narrated in the *Iliad* and *Odyssey*. Hence a play must have an action that "is easily imprinted on the memory." With the models of the great tragic poets in mind, Aristotle is thinking of an action that does not exceed twenty-four hours in length. As he puts it, "Tragedy seeks, so far as possible, to remain within one revolution of the sun or to exceed it by little." That is a short span of time, which should probably be conceived as extending from sunrise to sunrise, that is, twenty-four hours. As a result of the authority posterity granted Aristotle, as "the philosopher," this pragmatic rule based on experience was erected into an absolutely valid precept requiring "unity of time" on the stage. If a playwright failed to observe this rule, he lost all claim to be a classical author.[3]

To the unities of action and time, which are very closely related, was later added, in order to complete the triad, the "unity of place," which limited the change of settings on the stage. At any rate, the more a dramatist wanted to be counted a classical author, the more he had to make "the three unities" (in France, *les trois unités*) the center of the Aristotelian poetics that acquired canonical status in Europe from about 1550 onward.[4]

As we have seen, in Aristotle's *Poetics* twenty-four hours are prescribed as the limit for a dramatic action—one day and the following night, or as he puts it (in his pre-Copernican language), the time from sunrise to sunrise.[5] For the French dramatist Pierre Corneille (1606–84), the same twenty-four hours last two days. Corneille, whose play *The Cid* (*Le Cid*, 1636) made him famous in France, was a respectful reader of Aristotle and an adherent to his poetics. But he came from Normandy, whose inhabitants are known for their peasant wiliness. So in *The Cid* he cleverly spread the period Aristotle allowed him—too short to achieve his poetic goals—over two days. He managed this trick by calculating the twenty-four hours from noon to noon, so that he had the afternoon of the first day and the morning of the second day, along with the intervening night, into which to fit the action of his play.[6]

During such a night, much can happen that completely changes the situation, and that is exactly what happens in *The Cid*. The night falls between the third and fourth acts. Thus this "tragi-comedy" (as Corneille sometimes called it) can consist of a tragic part and a non-tragic part, and finally end in a reconciliation without a catastrophe.

Corneille's play is set in Spain, at the time of the Reconquista. The Moors and the Christians are fighting for control of the country. Near Valencia, the opposing armies are preparing for battle. This takes place at night, under cover of darkness. In the early morning hours, a decisive battle is fought, resulting in a complete victory by the Christian Spaniards. Their leader, Don Rodrigo (in French, Rodrigue) henceforth bears the (Moorish) honorific title of a *Cid* ("lord").

In this play, Rodrigo is not only a glorious hero but also a young lover. He loves Jimena (in French, Chimène), who for her part "does not hate" him.[7] Her father has given his consent to their marriage, and the wedding is soon to take place. But suddenly tragedy unexpectedly breaks into this idyll of family concord. The two fathers get into a violent argument that ends with Jimena's father publicly boxing the ears of Rodrigo's more elderly father. This is a terrible insult. Honor is involved.

The rest of the action on this first day of the drama follows the relentless laws of honor point for point. Spain is, after all, the ancestral homeland of honor in Europe. Since Rodrigo's father is too old to defend his honor by force of arms, this duty falls to his son. Rodrigo must not hesitate or wait a single unnecessary moment before "washing away with the blood of the offender" the stain his elderly father has incurred through his public humiliation. He kills Jimena's father in a duel.

So now Rodrigo has involuntarily become Jimena's mortal enemy. She also has a "lofty soul" (*l'âme haute*), and she is well aware of what honor demands of her in a situation where her father has neither brothers nor sons to avenge him.[8] Contrary to her innermost feelings, she must take revenge on her father's "murderer," even if—as a woman—she cannot do so with her own hand. This is the tragic predicament constructed in the brief action-time of the first part of the play, and it seems to all persons of honor an insoluble dilemma. Thus in his famous monologue Rodrigo complains, "On both sides I face infinite disaster" ("Des deux côtés mon mal est infini").[9] But Jimena unhesitatingly obeys the "point of honor" and does not ask whether honor, when it conflicts with love, is undoubtedly the higher value. Thus in this conflict neither party can abandon honor and surrender to love. Is there no way whatever to escape this tragedy?

Fortunately for both parties, night comes. The night adds a few hours to the narrowly limited time of the dramatic action. At first light, there is even still time for the decisive battle against the Moors, which Rodrigo, serving as a commander, makes into a glorious victory for the Spaniards. And after this victory over the Moors, the king still has enough time to intervene in the affair of honor involving his nobles. As sovereign, he is not bound by the laws of the point of honor. Rather, all honor proceeds from him, and is only "lent" to other persons of rank. Thus the king stands above honor in the same way that honor stands above love. Under these conditions, the king can appear in the second part of the play as a *deus ex machina* and suspend the fatal principle of "blood for blood" (*le sang par le sang*) in a splendid act of forgiveness. The kingdom will be in need of Rodrigo's military prowess.[10]

In the same pronouncement, the king releases Jimena from the bonds of her duty to avenge her father, and she may hope soon to be united with Rodrigo—though not immediately, within the short time of the play's action, but only after a year, when time will have healed these wounds:[11]

> Time has often made legitimate
> What seemed impossible without crime.

> Le temps assez souvent a rendu légitime
> Ce qui semblait d'abord impossible sans crime.

Has Corneille succeeded, as it seems, in using this elegant resolution of the dramatic conflict to eliminate all the problems of time in poetics? The author himself discusses this question, notably in the *Examen* of the play he wrote later on.[12] In the self-critical sections of this text he concedes that the rule limiting action to twenty-four hours gave him much difficulty in writing this play, since it forced him to unduly compress certain elements of the action ("la règle des vingt et quatre heures presse trop les incidents de cette pièce"). Had the work not been a play but rather an epic or a novel, he would not have needed, for example, to include royal audiences for Jimena in such quick succession, in the evening and on the following morning. Corneille is well aware that this haste contradicts every rule of courtly etiquette, according to which two audiences of this kind with a petitioner should be separated by at least a week of "patience," and in a narrative work enough action-time would surely have been available. However, because of the narrowly limited time of drama, such violations of protocol unfortunately became unavoidable. Literary criticism also showed patience and understanding for this argument, and learned from it: classical writers sometimes reckon time differently, but not entirely differently.

TIME OUT OF JOINT · Shakespeare, *Hamlet*

Our discussion of Shakespeare's *Hamlet* (1603) will be limited to consideration of it as a tragedy of short and dramatically limited time.[13] From the point of view of its dramaturgy, however, the play does not at first seem to involve conspicuous relationships to time. For example, Shakespeare handles rather loosely the Aristotelian "unity of time." The play covers an undefined period of a few weeks, which is used, however, less for the dramatic action than for the time-consuming travels of some of the *dramatis personae*. But these intervals do not detract from the "unity of action," which Shakespeare, as a playwright and actor, considers very important.

Within this rather inconspicuous time frame of Shakespearean dramaturgy, an inner drama of time unfolds in the play that has already begun long before the curtain goes up. A terrible crime has been committed in Denmark. The old King Hamlet has been secretly murdered by his brother Claudius. Now the murderer himself rules over the land as its king. Here we must pay close attention to the circumstances of this fratricide. As King Hamlet slept unsuspecting in his garden, the murderer surreptitiously poured a fast-working poison into his ear. His victim never awakened again. The murderer did not give his victim even the smallest length of time for repentance, atonement, or confession before this sudden death. Had the king perhaps burdened his conscience with a "mortal sin"? Then his sudden death would have deprived him not only of earthly life but also the eternal salvation of his soul. This possibility of an inevitable consequence of his act the murderer willingly accepted, as modern jurists say, and may even have intentionally planned such a "soul murder " to be part of his act.[14]

Did King Hamlet in fact have to go before the Divine Judge with a mortal sin outstanding on his salvation account? Fortunately, in his lifetime he had committed only venial sins that can be atoned for in Purgatory, that is, through a punishment limited in time, as we have learned from Dante (see above, chap. 3, sect. 2). How do we know all this so precisely? We learn it as readers or spectators of the play, from the words of the "ghost" or "spirit" who appears in two important scenes and reveals to Hamlet the truth about this "murder most foul."[15] But who is this spirit, and where does he come from? He tells us himself:

> I am thy father's spirit,
> Doomed for a certain term to walk the night,
> And for the day confined to fast in fires,
> Till the foul crimes done in my days of nature
> Are burnt and purged away.

In the framework of the theology of the Elizabethan period, this statement is unambiguous. Old King Hamlet's spirit, which appears around midnight, that is, at the witching hour, cannot come from Hell. He is a "poor soul" from Purgatory, as is indicated by the three expressions he uses to describe his punishment: "for a certain term," "fires," and "burnt and purged away." These clearly determine his abode as Purgatory, understood as "a temporary Hell" (Le Goff), and cannot be attributed to any other part of the Beyond. From this we can conclude that the murderer's "hellish" intention to deny his victim even the smallest time to concern himself with his eternal salvation succeeded only in part ("temporarily"). But at the same time, this enables the spirit, as a revenant allowed to return to Earth for a strictly limited time at the witching hour, to uncover the crime retained in his memory even after death.

The "foul murder" of his brother is not Claudius's only attempt to make time an ally in his intrigues. He reveals another battle over time immediately after the murder.[16] He quickly usurps the throne. Hastily, without respecting a decent—though in his case, feigned—period of mourning, he immediately marries Queen Gertrude who, as the king's widow, apparently does not know that Claudius has murdered him. In the speech from the throne given early in the play before the assembled court, the new king justifies taking power after so short a span of time by referring to the war that currently threatens the Kingdom of Denmark. "Haste" is therefore called for, and this state of emergency supersedes all longer-term concerns. Let us note how quickly this unscrupulous strongman is able to act politically. His murder is an act that fundamentally changes all temporal relationships in the state. From this moment to the end of the play, when fate finally catches up with this royal scoundrel as well, the only time that counts is time shortened by violence, a time of which Claudius, as the new king, has made himself the master.

.   .   .

In contrast to his criminal antagonist, Hamlet has a sense of time that has grown—in accord with the psychological and medical theory of humors, which Shakespeare knew well—out of his melancholy temperament.[17] Part of this temperament is the "old," Saturnian time, which extends over long cycles in life. The "new" time, calculated in short periods, is alien to his nature. Thus since the strongman Claudius has ruled Denmark, Hamlet has been a stranger in the country, and he can't stop thinking, prudently and sometimes obliquely, taking time to make decisions that are heavy with consequences, and always acting somewhat later than the new reason of state requires of a prince and pretender to the throne.

In the five scenes in the first act of the play, in which the dramatic situation is set forth, Hamlet is immediately confronted by the accelerated temporal relationships the new king has put into effect. Thus what most angers him at the beginning, when he still considers his father's death an accident, is the "most wicked speed" with which his royal mother married again after his father's death: "Frailty, thy name is woman!" Never will he understand what has happened in so short a time in the soul of his still beloved mother—and the reader can't understand it either.

However, Hamlet immediately understands one thing after the spirit of his dead father has revealed Claudius's "rank" crime and left him with the words "Remember me!" It is instantly clear to Hamlet what these words mean for him as the son and legitimate heir to the throne: "Haste me to know't, that I with wings as swift / As meditation or the thoughts of love, / May sweep to my revenge!" Thus Prince Hamlet knows that blood must be avenged with blood, immediately, in the shortest possible time, as a prince's code of honor demands.[18]

Nevertheless, Hamlet cannot betray his slow nature. He still has doubts that prevent him for a while from carrying out the task assigned him without delay. He is also not sure how broad his revenge should be. Did his mother know about the murder, or did she consent to the new marriage "only" out of womanly weakness? Hamlet needs time to put his thoughts in order, and at first he hides behind a veil of ambiguous words and confusing acts. But all the time he is well aware that long hesitation and delay are unworthy of a prince and can disgrace him. That is how we should understand his bitter complaint about time at the end of this scene:

> The time is out of joint, O cursèd spite
> That ever I was born to set it right.[19]

The dark melancholy expressed in these verses is noticed by King Claudius, and the suspicions it awakens drive him to act still more quickly. First, he orders Hamlet to seek distractions. "Pleasures" and "pastimes" are to keep him at a safe distance from the shortened time of which the king is master. Hamlet, who soon sees through these ruses, decides to play along and acts as if he had plenty of time. Thus, for example, he walks about the castle with a book in his hand, reading "words, words, words" as if he had nothing better to do. He jokes with the courtier Polonius and flirts with his daughter, Ophelia. He seems delighted when a theater troupe is brought in to cheer up the court.

Hamlet takes advantage of this opportunity to shape the play in his own way. During a rehearsal, he arranges with the actors to modify the script in such a way as to cause consternation in the king and queen, and through this "play within the play" the king is unmasked. This *demonstratio ad oculos* dissipates Hamlet's remaining doubts.[20]

What obstacles can now prevent Hamlet from immediately taking revenge on his father's murderer? "Spiritual" obstacles. We see here again how the frightening theological idea of death without a short time for repentance and grace, as a "soul murder" for all eternity, plays a role in the dramatic action. The passage to keep in mind in this respect identifies the favorable opportunity (kairos) Hamlet fails to seize when he comes upon the king praying alone in a room in the castle.[21] Just as he has raised his dagger to strike the fatal blow in this isolated place, it occurs to him that even a treacherous murderer, if he dies unexpectedly but while in reverent prayer, has a claim to merciful forgiveness in the Beyond. This murderer must not die with such a guarantee of grace, since he himself denied the victim of his crime any opportunity for remorseful prayer. Thus Hamlet lets this unique moment for taking his revenge pass. By an irony of fate, he does not hear (although the theater audience probably does) the words Claudius murmurs as he rises from his knees: he has not been able to summon his soul to reverent prayer, and thus according to theological judgment would have been, in the event of his sudden death, condemned to eternal damnation.

Now it's Claudius's move again. In another conspiracy against Hamlet's life, he urges young Laertes, whose father Polonius Hamlet has accidentally killed, not to let his legitimate need for revenge cool by any kind of delay. In this exchange, the king makes it clear that the natural course of time is hateful to him because, with its "abatements and delays," it can calm "the spark and fire" that lead to prompt action.[22]

However, in the later course of the action Claudius does not rely solely on Laertes, and he uses the power of limited time against Hamlet in still another way. Hamlet's former fellow students in Wittenberg, Rosencrantz and Guildenstern, willingly agree to help the king by taking the prince off to England in great haste and there arranging for him to be immediately killed ("our hasty sending," "with fiery quickness," "this speedy voyage," "delay it not"). To this end Claudius gives Hamlet's traveling companions a secret letter urging the English king to have the prince immediately beheaded ("no leisure bated") upon his arrival in England. The executioner should not even take time to sharpen his axe. Everything is to be done so quickly that Hamlet loses his life without having a chance to repent ("not shriving time allowed.") Thus for him, as for his father, "murder of the soul" is part of the plan.[23]

The plan misfires. The (slow) Danish boat with Hamlet on board is overtaken by a (fast) pirate ship. As a result, after a few turbulent episodes the prince returns to Denmark earlier than expected. Unscathed, he enters the royal court again. Hamlet has won this battle over time by luck. But will he retain his advantage?

The last act of the play begins with the highly poetic scene in the cemetery, at the grave of the court jester Yorick, whose antics long amused the royal court. Holding Yorick's skull in his hand, Hamlet sees himself at the limit of his life-time. But he still discovers, in the tight temporal net of intrigue and pursuit Claudius never tires of weaving, a narrow window of opportunity of which he has to take advantage: "The interim is mine."

In fact, at the end of the play the prince still has time to engage in a final duel that neither he nor his opponent will survive. Yet in their last words, both he and Laertes call upon Heaven and agree to forgive each other, in the Christian manner. Thus they can die with trust in God. On the other hand, Hamlet's mortal enemy, King Claudius, though he also has at the end a small amount of time, does not use it to seek salvation. Not realizing that Hamlet has struck him with Laertes' treacherously poisoned rapier, he thinks he has "only" been wounded ("I am but hurt")[24] and carelessly fails to make the quick prayer that might have still have saved him at his last breath. Thus, in accord with the law of retribution (*lex talionis*) and through an irony of fate, the life of this criminal ends without a trace of remorse or atonement, and thus also without rescue from eternal damnation, an outcome he himself had vainly intended for his victims.

SALADIN LEARNS TO TAKE HIS TIME · Lessing, *Nathan the Wise*

The Sultan Saladin is a powerful man. However, he is short of money ("tiresome, desired money!") to wage war and to hold court as ruler. Thus it occurs to him to borrow money from Nathan, a Jew also known as "Nathan the rich" or "Nathan the wise." But the thing must be done without too much delay, for the powerful man is not only short of money but also short of time.[25]

So he has the Jew sent for. Nathan is to come to him quickly. Saladin is already impatiently waiting on his throne, and he receives the visitor in a curt manner that augurs no good: "Come closer, Jew! Closer! All the way! Don't be afraid!" All his words of greeting are commands, and the latter is a threat. Nathan understands these signs very well.

Then begins a conversation directed by the sultan. "Your name is Nathan?" "Yes." "The one people call the wise?" This is the ruler's way of confirming that Nathan is indeed the man of whom he has heard. Nathan keeps a low profile and answers Saladin's questions prudently and as humbly as possible. Thus the sultan gets the impression that he doesn't need to waste time on unnecessary courtesies. Lessing's stage direction: "He leaps up." Then comes the familiar formula that comes so easily to the lips of the powerful and announces that their patience is at an end: "Let's get to the subject!"

Now we're probably going to talk about money, Nathan surmises. Carefully, he holds out the prospect of a favorable price ("a price for a friend"). But for the time being, the sultan rejects this subject. The sultan also seems uninterested in discreet reports about the machinations of his enemies that the widely traveled Nathan might be able to provide. Using another formula for cutting short discussion ("In short!") he tells the merchant, to the latter's surprise, what he seems to want to talk about: "Since you're so wise, then, tell me: Which faith, which Law do you find most credible?" To justify this question—unusual for a sultan and amazing for a merchant—Saladin explains that the pressures of governing have not so far given him time to "ponder" this question. Generously, it seems, he even gives the Jew time to think and leaves him alone for a few moments. But even in making this concession he remains the ruler who is in a hurry: "Quick, think about it! I'll be right back!"

Nonetheless, Nathan now has a short time to reflect. He senses a trap. He knows that among strangers it is not common to bring up, just like that, such an explosive philosophical and theological question. And it is certainly not fitting to blurt out what one is after. For questions of this kind, more time is required: "There's a knock at the door, but it's only heard when someone comes as a friend." So he remains more than ever on his guard, and does not take the sultan's words "at face value."

After a short absence, which is just long enough for the merchant's monologue, the sultan, who had gone only into the next room, comes back. Once again he uses a formula to cut off discussion, this time, however, cunningly attributing it to the merchant: "I didn't come back too quickly for you, did I?" It's time for Nathan to tell him "the truth."

This removes Nathan's last doubt that in this question the stake is high, namely: "Life and limb! Good and blood!" But now the opportunity has also come for his wisdom to prove its worth. Humbly, the Jew advises the sultan to raise the question about the truth value of the three monotheistic religions not directly, but rather—taking a little time—indirectly: "Would you permit me to tell you a little story (Geschichtchen)?" Note that Nathan uses a diminutive to refer to his parable of the three rings. Saladin is oriental enough to swallow this bait and immediately falls into a trap that we can call the patience trap. He tells Nathan that he must "tell a good tale" and impatiently urges him to begin: "Go on! Tell the story! Tell the story!"

His listener's impatience is very convenient for Nathan. He uses it to purchase what he needs most for a good story: permission to tell his story in great detail. Now he has gotten time on his side, and he begins his tale in a leisurely fashion: "Many, many years ago there lived a man in the East . . ." He goes on to say that this man has a precious ring, every detail of which is worth describing, for instance, that the ring is set with an opal in which "a hundred beautiful colors play." We also learn that the man wants this precious ring to remain in his family and to be bequeathed to that son in each generation who is dearest to his father. Thus the hard-pressed Jew uses up a great deal of narrative time: "And so it happened, so long as it happened." But in its long wandering "from son to son" the ring is finally lost. However, the father to whom this misfortune happens, and who moreover loves each of his three sons equally, secretly has three copies of the ring made, and bequeaths each of them a ring that he claims is authentic.

Is this Jew ever going finish his story? The sultan becomes impatient again: "Now come quickly to the end.—Will it be?" But the story is actually over. Only its moral remains: The three religions are like the three rings: it cannot be proven which of the three is the sole true one. Indeed, so goes Nathan's wise counsel, we must wait a thousand times a thousand years before the truth of the world comes to light. That is Nathan's definitive longest time, which he brings into the field against Saladin's short time.

In addition, at the end of the story money finally claims its rights as well. It turns out that Nathan has fully understood the real ground or background of Saladin's dangerous question about the truth-value of the three great religions, namely money. The philosophical question served only the treacherous goal of leading the Jewish merchant to make a careless statement that could ultimately be used to extort money from him. In this way, the sultan would probably get his money at the cheapest rate, and even perhaps for nothing. Generously, and still wisely, Nathan finally offers the sultan, whose "trap" he has escaped by telling his little story, a loan on favorable terms. One has to go easy on people one has bested.

There is one thing left to mention in Lessing's play, a scene that precedes the events already described. In it, the sultan talks with his sister Sittah. He explains to her how he plans to render the Jew compliant by means of "little ruses." He's not entirely comfortable with this plan, because it involves using weapons he has never learned to wield in his life as a soldier. The prudent Sittah smiles at this, for acting as her brother cunningly proposes is just what pleases her "womanly mind." Nonetheless, Lessing does not present her character in an unfavorable light. He shows her as having no doubt that Nathan will certainly find a clever way to escape the trap, insofar as he is really a good and wise man, and she is convinced he is. Thus she hides in the next room and secretly listens in on the sultan's conversation with the Jew, "in order to hear how such a man talked himself out of a jam." So far as time, wit, and wisdom are concerned, as a woman she has long been on the Jew's side. In Western male-dominated society, women and Jews have always shared a role in which they play the weaker and slower parts in the hard, hurried dealings of men. So they are both right to traffic with storytellers and to learn from their longer art.

TIME AND THE OEUVRE · Proust

The search for lost time that Marcel Proust's novel *A la Recherche du temps perdu* keeps going over more than three thousand pages seems to turn out well, since the seventh and last part of the novel is entitled "Time found again" (*Le Temps retrouvé*).[26] Yet both titles are in a certain way misleading. The time lost in this novel—which is not clock and calendar time—is not consciously sought during long stretches of the first six parts of the novel, since any goal-oriented, intellectually directed, and to that extent voluntary search for it would be futile. The memory stored up in lost—because inexorably past—time will not open its treasures to any searcher who approaches it with zeal and effort.

Memory rejects with special obstinacy the efforts of the sense of sight, which in the rhetorical tradition of the art of memory (*ars rhetorica*) is considered the "most acute sense" (Cicero) in searching for lost time, and hence was for ages especially recommended for exercising the memory.[27] Instead, we must draw upon the duller senses, namely the senses of smell, taste, and touch, which can serve as more reliable vehicles of memory—but always on the condition that they do not willingly allow themselves to be pressured to do so by the intellect. A memory arising out of the depths cannot be forced. Stubborn as it is, it comes only to those who are not looking for it. Unexpected and unforeseen, it appears almost out of nothing and is sometimes contained in the smell of hawthorn, sometimes in the taste of a teacake or in the bodily sensations of a muscle that has cramped while one was lying down. However, if the memory occurs involuntarily in the way just described, then a person who lets it work on him will be granted a long-lasting state of consciousness accompanied by an experience of kairos that enriches him. The latter is a happy gift from a time raised up out of long oblivion and presented anew.[28]

In the last part of the novel, the relationship between sought time and found time is reversed. It is no longer concerned with time that is preserved in memory and must be raised out of its depths. Instead, what is now at stake is the outline of a time of waiting oriented toward the future. One morning it just happens to occur to the first-person narrator—now older—that from now on he should willingly move closer to time through the instrument of a book that is to be written. Using this new way of searching, will he actually find time, as the title of this part of the novel suggests?[29]

At first, it seems that he will not. Involuntary images of ideas are what initially force themselves upon the narrator's consciousness. For the first time, he perceives his own aging, as a result of seeing "the artist Time" at work in the faces of other people he meets every day—a time that continually repaints the features of their faces in a slow but noticeable process. Is he perhaps himself—let us call him Marcel—called upon to be a painter of time, and mustn't he hurry, so that darkness doesn't break in and tear the brush from his hand?

Since that memorable morning on which the theme of time pen-
etrated his consciousness in the form of a spur (*aiguillon*) and idea
(*idée*), the narrator has been in the grip of great uneasiness and concern as to whether the time that remains for him to live (*le temps*)
might not be long enough for him to complete his great work on Time
(*le Temps*). In the interim, this time is present to his mind only as an
idea or representation, and is still far from being "safeguarded" (*mis
en sûreté*) in a book or oeuvre. This creative spirit inhabits a body and
shares with it all the dangers to which such a fragile dwelling is ex-
posed, and which can put a sudden end to it. Painstakingly, Marcel
lists all the injuries that his body could incur as a result of hazards
or accidents. The danger might come from outside (an absurd traffic
accident) or from inside (a failure of memory): both events that from
one moment to another could affect his life or extinguish it. Thus in
relation to the book to be written, his creative power is comparable to
a besieged fortress whose fall is probably far more likely than the successful completion of the book, the oeuvre.

Simply planning a search for lost time—a search that has a literary motivation and is therefore directed by the mind—has granted the
narrator an important—perhaps the most important—experience of
time: time is short. That is something Marcel did not know, or at least
had not yet recognized clearly enough, when earlier in his life he was
vouchsafed a fragment of rediscovered time. But now that he has in
mind a literary work that certainly means time-consuming labor, he
realizes that the span of time that remains to him to complete it is limited, and above all that it may not be long enough for this great end. It
is clear to him that he must immediately set to work, for it is already
"high time" (*il est grand temps*).

Furthermore, the time needed to create such a work must be precisely calculated. Perhaps a few months? Naturally, the nights must be
included in the calculation. But how many of them? Perhaps a hundred? Or a thousand? Turning over these numbers, the narrator re-
members the thousand and one nights of Scheherazade, during which
she had to tell her stories—like him, under a thousand times repeated
threat of death. Throughout the world, that small portion of time
seems to be the "cruel law of art" (*la loi cruelle de l'art*).

Under such menacing circumstances, the narrator cannot avoid
calculating comparatively the shortness of life and the length of art.
His remaining life-time will probably be short, whereas the work

to be produced by his literary art will be long in the writing (*long à écrire*), and creating it will certainly require a much longer time than is granted an individual to live. Thus it is likely that this work will ultimately remain uncompleted, in that respect comparable to so many great "cathedrals" that were never entirely finished.

However, we cannot know this with precision, since we cannot see time. As a painter of time, Marcel at the same time imagines how good his sense of time would be if in painting a person he could make visible not only the "length of his body" (*la longueur de son corps*) but also "the length of his years" (*la longueur de ses années*). If there were such a point of view, it would have to be a perspective from above, looking out of brightly illuminated heights down on a dark abyss.

Gazing into such depths, the narrator notices a few visible signs that suggest that the time that still remains for him to live is very short. Hasn't he just recently stumbled on the stairs, three times? That was an alarming sign of the poor state of his health. Since then anxiety about time has taken full possession of him, and the thought of death has made its way into his soul, in which henceforth only fear and anxiety rule, an almost Heideggerian condition of the soul a few years before *Being and Time* was published.

Did Marcel, the aging narrator, in fact live long enough to "safeguard" his work on time within the pages of a book? The text does not say, for the last sentence the narrator formulates is in the conditional mood, and begins: "At least, if strength were granted me long enough to complete my work . . ." ("Du moins, si elle [la force] m'était laissée assez longtemps pour accomplir mon oeuvre . . .").

Thus at the end of the novel the cathedral of time remains unbuilt before the narrator's inner eye. He must still carry out the actual construction. But with this conditional sentence, Marcel Proust, the author, has just completed his work on time lost and ultimately found again, nine years after beginning it. Since 1927, five years after Proust's untimely death, the reading public has also had access to the book. And its last word is "Time" (*le Temps*, with a capital T).

7

Finitude, Infinity

If life is short and art is long or even very long, can an art ever be mastered in a single human lifetime? By what unheard-of efforts could this race still perhaps be decided in favor of individual life? This question was made significantly more pressing by the growth of knowledge during the period of the Renaissance and Humanism, and it entered a critical phase in the seventeenth century.

What precisely is the impulse behind this rapid and accelerating development? It has an unlikely name: curiosity, the Latin *curiositas*. What does that mean? Here we need to examine briefly the conceptual history of this word, and Hans Blumenberg's comprehensive monograph on the subject ("The 'Trial' of Theoretical Curiosity") will be of great use to us.[1]

At the beginning is a maxim in Aristotle: "All human beings are by nature curious."[2] This maxim is recalled by everyone who sees in curiosity and the thirst for knowledge a positive impulse that ultimately becomes the most powerful force driving scientific research. In Rome, Aristotle's judgment in favor of the "insatiable" and "ingenious" thirst for knowledge was adopted and disseminated above all by Cicero and

Seneca. Yet in the world of the late Latin romance (Apuleius) attention is also given to a restlessly roaming curiosity that takes an interest in anything strange.[3]

In Christian times, the most important church fathers discuss *curiositas* in an unfavorable light. Tertullian believes that human beings, to whom Christian revelation has been granted, can dispense with any kind of curiosity: "Since Christ, we no longer need to be curious" ("Nobis curiositate opus non est post Christum"). Curiosity is above all feared as the source of all heresies. Augustine is chastising himself even when he includes "idle curiosity" (*vana curiositas*) in the Christian catalogue of vices to which Montaigne, Pascal, and Rousseau will later refer. It is interesting that Augustine warns against curiosity chiefly on the ground that it wastes valuable time on useless matters, for example, star-gazing, whereas only one thing is truly important: the salvation of the soul.[4] After these pious admonitions, *curiositas* first comes up again in Dante, who—alluding to Aristotle and Cicero—counts "the natural thirst which is never quenched" ("la sete natural che mai non si sazia") among the spiritual forces behind his journey through the Beyond, but then qualifies this by noting that the Samaritan woman in the Gospels to whom Jesus gives a drink of water shows that she knows a superior beverage, the refreshment of grace that better satisfies any thirst (for knowledge) than life-long devotion to science.[5]

This Samaritan, who wants to know no more about the world than what she can learn from Jesus himself, is nonetheless an exception among women. All the authors of antiquity and the Middle Ages—and many later authors as well—agree that curiosity is a vice to which women are especially prone. In the biblical world, this is exemplified by Eve's fateful curiosity in the Garden of Eden, and for the pagan world by the equally disastrous curiosity of Pandora (in Hesiod), who by curiously opening the casket she has been given sets free the vices that had been imprisoned within it. In Charles Perrault's tale "Bluebeard," the king is the villain, of course, but his many wives fall victim to his murderous desire because of their restless curiosity. Knigge sees the matter the same way: "Curiosity is a major element in the female character." In the persistent opinion of men, women are naturally curious because they are constantly asking questions that are tiresome to answer and that distract attention from things, whose masters are men. Thus Lohengrin is the hero of a mysterious myth, whereas Elsa of Brabant, who insists on asking questions, is a heroine of curiosity.[6]

With this ambivalent prehistory, well into the seventeenth century *curiositas* was able to force its dilatory-curious side into the "knickknack cabinet" (*Kuriositätenkabinett*) so that the thirst for knowledge as "theoretical curiosity" (Blumenberg) could be erected into a primarily male virtue that became the enduring drive behind modern science. Let us briefly examine this decisive step in the history of modern science.

So long as it could still seem that the knowledge most important for human life was stored up in books and could best be brought to light by patient labor on classical texts, philologists were needed. It was incumbent upon them, by extending study time to the maximum in what might be a final and definitive effort, to keep the arts under control. In this effort, as always, a concept of art was used that, as "knowledge expressed in rules," could hardly be distinguished from the knowledge gained from reading books. Polyglot philologists and other prolific writers determined to what extent the ideal of broad knowledge (*polymathia*) seemed attainable. In Germany, the philologist F. A. Wolf was one of these polymaths. In the history of scholarship he is known as a specialist in Homer. But what there is to know about Homer can by itself fill a human life. So Wolf made, as Judith Schlanger has shown, superhuman efforts to master all this knowledge within the bounds of a lifetime too short for the task.[7] In France, François Rabelais finds in this subject a wealth of material for his grotesquely exaggerated novel, in which the heroes (Gargantua, Pantagruel) are giants, as they must be, because they devour in a finite lifetime a gigantic amount of knowledge and have to digest it as well, so far as they can. To this end they subject themselves—as Leon Battista Alberti already had done (see above, chap. 1, sect. 3) to a strict temporal discipline that leaves not a minute of the day free from the timetable (*horarium, horaire, Stundenplan*). Toward the end of the first part of the novel, however, Rabelais takes his heroes to the utopia of the Abbey of Thélème (from Greek *thelema*, "free will"), where every resident can finally do whatever he wishes, and all clocks are banned. Evidently it is impossible to pursue art and science all the way, once and for all, by merely accumulating knowledge.[8]

. . .

At the end of the sixteenth century, this impossibility is explicitly acknowledged by Torquato Tasso in his dialogue *Porzio, or on the Virtues* (*Il Porzio ovvero de le virtù*, 1593), which highlights mathematics and the rising natural sciences in the reflections of the dialogue partners. Can the goal and end of art ever be reached in these and other branches of knowledge, so that it is possible to build on this certain knowledge? This question is answered differently by the two dialogue partners. The man who gives his name to the dialogue, Simone Porzio, still believes it can, while his skeptical interlocutor, Muzio Pignatelli, considers this goal unattainable within the lifetime of an individual man, arguing:

> Wherever I turn, the road stretches out almost endlessly in front of me, and the difficulties are also endless, so that it seems to me that toil engenders further toil and one never reaches this goal and end of the sciences.

> Dovunque me volga, veggio quasi infinita la strada e infinite le difficoltà; la onde mi pare che da le fatiche nascano fatiche e che mai non si arriva a questo fine de le scienze.[9]

. . .

From Italy we turn now to Germany, and in doing so must take into account a significant historical belatedness, which is nonetheless compensated by a greater acuity in reasoning, at least in the case of Leibniz. In addition to his great philosophical works, Gottfried Wilhelm Leibniz (1646–1716) also wrote a small and relatively neglected note, *De arte inveniendi* (1669).[10] In this note, Leibniz discusses a problem that actually lies one step beneath his level as a scientist, namely the "art" of rhetoric. The first subject of study in rhetoric—and this art was still generally known in the seventeenth century—was "invention" (*inventio*). This part of rhetoric taught in which "places" (Greek *topoi*, Latin *loci*) in the memory the speaker is to find the arguments he needs for his speech. The philosopher would be wise to glance at this art now and then, for example with the help of Aristotle's *Topics*. For that reason Leibniz does not despise the rhetorical doctrine of invention, but he nonetheless assigns it, as *inventio analytica*, a subordinate rank in the intellectual world.

The rhetorical art of invention's more noble sister, the art of "synthetic invention" (*inventio synthetica*) has for Leibniz an entirely different rank in intellectual life. Whereas the former is satisfied to gather from the store of topics arguments suitable for replying to questions that have already been asked, the task of the art of "synthetic invention" is constantly to find, or rather to "discover" (as the Latin verb *invenire* must henceforth be translated), new questions.

By taking this apparently small step from the analytic to the synthetic, Leibniz has left the art of rhetoric far behind and thrown wide open the door to science in the modern sense of the word. There is no longer a limited store of already existing questions that could, by means of art, be worked through in a calculable length of time. Instead, every question that is more or less good but has never been exhaustively answered opens up a new horizon of questions, whose production is in fact the first and noblest task of the scientist. An end to this process in time cannot be foreseen, since science itself constantly renews its store of problems, without ever flagging in its endless "global curiosity" (*Weltneugierde*, Blumenberg). In a novel published in 1864, the French writer Victor Hugo put this point with unsurpassable succinctness: "Science seeks perpetual motion. It has found it, and it is itself" ("La science cherche le mouvement perpétuel. Elle l'a trouvé; c'est elle-même").

A NOTHINGNESS OF TIME IN EXCHANGE FOR ETERNITY
Pascal, Emily Dickinson

At approximately the same time that in Germany Leibniz was grappling with the problem of infinity, Blaise Pascal (1623–62) was doing the same in France.[11] Pascal, who is known in literature chiefly for his *Pensées*, is known in science chiefly as a mathematician. In his mathematical thought Pascal was most stimulated by geometry, which in its ancient form as a Euclidean art provided the classical model of a doctrine firmly based on axioms, as was favored by the *esprit de géométrie*. But Pascal is forced to acknowledge that even such a geometry is based on a certain number of propositions that are themselves based on other propositions, and so on and so on, in an endless movement of thought that constantly renews its own impulse. This seems also to hold for all other disciplines, so that in his *Pensées*—short aphorisms not unlike those of Hippocrates—he can already write:[12]

> We see that all the sciences are infinite in the extent of their research: for who doubts that geometry, for example, has an infinity of an infinity of propositions to state?

Nous voyons que toutes les sciences sont infinies en l'étendue de leurs recherches: car qui doute que la géométrie, par exemple, a une infinité d'infinité de propositions à exposer?

It is plausible that Pascal is referring to an epistemological-methodological infinity here, one that arises from the fact that the process of searching or researching not only cannot come to a natural end but also does not want to, since "we never seek things, but rather the search for things" ("nous ne cherchons jamais les choses, mais la recherche des choses"). Under such conditions, it would be a fatal misunderstanding of the nature of his profession were any scientist to think he could ever arrive at a point where there would be nothing new for him to know (Wagner in *Faust*!). There will always remain infinitely much for him to know (*il vous reste infiniment à savoir*).[13]

In his further reflections, the idea of infinity does not leave the mathematician Pascal in peace. But as a geometer he applies it chiefly to spatial relationships and develops from it his suggestive theory of the two infinities, namely the infinitely great (*infini de grandeur*), which manifests itself in the heavenly macrocosm, and the infinitely small (*infini de petitesse*). Man stands bewildered between these two infinities, a nothingness (*néant*) in relation to either of them.[14]

In a small but important passage of the *Pensées*, there are also statements in which Pascal translates this theory from geometry into chronometry. In doing so, however, he must struggle with the difficulty that for infinitely great time a recognized concept is available: eternity. On the other hand, for infinitely small time he must make do with a description: "a nothingness of time" (*un néant de temps*), but he sometimes also uses the concept "instant" (*instant*). Once again, between the two stands man, with the "short duration" (*petite durée*) of his temporality, which is heedlessly absorbed (*absorbée*) into the infinitely great. Thus Pascal writes about man in this situation:[15]

Isn't he always infinitely distant from the end, and isn't the duration of our lives equally infinitesimal in eternity even if it lasts ten years longer?

N'est-il pas toujours infiniment éloigné du bout, et la durée de notre vie n'est-elle pas également infime dans l'éternité, pour durer dix ans davantage?

This reflection makes it clear that for Pascal, ten years more or less life-time is completely insignificant with respect to the infinite duration of eternity, which is among the fundamental attributes of divinity.

It is between the finite and the infinite in its temporal garb, that is, between the short and limited nature of human life and the participation in eternity promised by God, that we encounter the much-discussed "wager" (*le pari*) that Pascal recommends to the agnostics and skeptics among his readers.[16] In modern terms, the wager is a game-theory risk calculation that in its structure reminds us of many earthly games of chance, but it is one in which not money but rather time is played for. The rules of Pascal's game stipulate that a bettor, man, stake his small account of life-time on the—admittedly—uncertain playing field of belief. As his transcendent partner in the game, God offers in return nothing less than participation in eternity. However, this overwhelming prospect also remains uncertain, since it is based only on belief.

When the game begins, the human player has an equal chance of winning or losing. But like any earthly gambler, he can weigh up the chances and the risks. If man wins, because God's promise turns out to be true, then he has won "an eternity of life and happiness" (*une éternité de vie et de bonheur*). But if he loses, he has lost almost nothing, at most a small amount of life-time, which doesn't represent pure happiness in any case and cannot compare with eternal bliss. Given these extremely unequal conditions, according to the infinitesimally calculated advice given by the mathematician Pascal, no one should hesitate to discard all skepticism and take the insignificant risk involved in this wager, since such a tiny loss on earth is amply and even excessively counterbalanced by the hopeful expectation of an infinite gain in heaven.

However, in reading Pascal let us not forget that this game of chance is recommended, not to convinced Christians, but rather to unbelievers and those of little faith, as a calculable spiritual adventure that should as quickly as possible find its goal and end in belief in God.

Should we engage at all in a wager with God about our salvation if it involves such a despicable kind of calculation? Many critics, Paul Valéry being the most acerbic, have considered Pascal's wager "a slander on religion and a scandal for science."[17] However, during the night of November 23, 1654 Pascal received a visionary message of salvation, which he described in his *Mémorial* and carried with him to the end of his life. In this private document of his belief, he thrice appeals to the

divine eternity for which he had gladly wagered the small happiness
of his finitude.[18]

. . .

Now we have calculated and speculated enough, and I close this section with a contrasting view of a great American poet who led a pi-
ously puritanical life in the most extreme seclusion: Emily Dickinson
(1830–86).[19] In her deeply felt verses she sometimes also calculates
lengths of time, but entirely differently from the mathematician Pascal, as for example in this poem:

> I reason, Earth is short—
> And Anguish—absolute—,
> And many hurt,
> But, what of that?
> I reason, we could die—
> The best Vitality
> Cannot excel Decay,
> But, what of that?
> I reason, that in heaven
> Somehow, it will be even—
> Some new Equation given—
> But, what of that?

Emily Dickinson knows, in her religious thinking, that human life
("Earth," "Vitality") is short. This does not much grieve her, and she
does not begin to count the days. On the other side of death Heaven is
waiting, where a new and just reckoning ("even," "Equation") will be
made, from which her Christian soul may hope something. But that
does not count for much either.

TOO LITTLE TIME, TOO MUCH WORLD · Blumenberg

After Martin Heidegger, in his fundamental work *Sein und Zeit* (1927),
brought Being back out of transcendence and into the "lifeworld" (Hus-
serl: *Lebenswelt*), the opposite operation became imaginable. In the
latter, life projects its short life-time ("Being towards death, *das Sein*

zum Tode) onto the world and witnesses with distress its boundless otherness. This idea is discussed from various points of view by Hans Blumenberg (1920–96) in his widely read book *Life-time and World-Time* (*Lebenszeit und Weltzeit*, 1986).[20] As a young man, Blumenberg was subjected to an oppressive experience of the brevity and finitude of human life: bearing the stigma of being a "half-Jew," he narrowly escaped the Holocaust. After the war, as Professor of Philosophy in Gießen and Münster, he became well known as the author of many books written in elaborate prose, and his fame has continued to grow since his death.

Hans Blumenberg was a tireless reader. During his lifetime, no other German philosopher could match him in literary culture. And so of course he was also familiar with Hippocrates, whose first aphorism he often cited as proof of the incongruencies pre-programmed in human nature when the "shear" (*Schere*) between life and art, between life-time and world-time (*Weltzeit*) opens wide. In these statements we see that Blumenberg has sharpened and put a point on the Hippocratic problem in his own way, by opposing the shortness of our life-time, not to the long time of art and science, but directly, without intermediate stages, to a superhumanly increased world-time, which shares many characteristics with Leibniz's and Pascal's infinity, since the more one approaches it, the farther it recedes. To that extent world-time is the greatest of all life-time's opponents; its "immense" magnitude far exceeds all earthly lengths that were ever considered for long art or science. And so we see here with impressive clarity "the human organism's constitutive lack of time."

In Blumenberg's work, world-time appears in three forms, and in all three disposes of such an immeasurable supply of time that it can "lord it over" humans. Thus for Blumenberg, world-time is first of all a time that can be calculated only in millions of years and that takes nature as the field for its movements and transformations in the cosmos, far beyond any life-world ideas of length and size. Secondly, in Blumenberg's book world-time is the time of world history, which can at most be matched with human time in secular dimensions. Thirdly, however, he considers world-time above all an open horizon of possibilities and virtualities that offers, or seems to offer, a surface onto which we can project our most excessive wishes and claims, together with our often insatiable "global curiosity" (*Weltneugierde*). Should we meanwhile want to make an attempt to demand that the world actually redeem these projections, then it immediately turns out, to our disappointment and frustration, that the great world does not give the slightest thought to allowing human beings to share in its temporal splendor. Instead, the limitless rivalry between life-time and world-time remains irreconcilable, given their incommensurability (*Unverhältnis*) and the abyss that separates them, so that Blumenberg must soon abandon the metaphor of the "shear" between life-time and world-time that he introduced at the outset. He can now only note the shattering of the shear's blades. Blumenberg's central proposition, "The world costs time" (*Die Welt kostet Zeit*), can therefore be seen as a resigned summation, after which we must lay down our pencils, because no satisfactory solution can be calculated for a creature "that with a finite life-time has infinite wishes."

What do humans do, then, if on the way through their short lives they are forced to notice that they "always have a diminishing amount of time for an increasing number of possibilities and wishes?" Will they suffer from their finitude and fall, for instance, into a deep melancholy? Or will they, as life-artists (*Lebenskünstler*), seek to make themselves at home in the world as it is, in order to work on producing little comforts within the limits of their *conditio temporalis*? Might the longevity that humans have with some success achieved since Hufeland be of aid? Blumenberg bases no hopes on this, and even expressly refers to a "failure of macrobiotics."

But what else can help, then? Perhaps art itself—understood as *technē*, that is technology—can come to our aid. Among his contemporaries, Blumenberg notes a tendency to compensate for the shortness of life-time by accelerating everyday life in various ways great and small. That is an idea that many other authors came upon and developed at the same time he did, in particular Reinhart Koselleck and Hermann Lübbe.[21] These observers agree that a large part of the discoveries whose advantages shape everyday life, especially in the areas of transportation and communication, have as the driving force of their technological activity the desired savings in time that can be credited if the daily erosion of time can be stemmed. Then, it is hoped, life-time, while just as short as it ever was, will at least be lived more intensely than before. As Blumenberg puts it, the "must time" (*Mußzeit*) that every human being has to devote to simply maintaining life, as he always did, can be minimized in the interest of a more pleasant "can time" (*Kannzeit*). The latter, however, is to be understood in Blumenberg's work not as the leisure time of our fun-loving society but rather as Seneca's ambitiously defined "time for oneself." Blumenberg even mentions the hope that in the future the relationship between "must time" and "can time" will shift to the advantage of the latter. In this way more reality might be brought into human time—though still short or perhaps somewhat prolonged through longevity—and experienced by humans as an increase in the quality of life.

That is, however, a rather optimistic view not particularly in accord with Blumenberg's rather darker temperament. In fact, his confidence is soon transformed into a pessimistic variant, according to which time-saving technologies, instead of serving human beings peacefully and patiently in the "garden of wishes," produce with increasing speed new demands whose excessiveness leaves any possible "can time" far behind. Ultimately, little humanity still stands there blamed, because when it seeks to be measured against the great world-time, it elicits nothing more than a sardonic laugh.

Many questions of this kind are more raised than answered in Blumenberg's book—although, as we know from Leibniz, asking questions does not necessarily indicate a lack of scientific rigor. In any case, we easily discern in his work a great and perhaps suppressed love for the astronomical dimensions of world-time, and a lesser love for the somewhat more meager dimension of human time, which with grim humor he sometimes lets run on in the void. For that reason Blumenberg always supported the natural philosopher Thales, who observed the stars from a hole in the ground, rather than the Thracian maid who was philosophically scolded because she shrieked with laughter on witnessing what she considered a comic sight.[22]

Nonetheless, we cannot conclude these remarks without mentioning that Blumenberg's book on life-time and world-time contains a short section that inexorably confronts all the reader's ideas—though in dialogue with Blumenberg they may sometimes tend to play between the poles of life-time and world-time—with reality and its extreme cruelty. It may even be that the author really wrote his book for the sake of this little section. It has to do with Hitler.[23]

One may well wonder whether it is realistic to suggest that a man could be so blind as to seek, contrary to all the rules of reason, and through an act of extreme violence, to give his short life-time the superhuman magnitude of world-time, at least in the world-time dimension of world history. Sebastian Haffner was the first to find in the contemporary sources he consulted for his monograph on Hitler the idea that this must in fact have been Hitler's great paranoid fear during the war or at least during its final phases. Like Haffner, Blumenberg is convinced that at this point in the war, Hitler was obsessed by the idea that he alone had to manage, within his own lifetime, to achieve the great and ultimate focusing of world-time on the establishment of a German or Germanic world empire, and do so with the inordinate speed of a world war—otherwise this unique conjunction of life-time and world-time would be forever lost. Until the final days of his sub-terranean rule in the bunker at the Reich chancellery, Hitler seems to have nourished this apocalyptic hope. Blumenberg writes: "This forced convergence of life-time and world-time was the last of his monstrosities." In this frightening perspective of a perverse concep-tion of time we can discern, in addition to Hitler's rule of terror, what latent dangers may still lie in human calculations of life-time if vision-ary thoughts beyond the measurable facts of clocks and calendars are allowed to run amok in the immeasurable and the infinite.

ANTHROPOLOGICAL EXPERIENCES OF SHORTAGE · Odo Marquard

In his way of philosophizing, Odo Marquard (b. 1928) is in many re-spects comparable to Hans Blumenberg. But the basic tone of Mar-quard's philosophizing is skeptical. That includes his preference for thinking clearly about the shortages of life-time rather than the large formats of world-time as they are to be observed in the starry heavens, in world history, or in Faustian visions. And so in his writings he never tires of quoting Hippocrates' first aphorism, taking obvious pleasure in its coolly diagnostic view of human beings' *conditio temporalis* and "shortage of time."[24] Like the Greek physician, Marquard is fond of the short, concise form of the Hippocratic aphorism, and that is why he prefers to publish his own works in small-format but philosophically important paperbacks. For a skeptic who wants to retain his bond with humanity, this is undoubtedly the correct way to write.[25]

Marquard also much admired Blumenberg's book *Life-Time and World-Time*, but he read it against the grain, as it were, as an acknowl-edgement of the shortness of life and as a temporal phenomenology of human finitude.[26] Therefore in his discussion of this book, after a brief nod to world-time, he quickly turns his attention back to the little "niche in time" (*Zeitlücke*) in which human beings must get by on earth. In view of these conditions it is comprehensible that short time, which is available for human action only in such limited situations, is in general not sufficient for worldwide offensives and global upturns, even and especially if the splendid prospects of absolute changes are announced with much fanfare. Even if a few things that can be changed actually are changed, most must remain unaltered, since otherwise the changes that can in fact be made will misfire. As a result, real life takes place for the most part within the framework of "the usual ways"—ways that have always already been accepted, and at least for the time being must continue to be accepted, not because they have been so wonderful, but simply for lack of time.[27] About these usual ways one might further remark that most of them are social in nature and largely coincide with the contents of the "collective memory" (Maurice Halbwachs). For precisely that reason, in the course of his short life-time the individual is in most cases fairly powerless to escape the usual ways and to live in accord with absolute prescriptions. Thus the usual often also protects him against futility. Marquard's well-known book titles, *Farewell to Matters of Principle* (*Abschied vom Prinzipiellen*) and *In Defense of the Accidental* (*Apologie des Zufälligen*) pursue these reflections further, with many original ideas.

However, Marquard brings to bear on the tension between life-time and world-time a further noteworthy argument that had already been considered in other historical and philosophical contexts by Hermann Lübbe and Reinhart Koselleck.[28] Marquard asks what man's "mortality-determined brevity of life" implies for the tempo of that life. He gives two answers to this question. On one hand, Marquard finds it plausible that human beings do things in haste so that death doesn't "catch up with them" before they have made some respectable achievement. In fact, that is how modernity has used technological innovations to constantly increase the speed of life. "The modern world is fast," Marquard observes, and he discovers, in passing, a maxim for *homo modernus et oeconomicus*: "I hasten, therefore I am" ("Ich eile, also bin ich").[29]

On the other hand, however, the skeptic and "unabsolute philosopher" that Marquard still wants to be actually has little liking for speed and acceleration. How can all this daily running and hurrying pay off in terms of time, if it is certain that death still arrives faster than almost all desired or planned changes? In comparison to death, all human life is fundamentally slow. Therefore human beings, whether they want to or not, have to develop a "sense for slowness," for only through slowness can they acquire the ability to discern those changes that are both desirable and feasible. In Marquard this means, put more simply and in the language of the old moralists: Modernity requires humanity.

That is also how Marquard's other essay and book title, *The Future Needs a Heritage (Zukunft braucht Herkunft)*, should be understood. It corresponds to the recommendation that the reader smuggle into the rapidity of the modern world as much (postmodern) slowness as possible, combined with the cunning suggestion that everything new, because it is constantly overtaken by still newer developments, ages much faster than the old, and therefore after the brief excitement of novelty soon seems older than what is truly old. If consequently the newest things always quickly become old, then the chances are greater that the old, when it has aged with honor, will soon become the newest thing again: Hippocrates and Seneca, for instance, Leibniz and Pascal, Hufeland and Goethe, or finally Blumenberg and Marquard as the most recent philosophers of time whom we count here, to their honor, among the ancients, because they are able to reason as humanely as the classical authors and also write as well as they did.

8

Living with Deadlines

First, we must discuss clocks, which of all devices for measuring time are the ones that most give us the impression that time can not only be measured but also mastered. Even the Creator therefore came to be called, by the philosophical school of Deism, the "clockmaker" of the universe. This metaphor nonetheless already presupposes the existence of mechanical clocks such as were invented around 1300 in northern Italy and rapidly further improved. Since then humanity, at least in the Western world, has found itself a frenzied age of clock-time and has not let anything stop it from developing, through the regular progress of the art of mechanical and then electronic clock-making, constant time control to the point of perfection and obsession.[1]

Mechanical clocks, which at the beginning of the age of clock-time were large, public clocks on towers of churches and town halls, were modeled on sundials in their way of showing time. On sundials, which of course show the time only during daylight, the dial takes the form of a half-circle that mimics the arc of the sun's (apparent) movement from dawn to dusk. In mechanical clocks, which in principle can perform their task even at night and during cloudy weather, the half-circle is extended to form a full circle. The markings on the dial show the hours, minutes, and seconds, and over them moves a hand (later on, two or three hands) analogous to the position of the sun. After moving all the way around the dial, the hand begins a "cyclical" repetition of its circular movement. Thus day and night, we can now *see* the passage of time with our own eyes.

However, in considering these obvious advances in the measurement and indication of time, we must not however overlook the fact that sundials and mechanical clocks, which indicate simple points in time, are in some respects less effective than the water-clocks (clepsydras) used chiefly in monasteries in earlier times and candles of a regular length and thickness. These were better suited than mechanical clocks for indicating certain relatively short spans of time. This also holds for the sand-clock, which was invented in Europe at about the same time as mechanical clocks, and which could easily show the duration of sermons, speeches, and readings that were to be limited in time. In the form of the *hourglass* it must soon have taken on the emblematic function of symbolizing the transitory and limited nature of human existence. Consider, for instance, the hourglass held by the god Chronos/Kronos in Tiepolo's painting *Il Tempo*.

A remedy for an inadequate understanding of periods of time was soon found by combining public clocks with the bells in church and town hall towers (thus the English word "clock" corresponds to the German word *Glocke*, "bell"). Churchbells and chimes made mechanically mediated time audible at great distances, broken up into hours, half-hours, and quarter-hours. "Turret clocks" were capable of marking deadlines, and in addition to their greater precision in measuring time they also provided, by indicating short lengths of time, a more exact time control than their pre-mechanical competitors. Thus they were increasingly able to regulate everyday life and set the pace of work time, meal time, and leisure time. In this respect as well, the emblematic function of bells did not escape the poets. It was easily internalized by readers of Schiller's "Bell" (*Glocke*), who were often required to memorize the poem in order to strengthen their sense of time.

Today, we frequently make use of electronic clocks in everyday life. Their precision leaves little to be desired, but they are still structured just as cyclically. Newer digital clocks and watches, which have a window that shows the time in numerals instead of a dial with hands, at first give the impression, with the jerky advance of a temporal value expressed in numbers, of a linear time, but they also begin the daily cycle every twenty-four hours and to that extent are still cyclically organized devices for measuring time.

Since all mechanical or electronic clocks (including hyper-precise cesium atomic clocks) must have an energy source that is transformed by means of clockwork into a normalized expression of time, clocks can also be regarded as machines that produce a temporal product. This product is time, insofar as it is short.

■ ■ ■

For ordering and registering larger units of time, from the day onward, we use calendars. Let us discuss first the usual calendar, in the "classical" form of a tear-off calendar. In this kind of calendar, each day has its own page, printed in black for workdays and in red for Sundays and holidays. The page for a past day—and this says quite a bit about time—is torn off and thrown away, unless some important event (a wedding, birth, death) or the sage remark of a literary calendar-maker (Franklin, Brecht) makes the page worth keeping.

A full-year calendar of this kind has 365 pages (in leap years, 366), on which the date, day, week, and month are shown in fairly diverse ways. All the dates indicated are recurrent, that is, they come back after a certain amount of time, though the months first recur on the next year's calendar. Therefore we can say that in comparison with clock-time, calendar time is also conceived cyclically. This holds for the civil year as well as for the Christian ecclesiastical year, with its cycle of feast-days. Only the years themselves are identified by year numbers, which run from the birth of Christ into the unforeseeable future, or in reverse order from the same turning point in time. The year number—which provides the title and proper name, so to speak, for each annual calendar (e.g., "2005 calendar")—thus corresponds, as an individual numeric symbol, to a purely linear order, which mathematicians and natural scientists sometimes stubbornly present as the sole real time: a flying arrow of time that speeds from the Big Bang to the end of the universe.

The preceding observations have already shown that calendars regulate time effectively, but in a quite disorderly, not to say somewhat slovenly, fashion. All valid calendars are rather bizarrely cobbled to-gether in a way that French sociologists and anthropologists like to call "bricolage" ("makeshift"). But who did this makeshift work? We know a few names: the emperor Julius Caesar, the monk Dionysios Exiguus, Pope Gregory XIII. But the most general answer to this question is simpler: the calendar is cobbled together by history.

Let us look at the calendar day. In the Middle Ages, St Isidore, bishop of Seville, already complains in his *Etymologies* about the fact that one never is sure whether the word *day* means the period from sunup to sundown or the whole day, including the night, that is, from sunup to sunup. Since the sun can be seen only from dawn until dusk but always returns the next morning, both ways of interpreting the word seem equally justified.

Next, the week. Nothing in the firmament corresponds to this unit of time. The basis of the week, of Chaldean-Hebraic origin, is a purely religious or cultural. In the Bible, it is traced back to the divine act of creating the world. This is already indicated by the impractical but sacred number of seven weekdays, a number that cannot be equally divided unless Friday, Saturday (Sabbath), or Sunday are subtracted as holy days, so that only six days—a number that can easily be divided ($6 = 2 \times 3$) for practical purposes—remain.

In the case of months, we must once again look to the heavens, but this time not to the sun but rather to the moon, from which in fact the word "month" is derived. But so far as the temporal length of the month is concerned, once again it is history that cobbles together a solution: four months have thirty days, seven months have thirty-one days. February, finally, has twenty-eight days (twenty-nine in leap years). This was the reservoir of time on which the Roman rulers "Ju-lius" Caesar and "Augustus" Caesar drew in order to give their high summer months of July and August a full thirty-one days, in accord with their status, with the result that February was robbed of two days in the annual cycle and became the shortest month in the year.

Moreover, so far as the year as a whole is concerned, what counted in the agricultural contexts of earlier eras were above all the seasons, with their biological rhythms of planting time in the spring, ripening time in the summer, harvest time in the fall, and rest time in the win-ter. In the seasons, the calendar is closest to nature and takes as much time as it needs: enough.

. . .

After the old clocks and calendars had taken over the task of dividing up God-given time for the purposes of a laborious and meager but bearable life, the twentieth century is to be praised or blamed for having invented the appointment calendar. The latter (also called an "agenda" in several European languages) is a variable register that combines a calendar with a clock. In its commercial form, it takes the form of a book in which there is a page or two for each day of the year, organized by hours, and to that extent it amounts to a thin dial. In the appropriate time-slot on these pages are written "appointments" to do something (Latin *agendum*, pl. *agenda*) or to provide a certain service. The true dimension of the appointment calendar is therefore the future (*memoria futuri*).

If, for example, a contractor's calendar shows that in two weeks he has an appointment with the city building department, a period of time is defined that begins at the moment it is entered on the calendar and lasts fourteen days. During this time the contractor has to prepare for the meeting, for example by collecting and filling out the required documents. If he does not do this, or forgets the date or the time, the appointment "falls through," and he has to expect certain annoyances or other disadvantages.

This small example already shows that the appointment calendar is actually a calendar of deadline-periods.[2] As a rule, only a single point in time, the deadline (Latin *terminus*), is entered on the calendar, but it is understood that there is also a beginning point at which "the clock starts running." The calendar-user sees this intervening period of time every morning, when he looks through its pages, the starting point moving closer to the endpoint from day to day until it is finally reached. After the appointed action or service has been completed, the whole period of time can be forgotten ("erased").

This short description also allows us to see that in order to function, appointment calendars presuppose clocks and calendars, and complement them for the purpose of the more effective planning of time; that is why they are sometimes called "planners." Thus they also presuppose the elementary virtues of punctuality (by means of clocks) and good order (by means of calendars), and on this basis the new virtue of respecting deadlines (*Fristengerechtigkeit*) can fully develop.

DEADLINES IN EVERYDAY LIFE · *Tutti, con moto*

Short time has many faces. Under the complex conditions of industrial and post-industrial societies, with their highly differentiated managerial apparatuses, it appears with special frequency and with considerable dominance in the form of periods of time with deadlines—limited spans of time that are generally defined by their starting and ending dates, and before the end of which the person subjected to these deadlines is expected to perform a certain act or provide a certain service (or, on the contrary, to avoid doing something).[3] However, if a person himself determines the starting point of this period according to the context or the situation, then a beginning date may not be explicitly stipulated.

For example, if one wants to borrow a book from a public library, one must usually agree to a lending period of a few days or weeks within which the book must be returned. An unjustified failure to respect this agreement results in a (first, second, final) warning, accompanied by increasing fines. However, on petition the lending period can also be extended, if the book is not needed for other purposes or reserved. All this is known to the borrower from the rules that are given to him along with his (limited term) library card.

There can be no doubt that the existence of public libraries is a great advantage for users and a blessing for the society. At the same time, the necessary limit on the time for which a book can be borrowed is accompanied by a small amount of constraint. While he or she is reading the book, the reader must not only concentrate on its content but also keep an eye on the lending period and the "deadline" for its return. That is a temporal duty that is in many cases made easier to fulfill insofar as the borrower is accustomed to doing things punctually and in an orderly way, but a certain amount of attention is still required if the system of limited lending periods is to function as a mode of public interaction.

Like any other interaction, this problem can be viewed from two sides, in this case from those of the lender and the borrower. Both sides have a common but differently focused interest in having the lending period go "smoothly." On the lender's side, it is the librarians (insofar as they are not in charge of an infinite "Library of Babel") who are professionally responsible for ensuring that the rules concerning the lending period are not carelessly or deceitfully disregarded. On the other side, the borrower's interest is focused not only on getting a specific book but also on having access not only to this book but also to the next one he wants to borrow, and which another borrower now has, so that in the whole system of borrowing for a specific term a small part of the Kantian ethics of duty is involved.

Nevertheless, we must not overlook the fact that these two complementary roles in relation to lending periods are not equally assigned. The larger and immediately noticeable pressure of the deadline is exercised by the lender, and the individual library user has to subordinate himself to this pressure. This is a "classical" power relationship that may make some people quickly—too quickly—think of the division of roles between employer and employee (Marx: master and slave). But this comparison is unproductive insofar as in modern or postmodern societies such periods are so complexly interlinked that most who play one role in a given situation play the other in another situation. A class or class-struggle schema is not adequate to account for complicated temporal relationships in a society relying on such term-deadlines.

. . .

Next, it will be worthwhile to examine the system (and sometimes also the lack of a system) of term-deadlines from the linguistic point of view as well. In German, the word *Frist* (a determinate period ending with a deadline) is already well attested in Old High German (eighth century); in the Grimms' dictionary, it is connected with "first." This semantic connection is not implausible. Just as the gable of an old house rests on the ridge-tree (*Firstbaum*) as the "first" tree-trunk, so already in ancient Germany economic life was based to a significant extent on the delivery of goods and services within certain deadlines. However, at that time it was obviously not always easy to meet these deadlines and their conditions, so that *Frist* came to be sometimes understood less as a term-deadline than as the latter's merciful or unmerciful postponement. This can be explained by the fact that with a term-deadline understood as a shorter or longer span of time, the attention of the person who has to meet the deadline is focused chiefly on the deadline as the temporal endpoint, so that the meaning of the word, born by the wings of fear or desire, can easily fly over this borderline in order to achieve a lessening of the pressure of the deadline. But on the other side the person to whom some good or service must be rendered will take care that this postponement of the deadline (*First*; "ridge-tree") does not cause his house to collapse.

These observations can be complemented by a few brief remarks about other languages. In French, the term-deadline is expressed by the word *délai*, which in the form of a legal term migrated to England in the Middle Ages: "delay." Like their German counterparts, these words can be used to express not a period of time ending in a deadline but also the deadline itself, and even the failure to meet it, and this can be explained by their derivation from Vulgar Latin *dilatare* ("stretch," "expand"). Thus we arrive at expressions such as French *sans délai* ("without delay") and English "the plane is delayed." In Spanish there is a deviant construction. The Spanish word for term-deadline is *plazo*. This word goes back to Latin *placitum*, a legal term that shows that a deadline represents a quasi-contractual "agreement" or even a formal contract.

.   .   .

Let us return briefly to the linguistics of deadlines. There remain a few more important observations to make about the way language deals with deadlines. First of all, metaphorically: it is characteristic of the power relationships latent in a deadline that it is set by the grantor of the loan-period, etc. Thus the deadline-period is positioned in time, but at first gets going rather slowly. Only when a deadline-period has moved far beyond its beginning and is nearing its end does it move with increasing speed, until finally its "run" (German *Laufzeit*) has reached its end and the debt (etc.) "falls due"; cf. Italian *scadenza* and French *échéance*, both derived from Latin *cadere* ("fall"). If the grantor of a deadline-period is benevolent, when the deadline arrives its receiver may be able to gain a little more time by delay or postponement. But a dilatory receiver is always unwelcome, and at least a late-payment fee will be expected. Thus the deadline-period's running-time comes to its contractually agreed-upon end: it "runs out."

Therefore—as grammar will now show us—in the interest of caution it is prudent to limit a deadline-period more strictly, as calendars and clocks require *nach strengster Rechnung*. For this purpose, the language of agreements about deadline-periods uses temporal adverbs such as "at the latest" (*spätestens*) and "at the earliest" (*frühestens*), through whose restrictions it can be ensured that a deadline-period is not fully "exhausted."

Let us also observe that from a psychological point of view, all deadline-periods set boundary markers that sometimes make major demands on the memory. As a rule, grantors of deadline-periods make them as easy to remember as possible, so that they run, for instance, from the first of the month to the end of the month, dates that are easier to keep in mind than arbitrarily chosen ones. Another mnemonic technique that serves similar ends is known from the Christian calendar.[4] There used to be a series of saint's days that functioned as deadlines; thus people knew, without a written contract determining the dates, that certain services or payments fell due on St. James's and St. Philip's day (May 1), St. John the Baptist's day (June 24), St. Martin's day (November 11), or on "St. Matthew's at the latest" (September 21).[5] Easter was also a favorite deadline, for which people were able to prepare by using the money saved during Lent. For borrowers, the favorite was, of course, St. Never's day.

. . .

The lending periods in public libraries, which we have used as an example, are far from being the only deadlines that people have to deal with a hundred times a day. Rents usually have to paid by the beginning of the month, installment payments on the motorcycle bought on credit have to be made on time, and tax bills carry a due date.

In fact, among the current forms of deadline-periods, the most prominent is surely the one used in the credit system. We know how long it was in Europe before Christians were allowed to lend money and charge or offer interest and compound interest.[6] But modern economic life in the industrialized world is based to a significant extent on the principle that money must not remain idle, but rather—just like people—"work," in sense that it circulates in the global financial market, accompanied by obligations to pay interest and fees in accord with strict regulations regarding the periods of loans, going wherever it is most urgently required. There it will "hopefully" be of use, so that after a time, it can be repaid—sometimes in installments, but in any case by the agreed-upon deadlines, that is, without hesitation, so that it can be put back into circulation.

To that extent Benjamin Franklin is not in every respect correct when he warns against contracting debts in a frightening maxim: "He that goes a-borrowing goes a sorrowing." On the other hand, a maxim motivated not morally but economically (with full awareness of the risk) would have to read "Going into debt is necessary," because debt promotes economic growth and also puts—if all goes well—a nice profit in one's own pocket.

In the credit system as it functions in the modern industrial world, money is closely connected with time, and more precisely with the deadline-period. That for society this is a daring, risky, fortune-hunting connection is already shown by the fact that Benjamin Franklin's well-known saying, "Time is money," is not reversible. Although time (in the form of life-time) can easily be exchanged for money, according to the rules of labor and commerce, the money received cannot be re-exchanged for time. Life-time is a nonrenewable resource; it always decreases, never increases. Money, on the other hand, also often decreases, because it is used for living expenses and other purposes, but it is well known that there are many ways, some more honorable than others, of replenishing and increasing it. The result is the twofold appearance of deadline-limited time. In the financial world, it encourages people to borrow by providing funds for a limited time and only later demanding repayment, which can usually be easily made with the expected profits. Conversely, the creditor initially assumes the costs, and only later receives a profit through the surplus value of interest and compound interest. But in this way all participants have ultimately reaped a profit in terms of both time and money. The danger is that one might be tempted to squander funds acquired on credit without deriving any profit from them. In the fact that debts with deadlines must be paid first lies the unknown element that can make a daring merchant rich, if he has a little luck, but can also lead to insolvency, bankruptcy, and ruin.

DEADLINES IN LAW, WITH A BRIEF GLANCE AT "ABORTION LIMITS" · Civil Law, Criminal Law, Labor Law

Deadline-periods (*Fristen*) are an important concept in law, yet one which, because it is not used very differently from the way it is used in everyday life, easily escapes the notice even of jurists.[7] In German law, the essential points are found in section 4, paragraphs 186–93 of the German Civil Code (*Bürgerliches Gesetzbuch*) and in the commentaries on these paragraphs. However, the significance of legally relevant deadline-periods reaches far beyond civil law, appearing in three kinds of spans of time: statutes of limitations, prison terms, and expiration periods. All three concern, though in different respects, the shortness of time and may be differentiated as follows:

Statutes of Limitations (Verjährungsfristen). Statutes of limitations limit the period of time during which criminal prosecution or some other kind of legal action can be initiated. Depending on the subject matter, the time limit, which also determines the subordinate concepts of a limit on prosecution and a limit on enforcement, is temporally graduated. In the case of a simple theft, for example, the statute of limitations in German criminal law is three years (§ 242 StrGB). This limit means that between the point in time when the offense is committed and the beginning of prosecution—questioning of witnesses, etc.—no more than three years can have passed. If this period of time has elapsed, a criminal prosecution or enforcement is legally excluded (§ 78 StrGB). This kind of limitation is provided even for offenses that might result in life imprisonment. For the prosecution of such crimes, the statute sets a limit of thirty years. Thus in this case, a long or very long span of time is involved. And this is precisely the reason why justice here sets a due date for itself. A statute of limitations presupposes on good psychological grounds that after at most three years in the case of a minor offense, or after at most thirty years—the period of a generation—in the case of a major offense, people's memories may have faded to the point that a mistaken judgment cannot be excluded. Only for murder (§ 211 StrGB) and especially for genocide and other crimes against humanity (§ 5 VStGB) is no statute of limitations provided. In such cases no legal limit is set on the efforts of individual or collective memory.

Such limitations are important above all in criminal law and international criminal law. But this principle is not unknown in civil law. The German Civil Code contains a section (§§ 194–202 BGB) in which it is stipulated that the normal limitation is three years. However, at the absolute maximum, in the case of an exceptional statute of limitations, it can be set at thirty years—again, the length of a generation. In this we see once more the connection between time limitations and memory; the transition from one generation to another is a basic boundary of memory.

Penalty periods. By the expression "penalty period" we mean here a period of time for which a court has imposed imprisonment. According to the prescriptions of German criminal law, the legal minimum for a "short" prison term is one month, while the maximum is fifteen years. Life imprisonment can be seen as a limiting case, in which the (unknown) end of the prison term coincides with the prisoner's death. But as a rule, as soon as a significant portion of a life sentence has been completed, it is suspended on probation, under certain conditions. The result is that the prisoner is given a secondary period of time during which he is on probation, subject to certain restrictions (§ 59a StrGB).

We will first explain the temporal phenomenon of prison terms by examining the crime of arson (§§ 306, 306a–f). The legislature has prescribed different prison terms for this offense. Depending on whether it is a simple, aggravated, or especially aggravated case of arson, prison terms—in the imposition of which the court is usually granted some discretion—range from a minimum of six months to a maximum of ten years. In the case of arson resulting in death, the maximum sentence is life imprisonment.

Measured against the average length of a human life, a prison term can be short or long. But any prison term is in other respects to be regarded as "limited," since it is spent in a penal institution in which the prisoner's quality of life is restricted. People used to say that a prison sentence must be spent on "bread and water." This way of speaking expressed in a prototypical way the shortage of food that in earlier times was seen in famines and often resulted in a shortening of life-time. Although this kind of extreme shortage is certainly no longer characteristic of modern imprisonment, other forms of punishment—for example, the denial of a driver's license—clearly show the principle of restriction through which in prison life is systematically slowed down, with the goal of re-socializing the prisoner.

In many criminal offenses, as in arson resulting from simple negligence, German criminal law provides that a prison term determined by the court can be replaced by the payment of a fine. In legal requirements of this kind we once again see the equation of time and money. However, it is striking that a fine is generally regarded as less serious than the corresponding prison term. The reason for this is that in human life time represents a nonrenewable resource, whereas money is a renewable one, though usually not without effort.

Expiration periods. Expiration periods are chiefly a matter of civil law. In legal texts or the explanations accompanying them, a period of time is indicated during which something specific must be produced or claimed, if it is not to expire. In the Civil Law code, expiration periods are consequently treated chiefly as the determination of the beginning and ending dates for a legally relevant period of time. How the distinctions among workdays, Sundays, and holidays are to be made is also clarified.

All these detailed regulations show that expiration periods, in contrast to many statutes of limitations, are basically short spans of time, whose beginning and ending dates make considerable demands on the attention and memory of the people concerned, especially because the legislature has certain tendency to overregulate the whole system of such deadline-periods. This tendency is not unproblematic, because an erroneous or careless way of dealing with expiration periods can result in important legal disadvantages for the person concerned by the law.

■　■　■

After this general overview, we must now briefly examine criminal law, insofar as in it prison terms and expiration periods mesh in significant ways. I refer to the ominous "paragraph on pregnancy" (*Schwangerschafts Paragraph*) (§ 218 StrGB) that fueled a bitter controversy in Germany for decades until finally an acceptable temporary compromise was found. This controversy became known in public debate under the name of *Fristenlösung* (termination of pregnancy). The course of this legal battle shows how in a democratic political system legality not infrequently shifts from the morality of penalty to the temporality of expiration dates (*Ausschlußfristen*), in order to seek in the latter a pragmatic solution (*Lösung*) for a political and legal problem of a more basic kind.[8]

In this political, moral, and theological legal debate, the question was whether the prohibition in paragraph 218 of the German Criminal Code (*Strafgesetzbuch, StrGB*) outlawing the termination of a pregnancy ("abortion") when termination is not indicated for medical or social reasons, along with prescribed prison terms of several years, should remain in force without restriction, or whether criminal law provisions regarding "the protection of unborn life" under certain, legally well-defined conditions should be abolished or loosened. For a long time, the two sides in this debate, one religious-conservative and the other secular-liberal, remained unreconciled and irreconcilable. This controversy was set aside or at least calmed only by resort to the temporal category of the deadline-period (*Frist*). The compromise formula thus arrived at and used in the paragraphs (218a–218c StrGB) inserted into the criminal code recognizes that "serious difficulties" (*Notlagen*), "conflicts" (*Konfliktlagen*), or "limits to suffering" (*Opfergrenzen*) may arise that might justify not punishing the termination of a pregnancy, so long as certain expiration periods (*Ausschluß-fristen*) are respected (§ 218a StrGB). The most important of these is a three-month period, starting at the beginning of the pregnancy, to think things over, combined with a period during which the pregnant woman must be counseled ("at least three days before the operation") by a certified counseling committee. In sum, this is the substance of the "abortion limit" that has provided at least a temporary settlement of this controversy over the scope of the German Criminal Code.

■　■　■

In the framework of civil law, labor law is conceived in a way particularly dependent upon deadlines. In this area it is always a matter of expiration periods that must be respected by the persons and authorities involved. This is particularly clear in the German Industrial Relations law (*Betriebsverfassungsgesetz, BetrVG*).[9] In the version approved on September 25, 2001, and amended on December 10, 2001, this law consists of 132 paragraphs and requires respect for no less than 210 deadline-periods. That is approximately one third more than the number of paragraphs in the law. A layperson or even an expert who wants to act in accord with these deadlines must not only carry around in his head the text of the law and its many complicated regulations but also have an appointment calendar at hand if he does not want to become hopelessly entangled in this network of deadline rules.

For example, this law regulates "involvement of employees or their representatives in decisions regarding job terminations." The first two paragraphs of the law, which distinguishes between an ordinary and an extraordinary termination, read as follows:

> (1) The works committee must be heard *before any termination*. The employer must explain to the committee the reasons for the termination. A termination not accompanied by a hearing of the works committee is insufficient.

(2) If the works committee has objections to an ordinary termination, it must *within one week at the most* give the employer written notification of the reasons for its objections. If it does not notify the employer *within this time period*, it is assumed that it has given its consent to the termination. If the works committee has objections to an extraordinary termination, it must *promptly, but within three days at the most*, give the employer written notification of the reasons for its objections. The works committee should, so far as seems required, hear the employee concerned *before taking a position. . . .*

These and many other deadlines of the same kind are undoubtedly important in guaranteeing the employee the protection of the law. Fortunately, an employment relationship is usually not limited in time. But if in spite of that fact a job termination is declared or is to be declared, then a time limit is set to the employment relationship after the fact. Involving other employees in dismissal decisions provides some protection against just this kind of limitation, when it is unjustified, and that is one important achievement of a welfare state.

However, we must not overlook the fact that these protective provisions impose further deadlines, which are so numerous, so complicated, and often so pedantically overregulated that both employers and employees easily can become entangled and bogged down in them. Therein lies a problematic peculiarity of the contemporary system of deadline-periods, which we can call the welfare state's deadline irony. It consists in the fact that people with little power in society theoretically can use short deadline-periods to protect themselves against the long and sometimes threatening deadline-periods of those with much power, but they must accept the risk that ultimately it is always the specialized attorneys who know their way around in this confusion of deadlines and therefore can help their clients succeed with relatively little effort. "Deadlines are deadlines," they say.

". . . BUT FOR THE PRESENT, NOT YET" · Heidegger, Marquard

Up to this point in this book, we have frequently said, referring to a few master teachers of the philosophy of time, that human lifetimes are "short" compared with the "long" time of art. If we now disregard the comparison with art, it is still clear that human life-time is limited, or, as Pascal would have preferred to say, "finite." To put it this way is not to suggest that the measure of finitude could be otherwise appraised than in accord with general experiential values. But it is certain *that* death awaits us at the foreseeable end of the lifetime of every living creature. But no man knows *when* this end will come. For that reason the Bible warns: "Watch therefore, for ye know neither the day nor the hour."[10]

This idea is also found, in a secularized form, at the center of Martin Heidegger's (1889–1956) philosophy of time, especially as it is set down in his magnum opus, *Being and Time (Sein und Zeit*, 1927).[11] Here we will read this book selectively and only insofar as it is concerned, from the viewpoint of "temporality," with human existence or *Dasein*. Heidegger sometimes writes this latter term with a hyphen (*Da-sein*) in order to give both its elements, *da* ("there") and *sein* ("to be") their full semantic weight even when they are combined. For our investigation the adverb *da* is of special importance. In this *da* the idea of the temporal limitation, shortness, and finitude of human life is concisely contained. As Heidegger suggestively puts it, to that extent every *Dasein* is a *Sein zum Ende* ("being toward the end") or, less often, a *Sein zum Tode* ("being toward death").

However, in the everyday consciousness that "one" (*man*) has of the course of life, the consciousness of an end awaiting *Dasein* is demonstrable only in traces. Obviously, men are sufficiently occupied with the "urgencies and possibilities of proximate, everyday life," as Heidegger says, and they have no leisure to think about their potentially imminent end. No doubt every human being knows in principle that some day death will stand on his doorstep. But "one" thinks that will probably not happen—to quote Heidegger verbatim—"for the present, not yet."

Yet without reflection on the end, a *Dasein* that does not want to persist in the mode of banality and inauthenticity must be regarded as in deficit and as an "incompleteness." The question is in which form the end of life can be brought into the search for the meaning of existence (*Dasein*), if as humans we can have at most a consciousness of the death of others, never of our own as such, since this consciousness will of course disappear along with the extinction of our individual existence. That is an existential question that Western philosophy of time before Heidegger, with the possible exceptions of the religious philosophers St. Augustine and Kierkegaard, had never raised in such an acute form. And the answer cannot consist in regarding existence as a (quasi-spatial) road or line running "between" a beginning and an end, and requiring only the fulfillment of an uninterrupted series of "nows." In that way one arrives at most at the death of others, not one's own, unmistakable death.

On these grounds, *Dasein* has as its attributes not only its limitedness and finitude but also datability, with the ending date being more important than the beginning date. For that reason, in his philosophical language Heidegger avoids the expression *Frist* (deadline-period), which implies a datable beginning and end. But he often comes close to this expression when he speaks of *Dasein*'s "span of time" or simply "span," although this always also succinctly implies the "expectancy of time" that emerges in *Dasein* through a certain ex-stasis or "being pending." Then what in it is still pending? The end is pending, yet not as a "pure one after the other," but rather—and this is very close to a latent concept of a deadline-period—as "the remainder of a still to be received payment of a debt." In this "omission" (*Vesäumnis*) lies the "being-indebtedness of *Dasein*" (to be understood existentially, not morally), which is imposed on every *Dasein* in the form of "care" (*Sorge*).

Heidegger stresses this ontological outcome at various points in his book—with variable but substantially similar semantics—by means of his favorite preposition, *vor* ("before"). With its help, he implants in the Being of Being-There (*im Sein des Daseins*), as its "temporality," an existential *Sich-Vorweg* ("Before-itself") manifested as *Vorgriff* ("foreconception"), *Vorhabe* ("fore-having"), *Vorgabe* ("present/gift"), *Vorweisung* ("production"), *Vorsicht* ("fore-sight"), *Vorrufen* ("call forth"), *Vorwegnehmen* ("anticipate"), and—with special predilection (*Vor-Liebe*)—as *vorlaufende Entschlossenheit* ("anticipatory resoluteness"). About these structures of possibility, which include "No-longer-being-able-to-be-there" (*Nicht-mehr-sein-können*) as a short- or long-term "pending" (*Bevorstand*), it can be generally said that "the *vor* and *vorweg* indicate the future." Therefore it is consistent that Heidegger sees an extremely close connection between temporality (*Zeitlichkeit*) and the Being of Being-there (*das Sein des Daseins*; as George Steiner puts it, "Being and Time are as one"),[12] and that among the three "ex-stases" of temporality, he assigns existential priority (*Vorrang*) to neither the present nor the past (Heidegger calls the latter *Gewesenheit*, "completedness") but rather to the future.

At this point we must recall that in his introductory description of an "inauthentic" understanding of Being, Heidegger had already said that humans stubbornly evade their Being-towards-death, since death will probably not occur right away (*vorläufig noch nicht*; lit., "for the time being, not yet"). Here Heidegger has cunningly smuggled the word *vorläufig* ("for the time being") into everyday speech in such a way that it can serve as a stand-in for a central theorem of his philosophy of temporality. This word keeps *Dasein's* way out (*Ausweg*) open, "for the time being," and here that means in concrete terms "running ahead" (*voraus-laufend*) into the "resoluteness" of an existential analysis of *Dasein* while still in the midst of the cares of everyday life, in order to acquire an authentic consciousness of one's own finitude and mortality.

Pursuing Heidegger's ideas and images further, I would like to translate a few of the things he said about time in short supply and about life subject to deadlines into a short, picturesque story situated in his Black Forest. Let us imagine a certain mountain path, on which a hiker sets out from a hut near Todtnauberg. Fog blankets the landscape. The hiker can find his way only with difficulty. But so far as he can tell, he is on a *Holzweg*.

At this point, we must explain what a *Holzweg* is. It does not refer, for example, to the common German way of saying that someone is *auf dem Holzweg* ("on the wrong track") when he is in error. Here, a *Holzweg* is a technical term (as we can see in Heidegger's work entitled *Holzwege*, 1950) designating a path used primarily by forestry workers.[13] In the preface to his book *Holzwege*, Heidegger offers the following description:

> "Wood" (*Holz*) is an old word for forest. In the forest there are paths, most of which suddenly peter out. They are called *Holzwege* (lit., "wood paths"). Each one goes its own way, but within the same wood. Often it seems that one is just like another. But it only seems so. Forestry workers and people who live in huts in the wood know the ways. They know what it means to be on a *Holzweg*.

Our hiker finds himself on such a *Holzweg*, which probably leads into the wood but does not lead out of it on the other side. As he walks along, he thinks about what is ahead of him (*das Sich-vorweg*) on his hike and the possible endpoint (*Frist-sein*) of his life's journey. The higher he climbs, the thicker the fog gets. He can see only a few steps ahead, just far enough to follow the path and to be able to know where to put his feet for the next few steps. He also has a little past experience that tells him that a *Holzweg* follows a route that can somehow be anticipated, and that it must reach a certain height before it comes to the wood-cutting area. All this is enough for the hiker to continue along the path undeterred, for this *Holzweg* will certainly "suddenly" end somewhere, "but not right away."

It may happen that the fog suddenly lifts. It is even conceivable that the hiker has made his climb under such unfavorable conditions precisely in order to have at least once—perhaps in a clearing (*Lichtung*)—the overwhelming experience of light and clarity suddenly appearing out of the fog. But then the wood-cutting area may already be right in front of him.

As told here, this story is not to be found in Heidegger's writings, neither in *Sein und Zeit* nor in *Holzwege*. Thus it does not give us certain insight into Heidegger's ideas about the Being of *Da-sein* and about the possibility of a deadline (*Seinkönnen des Frist-seins*). Hence, on the basis of what I said earlier about the confusion and tangled undergrowth of the many small and middle-sized, generally hardly comprehensible time limits in everyday life, we may imagine that the story takes a quite different course:

On one of these wanderings of Being in the Black Forest, it happens that the fog suddenly lifts. Delighted, our hiker confidently looks in front of him, but sees no clearing there. And so he can determine the further route of the path no more easily than he could in the fog. Thick and tangled, impenetrable undergrowth prevents him from gaining a clearer view of the wood and makes further advance along the *Holzweg* impossible. The hiker must turn around. On his way back, while he is thinking about the strangeness of finite times and short deadlines, he involuntarily recites in time with his steps a little ditty:

> Often we can't see
> The looming death-line
> For all the tiny
> Daily deadlines.

Later on, the hiker calls this little ditty his *Holzweg*-rule. But it might also just be a catchy tune.

. . .

Since there is nothing in Heidegger's work about a hiker on a foggy *Holzweg* in the Black Forest, to complete this report let us follow, for a short stretch of the way, another wanderer between being and time: Odo Marquard.[14] Marquard is, like myself, a critical and attentive reader of Heidegger, but as a philosopher, he reads in a different way, namely as if there were no fog. Thus in his article "Zeit und Endlichkeit" (1991) he discusses Heidegger's philosophy of time expressly in terms of the temporally limited nature of human existence. The latter is, in Marquard's words, a *todbegrenzte Lebensfrist* ("a period of life limited by a deadline"), and in another part of his article he is even led to use the aphoristically abbreviated formulation: *Zeit ist Frist* ("time is a deadline-period). There are—fortunately, I would say—times and spans of time that are not deadline-periods: open, gliding, flowing, or fleeting times as well as the incomparable *kairos*, which is certainly not to be seen as a span of time with a deadline and without extension. However, we have to concede that in post-industrial civilization an increasing amount of time is consumed in the form of deadline-periods. I nonetheless maintain that in a deadline-period (*Frist*) in the strict sense of the term, there are two datable temporal limits, of which the second is the more important. This is a condition of life-time only insofar as we know *that* at the end of its course there is an end, that this end's name is death, and that this final date will not forever remain latent, but is only hidden from the living "for the time being," just as in history books a person's year of birth is sometimes given while the year of death is left blank. For that reason I believe that in discussing the Heideggerian *Dasein* Odo Marquard may have wished away the mists of the Black Forest a bit too forcefully. To sum up our brief encounter with Heidegger and Marquard, we may say that our merely latent, not apparent finitude as human beings is inevitably a trek through the fog during which no one knows whether he will be carried off before reaching the wood-cutting area.

9

Short Stories about Short Deadlines

SAVED FROM DEATH AT THE LAST MINUTE

Thousand and One Nights; Shakespeare, *The Merchant of Venice*

Short deadlines that must be respected to the day and hour are a serious matter. They can cause real problems for someone who is unfortunate enough to be subject to them. What happens when such a deadline is not respected? Can one expect a further extension that will result in salvation by one's own efforts or by those of others? Or is this already an extended and now irrevocably final deadline, after which time will have definitively run out?

What the pressure of a deadline of this kind, with its incalculable risks, might mean for someone can hardly be described with abstract concepts. In this case, only narrative can provide reliable information, drawn from real or from fictive sources. Thus in literature we find more than a few stories that represent time in short supply under extreme conditions, namely on the brink of death. We may take comfort from the fact that such narratives, by making intimate perception of the anguish and perils of deadlines possible, often lead to salvation from their most extreme dangers.

Thus the following story is told about a rich Asian merchant who often made business trips to collect money owed him. On one of these journeys, he rested in the shade of a tree and ate a few dates he had brought along, throwing the pits in a wide arc around him. An enormous demon suddenly appeared before his startled eyes and threatened him with a sword. He must die, the demon said, because one of the date pits had killed his son. The merchant vainly protested that he was innocent. Fearing that he was in mortal danger, the merchant finally beseeched the demon to grant him a reprieve of a few months so that he could set his affairs in order at home and say farewell to his family. Allah would be the warrant that he would return on New Year's day to pay for the accident with his life, even though he was guiltless. The demon accepted the warrant and granted him the requested postponement.

After the merchant had set his house in order and with much weeping bidden his family farewell, he delivered himself up to his enemy, punctually on New Year's day. Just then three sheikhs came along. They felt sorry for the merchant. In order to save him, they persuaded the demon to make a wager. Each of them would tell a story, and if they gave the demon the greatest pleasure, as a reward he would let the teller have one third of the blood that he demanded from the merchant as atonement. The demon accepted, and each of the three sheikhs told a story. The stories so delighted the demon that he gave each of them one third of the merchant's blood. By means of the three sheikhs' storytelling skills the merchant was freed from the deadline he had accepted and escaped a cruel death.[1]

The story briefly summarized here, along with the tales the sheikhs tell, is found in the *Thousand and One Nights*. The stories in this collection go back to the most ancient times and were initially handed down through oral tradition. Perhaps only the individual themes were very old, and were assembled in this story cycle at a relatively late date, during the flowering of Arabic literature in the eighth century. The dates given are all quite uncertain, however, and experts in the field disagree about them. What we do know is that this masterpiece of Oriental narrative art became known in the West only at the beginning of the eighteenth century. The French orientalist Antoine Galland was in this case the great mediator between East and West. In his translation, the *Thousand and One Nights* became a "classic" in Europe. In Germany, the stories were first translated from the French version by Johann Heinrich Voß; in England, by Sir Richard Burton.[2]

The little series of stories about the Oriental merchant and the evil demon shows *in nuce* something that is characteristic of the *Thousand*

and One Nights as a whole. The book's leitmotif is an acute mortal danger whose short-term menace is repeatedly put off by means of the ruse of artful storytelling until it is ultimately, but really only at the happy ending, completely averted.

In the overarching frame story, this turn of events and salvation also takes place through storytelling. There, the threat of death proceeds from King Shahryar, who has himself become a kind of demon as a result of painful experiences with an unfaithful wife. Every day he marries a virgin and after a night of lovemaking has her immediately killed so that she cannot be unfaithful to him. This is also to be the fate of his vizier's beautiful daughter Shahrazad, whom he marries for the short time of a single night. But Shahrazad is a clever woman and a gifted storyteller, and night after night, after she has lain with the king, she tells him such fascinating stories, breaking off her narrative at the most interesting point as dawn approaches, that the king keeps postponing the execution he has commanded, and which the vizier, who has already prepared his daughter's burial shroud, repeatedly expects. The stories told by the three sheikhs who saved the merchant from the demon's fury are stories of this kind; cunningly told by Shahrazad over several nights, they also save the vizier's daughter.

After precisely one thousand and one nights, this mortally dangerous game against the repeatedly postponed deadline for execution comes to a happy end. After telling her last story, Shahrazad can bring out, instead of more stories, the three sons who have been born to her over the narrative time of a little more than three times nine months. As deeply moved by the sight of his three sons as he is delighted by the memory of the precious stories he has heard over this long period of time, the king finally overcomes his thoughts of revenge and celebrates with great pomp and ceremony his marriage to Queen Shahrazad.

Thus at the end all deadlines for execution of the death sentence are easily cancelled in the broad frame story as well. The art of storytelling, which is essentially connected with unlimited time, has achieved this miracle.

∎ ∎ ∎

These stories from the *Thousand and One Nights* in many respects remind us of Shakespeare's play *The Merchant of Venice* (ca. 1597). This is not surprising, since such motifs are widespread and their precise itinerary is hard to evaluate.³ In Shakespeare's comedy—if it *is* a comedy—the role of the demon is played by the rich Jew Shylock ("this devil"). But the rich man takes on this role unexpectedly, in the course of the play. At the outset, he appears extremely philanthropic and responds with generosity to the Venetian merchant Antonio ("the honest Antonio") when the latter asks for a loan, not for himself, but rather for his feckless friend Bassanio, who needs the money in order to court the rich heiress Portia. Generously, without demanding interest, Shylock loans him three thousand ducats for three months. But the debtor must strictly respect the deadline for payment, witnessed by a notary; if he does not, the Jew will have the right to cut a pound of flesh from his body.

However, this harsh condition is imposed by the lender only in jest ("this merry bond," "a merry sport") and is therefore not taken seriously by the debtor Antonio, because he blithely assumes that in less than two months his ship will sail into Venice's harbor loaded with rich cargo. But two fatal mishaps thwart this calculation. All of Antonio's ships are wrecked by a storm at sea. He is incapable of paying. Shylock suffers a still worse misfortune: his beloved daughter Jessica runs off with a Christian lothario and takes advantage of the opportunity to plunder her father's moneybox. As is fitting in a comedy, Shylock at first bemoans the loss of his daughter and that of his ducats with equal distress. But we soon hear him say, in a heart-rending tone: "My daughter is my flesh and my blood." At precisely this point the comedy shifts into a tragic register. In the Jew's soul dark thoughts of vengeance are now awakening. Has the Christian debtor Antonio not staked as his bond for the loan a piece of his own flesh? The light-hearted joke suddenly becomes deadly serious. After the loss of his ships, Antonio obviously cannot repay the debt, and his creditor implacably insists on his paying the agreed-upon pound of flesh. Even when Antonio's friends offer to pay twice or thrice the amount he owes, Shylock will not relent: "I stay here on my bond" and "I'll torture him."

In this oscillation between comedy and tragedy, is there any character who could still use his storytelling skill to check or wholly avert disaster? There is not, and unlike the stories from the *Thousand and One Nights*, Shakespeare's play is not a paean to the lofty art of storytelling. But there is—as the end of play, which is not always equal to the height of the emotions churned up so far, will have it—an intervention on the part of a *deus ex machina*. This role is assumed by the Duke, who has his legal advisors prepare pettifogging arguments so that he can simultaneously agree with and contradict the cruel creditor. According to these arguments, the Jew may in fact cut the pound of flesh from the Christian's body, as was agreed, but woe to him if in doing so he sheds a drop of Christian blood. Thus the forfeited pound of flesh cannot be collected, and Antonio finds himself saved at the last minute from a mortal threat. The audience can heave a sigh of relief. At the end of the play, it is only the Jew Shylock who is cheated and ridiculed as if he were only a marionette in a comical play based on a folktale—and a Christian audience could take pleasure in this at a time when it was perhaps not yet so clear as it is today that pointed and light-hearted speech can quickly turn deadly serious.

A BALLAD ABOUT FRIENDSHIP AND DEADLINES
Schiller, "Die Bürgschaft"

Schiller's "Die Bürgschaft" ("The Pledge," 1799) is a standard example of the classical German ballad.[4] This poem in twenty stanzas used to be a fixture of the middle-class cultural canon taught in German high schools, and generations of German students had to learn it by heart. Memorizing Schiller's ballad and other similar texts was supposed to teach them that even long texts can be stored up in memory by someone who must or wants to do so, and as actors constantly have to do. However, to compensate for the effort of learning them, many generations of high school students have parodied Schiller's verses. In fact, it is hard to consider this ballad a good poem. But indirectly, through techniques of memory and their parodistic consequences, the "exciting" action of Schiller's ballad has helped give students a more acute awareness of deadlines and an opportunity to make use of it in learning.

The ballad's first stanza contains the exposition. It tells of an unsuccessful attempt on the life of Dionysos, tyrant of Syracuse. The would-be assassin, a noble youth named Damon, is seized and condemned to death:

> Toward Dionysos, the tyrant, crept
> Damon, a dagger under his cloak;
> His pursuers clapped him in irons.
> "What were you going to do with the dagger, speak!"

The hot-tempered youth replied darkly.
"Free the city from the tyrant!"
"You shall rue that on the cross."

Zu Dionys, dem Tyrannen, schlich
Damon, den Dolch im Gewande;
Ihn schlugen die Häscher in Bande.
"Was wolltest du mit dem Dolche, sprich!"
Entgegnet ihm finster der Wüterich.
"Die Stadt vom Tyrannen befreien!"
"Das sollst du am Kreuze bereuen."

If readers of the ballad expect the following verses to tell them more about this "hot-tempered youth" and his presumably noble motives, they will be disappointed. Strangely enough, even as a historian Schiller seems to take no interest in the political motives of the planned assassination of the tyrant. He is interested only in the dangerous game played with the pressure of deadlines to which the would-be assassin now finds himself subject.

In the second stanza, we learn to our astonishment that the would-be assassin accepts the death sentence with resignation, but asks the tyrant—so much does he still trust this monster—for a reprieve of three days. Being obliged to play the father's role in his family, he must carry out a familial duty that was in earlier times considered extremely important, namely, he must "ensure that his sister is married." Thus he makes the tyrant an offer that is risky for everyone concerned: a true friend will replace him as a living pledge and will consent to be put to death should he not return within the short time of three days.

To the reader's surprise, the tyrant accepts this delay, but only with the treacherous intention of tempting Damon to leave his friend in the lurch in order to save his own life, thus proving himself to be a coward. Unsuspecting, the friend undertakes this dangerous role out of friendship for Damon. The latter, on temporary leave from death, hurries home and "quickly" carries out his peaceful mission within the family circle.

Only at dawn on the third day can Damon begin his return journey:

Hasting home with a heavy heart,
So he does not miss the deadline.

> Eilt heim mit sorgender Seele
> Damit er die Frist nicht verfehle.

Here, the surprising word "home" (*heim*) presumably means fulfilling the condition of returning by the deadline. But for the reader, the deadline is still far off. As an experienced dramatist, Schiller has built a few retarding elements into his ballad. Time-consuming obstacles of the most diverse kinds confront the hastening traveler and dramatically delay his attempt to arrive before the deadline. First, an "endless rain" pours out of the sky and turns the river Damon has to cross into a raging torrent. In this we can also see a symbol of rapidly passing time:

> And wave after wave races by
> And hour after hour runs out.

> Und Welle auf Welle zerrinnet
> Und Stunde an Stunde entrinnet.

Luckily for the traveler, the storm suddenly stops, and he hurries on, racing against time, which is growing shorter and shorter.

A second obstacle appears in the form of a band of highwaymen, which he is nonetheless able to fight off "with mighty blows." And finally, as the scorching heat of the sun, a third obstacle to his returning on time, threatens to utterly exhaust him, nature itself helps him by making a silvery pure spring appear right before his eyes.

However, battling these obstacles has consumed a great deal of time, and the deadline is inexorably approaching. In the nick of time, as the saying goes, Damon arrives in the tyrant's city by the deadline, just as his friend is being led in fetters through the gaping crowd to the place of execution. His friend's life hangs in the balance:

> "Strangle me, executioner!" he shouts.
> "Here am I, he is my pledge!"

> "Mich, Henker!" ruft er, "erwürget!
> Da bin ich, für den er gebürget!"

Today, it is difficult to bring to the ballad the naiveté that this "classical" poet requires. The cult of friendship at the end of the eighteenth century is so far outside our literary horizon that the two friends in this poem seem to have come from some other planet. Even Dionysos, who at the beginning of the ballad seemed evil enough to justify assassinating him as a tyrant, bears within himself, as a man and a Greek, the seed of noble friendship. He is so impressed by Damon's courageous devotion that he relents, and asks the two men to be his friends. Thus in the innocently trusting verses of his ballad Schiller tells us only a beautiful fairy tale.

Yet it cannot be denied that this poem also has a certain elemental power. With his outstanding sense for historical drama, Schiller instinctively realized that the genre of the ballad was best suited to the dynamics of short spans of time. When at the end of the ballad only a few minutes and seconds remain, because the cross has "already" been erected, and Damon's friend is "already" being lifted onto it, the reader's mounting concern about the shortness of time and the approaching deadline is discharged in a rewarding moment of sympathy that a short period of German literature optimistically assumed might ultimately overcome even a tyrant's rage, and probably not only in far-off Syracuse.

A DEVIL'S PACT WITH DEADLINES · Chamisso

Charles Louis Adélaïde Chamisso de Boncourt (1781–1837), the son of a French count, could never have dreamed that he would someday become a German classical poet known as Adelbert von Chamisso. The French Revolution, which drove his family into exile in Prussia, sent his life down this unusual path. When the Prussians went to war against Napoleon's France, for a time Chamisso withdrew from the conflict between his two homelands, and in 1813 he wrote the "strange story" of Peter Schlemihl, the man without a shadow, which, even more than his poetry, made him a famous author in German literature.[5]

This story tells us that when he was a young, inexperienced fellow Peter Schlemihl let the Devil have his shadow in exchange for a purse that was never empty. Let us note the form in which the Devil appeared to him: the Devil is "the gray one" (*der Graue*), a unprepossessing little man in a gray frock who looks "like a bit of yarn a tailor has left on his needle." This "pale apparition" thus looks like the caricature and fairy-tale version of a poor tailor—yet it is the Devil, who now proceeds to take his unsuspecting victim's shadow as during a fitting a tailor might take new and dangerous measurements.

Once the Devil has rolled up the shadow and made off with it, the eponymous hero of Chamisso's strange story immediately becomes immensely rich. But the loss of his shadow causes him to experience the shortness of time as never before. Chamisso skillfully stitches the theme of time into the fabric of the story by making this pact with the Devil not yet concern Schlemihl's immortal soul, but—for the time being—"only" his earthly shadow. Thus at first, in accord with the intention of the Devil, who offers his advice here as an experienced jurist, there is only a kind of preliminary contract, to be followed by the main contract—in precise legal terminology—"after one full year" (*über Jahr und Tag*; lit., "a year and a day"). Thus Peter Schlemihl suddenly finds himself a millionaire in money but a beggar in time.

Peter experiences the year's time before the deadline set by the Devil as such a terribly shortened time chiefly because during its course he falls in love with the beautiful and demure Mina, whose hand he can win only if he gets his own shadow back. So day after day, "Count Peter," as people call him since he has become a rich man, looks forward to the end of the preliminary contract in the grim hope that his pact with the Devil can still be undone, even if he has to give up his wealth.

Chamisso further heightens the dramatic character of this expectation by having the impatient lover and his diabolical contractual partner interpret differently the date on which "the gray one" will turn up again. Schlemihl's calculation makes the period as short as possible, so that the contract comes to an end on the thirty-first day of the twelfth month, whereas the Devil, observing with greater legalistic precision the formal wording of the contract, does not arrive at the appointed meeting place until "one full year" has elapsed, that is, one day afterward, on the first of the following month. The disputed day during which Schlemihl prematurely awaits the Devil's arrival becomes for him the worst day of his shadowless existence and the quintessence of his hopelessly shortened time. The fear of having missed the deadline once and for all gnaws at his heart like a "tormenting worm," and we follow his shortage of time with sympathy after reading the following words of his confession:

> The fateful day approached, anxious and numb like a storm cloud. The eve of that day had already come—I could hardly breathe. I had

taken the precaution of filling a few chests with money, and stayed up waiting for the clock to ring midnight.—It rang.—I sat there, my eyes fixed on the clock's hands, counting off the seconds, the minutes, which were like so many dagger thrusts. At every noise I heard, I jumped to my feet; dawn broke. The leaden hours followed one another; midday came, evening, night; the clock's hands moved, hope faded, and nothing appeared; the last minutes of the last hour arrived, and nothing appeared; the first stroke of midnight rang, and despairing I fell back on my bed, weeping.

Finally, as Peter Schlemihl, "with death in his heart," sees the dawn of the following day breaking, the Devil appears—calmly, because he has arrived at the legally correct time—but only to reject Schlemihl's request for the return of his shadow in exchange for the purse. But at least the Devil extends the contract's duration, though for an even shorter three-day period (Schlemihl: "three dreadful days"), and then extends it again, and yet again, each time for a still shorter period, until finally the unfortunate Schlemihl, his nerves wracked by fear of the Devil's deadline, casts away all his wealth in money and property, without even having gotten the Devil to return his shadow. And so, deprived of his shadow and of the Devil's money, and of course also without the hoped-for happiness in love, Peter Schlemihl from that day on humbly and laboriously ekes out the remainder of his life. He even enjoys a certain serenity, since his time is finally no longer short.

THE TRAPS AND LABORS OF DEADLINES · Flaubert, Maupassant

Flaubert's novel *Madame Bovary* (1857) is not only about a great passion in a small city, but also about money, which first causes small problems and then great ones.[6] Emma Bovary needs money, a lot of money, to keep up her appearance in a French provincial town, and still more in Paris later on. There are all the little trifles (*fantaisies*) that an unhappily married woman needs in order to "make bearable the bitterness of her life." This feminine weakness is quickly discerned by a draper with the significant name of "Lheureux" ("the fortunate man"). He inveigles Emma, who has just received her inheritance, by offering her fine cloth at bargain prices. At first, he says nothing about payment. But as if it were a mere formality, he makes sure that every promissory note bears Emma's clearly legible signature. The date is also important to him: "And the date, please, the date!" These dealings seem to be without risk for Emma, since the notes with which she pays her bills are issued with a very long payment period (*une fort longue échéance*).

All the same, Emma thinks it worthwhile to learn something about financial matters, so that in negotiating she can use a few quickly acquired technical expressions which, trusting to luck, she inserts at random into her remarks. Her own husband is so impressed by this that he gives her full power of attorney over his assets, though the latter are none too extensive. He does so at Lheureux's urging: "a power of attorney would be convenient!" ("une procuration, ce serait commode!").

In this way, Emma succeeds for a time in meeting all her payment deadlines, making new debts if necessary in order to pay back the old ones whose payment period has elapsed. But the time soon comes for the crafty draper to tighten his deadline-period nets. He no longer bothers to conceal his evil game from the eyes of his careless debtor:

> Did you imagine then, little lady, that I was going to be your supplier and banker until the end of time, just out of charity?

> Pensiez-vous, ma petite dame, que j'allais, jusqu'à la consommation des siècles, être votre fournisseur et banquier pour l'amour de Dieu?

Now Emma's situation quickly becomes extremely critical. She resorts to pleading and begging: "I beg you, Monsieur Lheureux, just a few more days!" The merchant is unmoved: "I couldn't care less" ("Je m'en moque pas mal").

Yet the greatest humiliations for the tardy debtor are still to come. Emma swallows her pride and goes to ask her two former lovers to help her; formerly, they were prepared to lay their whole lives at her feet. But in this novel as well, when money is at stake love comes to an end. Another gentleman on whom in her extremity she has pinned her last hopes proves to be a shameless lecher who demands that she go to bed with him in exchange for his help. Nauseated, Emma also rejects this way out of her dilemma.

Nothing can now protect her from the threat of the approaching payment deadline. An official summons to pay her debt is delivered to her; it allows her a final period of twenty-four hours before the bailiff comes to seize the Bovary family's goods and thereby make their disgrace known to all. The trap snaps shut. Emma finds herself on the edge of an "abyss": "I am ruined" ("je suis ruinée"). As a result of the inevitable scandal, Emma's husband and their little daughter are caught up in her ruin. Emma poisons herself with arsenic. Death cancels all her deadlines. She dies with the "serenity of a duty fulfilled" ("la sérenité d'un devoir accompli"). But as he writes these final lines, the novelist Flaubert, who has put this destiny on paper, himself feels the bitter taste of arsenic on his tongue.

. . .

In Guy de Maupassant's short story, "The Necklace" ("La parure"), the tragedy of the deadline is of smaller dimensions and stops just short of death.[7] At the beginning, the life of Monsieur and Madame Loisel moves along regularly and peacefully. The husband is a minor employee in a Paris government ministry, where he contentedly performs his duties. But like Emma Bovary, Mathilde Loisel has learned about romantic raptures in her convent school, and in her modest family home she now dreams of an entirely different life in which luxury and happiness are the rule.

One evening—most of Maupassant's stories begin with some such "extraordinary event"—the husband comes home from work with a note in which the Minister and his wife invite Monsieur and Madame Loisel to an evening party at the ministry. This unexpected invitation causes the husband great joy but arouses despair in his wife. What should she wear? That problem she can deal with. But what jewelry should she put on? Mathilde Loisel has no jewelry. From her schooldays at the convent, however, she still has a wealthy friend with a great deal of jewelry. Willingly and without hesitation, her friend lends her a necklace made of sparkling diamonds. At the party, Mathilde is splendid in her dress and still more splendid with her precious necklace.

The tragedy begins on the way home. The necklace is lost. How can she explain this loss to her friend? There is nothing else to do; using money borrowed at risk, she must buy a new, identical necklace as soon as possible, and somewhat tardily give it back to the unsuspecting friend instead of the one she has lost. In fact, her friend does not notice the exchange. She is only somewhat annoyed by Mathilde's delay in returning her jewelry.

For the Loisels, that is the least of their worries. It requires only a few words of excuse. But now the real pressure of deadlines begins for the couple. They have to pay back the borrowed money in small installments that fall due one after another. All the money her husband earns at the ministry goes to pay the installments on their debt and to enrich a usurer, while Mathilde has to do menial labor of various kinds to make ends meet. In the end, after years of hard work in need and privation, all the debts are paid with compound interest. The final deadline is met.

Obviously aged and careworn, Mathilde goes again to see her wealthy friend, who scarcely recognizes her. Finally, she can tell her the long story of the lost necklace and the ten years of drudgery that have paid for it. The friend has trouble recalling the event. However, she is quite sure that the necklace she lent Mathilde was not made with genuine diamonds, but only with worthless imitations.

DEADLINES OF HONOR, PRUSSIAN STYLE · Theodor Fontane

The Prussian author Theodor Fontane's tale "Schach von Wuthenow" (1883) far exceeds, with its 153 pages, the usual length of a short story.[8] A modern publisher might even market it as a short novel. But the heart of the tale, which begins near the middle of the text after a long introduction dealing with the history of the times, can certainly be called a casuistic short story. The "case" thus narrated is so richly orchestrated with various lateral plot lines and fully developed dialogues that some interpreters have maintained that what is central to this tale is not so much the plot and the passions of the protagonists but above all a historical critique of Prussia's fading glory in the Napoleonic age.

Without contradicting that interpretation, we will read the tale—in accord with our subject in the present volume—as a text that gives expression to a dramatically decreasing time. However, we must first say as a preliminary to discussing the action, which the author has shifted from the end of the nineteenth century to its beginning, that among Prussian aristocrats and military officers of this period, honor meant everything for men, and beauty meant almost everything for women. But fate has already heavily intervened in all this. The still stunningly beautiful Frau von Carayon, who is part of the French "colony" in Berlin, has seen her equally beautiful daughter Victoire lose all her charm as a result of smallpox. Is there still a chance that Victoire, now deemed "unbeautiful" and deprived by fate of her triumph, can establish herself in this society through an advantageous and perhaps even romantic marriage? The Prussian cavalry captain Schach von Wuthenow, himself the very picture of masculine beauty, seems to be interested in her despite her scarred face. She is favorably inclined toward him as well, but is the captain really, as she expects, a man with character?

One "moment" of passionate attraction and "sweet intoxication" between the two protagonists sets the dramatic clock ticking, with a nine-month deadline that every one involved must keep firmly in mind if this brief episode of love is not to result in long suffering, and if honor is not to transformed into inextinguishable shame.

The aristocratic upbringing of Frau von Carayon, who is the center of the story's plot, has taught her exactly how to act in this situation. She demands that the captain immediately "legitimate the event." Saying goodbye "until tomorrow" and then showing up only occasionally is no longer permissible. Instead, marriage must follow "within a short time." The captain accepts this condition as his fate and unhesitatingly declares his willingness to marry Victoire as soon as possible. The engagement is set for a week hence, with the marriage to follow three weeks later. Afterward, they can take a year-long honeymoon trip that will blur all the exact dates.

At this point in the dramatically accelerated time of the action, Fontane skillfully inserts a retarding element. The love affair between Schach and Victoire has been discussed in the casino, where Schach's fellow officers do not let this marvelous opportunity for malicious gossip escape them. They cause defamatory pamphlets to be circulated in which Schach is mocked as an exotic "Shah" von Wuthenow, since instead of the beautiful mother, who is his own age, he has courted— why?—her unbeautiful daughter. Doesn't he realize that *her* face can cause him to lose *his* face? The vain captain is deeply wounded by this "conspiracy." He leaves the Carayons without saying farewell and retires to his family domain in Wuthenow. There peace returns to his soul, for in the Brandenburg countryside time still moves at a leisurely pace, in accord with natural rhythms and not with the fixed deadlines of society. After a few hours Herr von Wuthenow can already call out to his overseer: "Take your time, old man!"

This idyll doesn't last long, however, for the Carayons soon learn that Schach has taken "indefinite leave," which Victoire's mother sees as nothing less than a cowardly flight. So she sets out in writing a final deadline for the tardy lover to send her a confirmation of the engagement: "If I have not received it by Wednesday, I shall take other, completely independent steps."

Schach does not reply to this ultimatum formulated in legal terms. So on the following day—the deadlines are drawing near—Frau von Carayon sees no alternative other than to request an audience with the king. Once again Fontane inserts a retarding factor: the king is staying in the countryside. His petitioner goes to find him. With the help of a friend who is a high official at the court, she manages to meet the king while he is taking a walk in the park. Thus she is able to bring up her "dispute." His majesty finds the case "very unfortunate" and immediately summons the captain. He speaks with the officer laconically, the way superiors usually address their subordinates in Spartan Prussia. In the royal language of command, the case is put briefly and curtly: "You must make reparations, quickly, in fact immediately!" The captain must either marry or resign his commission, those are his alternatives. Nothing remains but for him to obey: "Yes, your Majesty!"

Now the last period of time during which the protagonists can act is running out. On Friday, Schach and Victoire are married. In the afternoon of his "day of honor," the captain puts a bullet through his head.

After the gestation period set by nature, Victoire brings a daughter into the world, a beautiful child, such as was traditional in both families until Victoire's misfortune. Since deadlines have been respected, honor is preserved for all concerned, at least a "false honor," as a few secondary characters in the story already know better than the main characters.

DEADLINES FOR HONOR IN IMPERIAL AUSTRIA · Arthur Schnitzler

As an imperial officer, Second Lieutenant Gustl knows, in the eponymous story by Arthur Schnitzler, what the code of honor requires of a man of standing.[9] If his honor is ever threatened and put in question by an affront, he must "stand firm" (*stante pede*) and defend it with his saber in his hand. Even the slightest offense, whether justified or unjustified, results in the immediate loss of his honor, and he regains it only when the offender has given him "satisfaction," preferably in a duel. Between these two critical points in time, which may not be far apart, extends the span of time that we can call a deadline-period for honor.

The very young lieutenant has recently fought his first duel, and he is about to fight another one. His last opponent was a First Lieutenant—a "serious opponent," he has to admit, but neither of them was wounded in the duel. He is soon to fight another duel, this time with a civilian—an attorney, but fortunately a professor with a doctor's degree, so that as in the case of the First Lieutenant, there is no doubt as to his ability to give satisfaction. What happened with him? The academic, obviously inclined to be ironic, had insulted the officer with some kind of witty rejoinder. So now blood must be shed in order to restore the military honor of Lieutenant Gustl and his caste. This second duel inspires no fear in the dashing young officer: everything will go well. Thus the evening before he can seek relaxation at a concert. An oratorio is to be performed.

Lieutenant Gustl grows very bored in the concert hall, and thus the story begins with him wondering: "How long is this going to go on, then?" But even the longest oratorio finally comes to an end. From that point, about eleven in the evening, until about seven the next morning, is the short time span of this story. It is also the short deadline-period that the narrator has set for the resolution of this case where his honor is at stake.

The delicate casuistics of this new case arise because on leaving the concert hall amid a crowd, Lieutenant Gustl accidentally bumps into an old man who in his annoyance calls him a "stupid boy." When the lieutenant's anger flares, the old man grabs the pommel of Gustl's saber. Thus he has "laid hands on his weapon," which according to the code of honor constitutes a clear case of infringement on his honor. But for Lieutenant Gustl it's an annoying matter: he knows the man—he's the baker Habetswallner. An artisan, and thus neither subject to the code of honor nor capable of giving satisfaction.

So what is to be done? At this point, the lieutenant is so much at a loss that he does nothing at all. Thus he fails to take advantage of the only propitious moment for spontaneous action. Only later, during the night, is his brain tormented by the bitter question as to what he could and should have immediately done in this situation, without reflecting, in order to punish the baker for his brazenness. But how could he have done such a thing amid the crowd, when his saber was held fast by a burly artisan?

The tormenting thoughts passing through the lieutenant's head during the long hours of the night are related to the reader in an "internal monologue." This monologue registers not only all the unfortunate hero's thoughts but also all the most hidden stirrings of his soul. What can he do now except finally acknowledge that his existence as a man of honor is over and, disgraced, give up wearing the honorable uniform of an imperial officer? But no, there is another, honorable way out for the lieutenant: he can without further delay put a bullet through his head. And the more he turns over his confused thoughts the more he becomes convinced that his disgrace can be erased only by committing suicide. His young life is to continue only for a period of a few short hours of the night, which don't count for honor.

During this short span of time, which he spends wandering aimlessly around the Prater, Vienna's great public park, the strangest ideas pass through the lieutenant's head, as we learn in detail through the hero's internal monologue. In the wild turmoil of his feelings, Lieutenant Gustl thinks about his fellow officers, his earlier and current girlfriends, the duel scheduled for tomorrow, and the debts he made yesterday, his mother, his cousin, his sister—and finally, it occurs to him that the following morning he will be dead: "How strange to be thinking of all sorts of things in this way when in a few hours one has to put a bullet through his head!" Naturally, he also considers the riddle of time since it has grown so short for him: "What does 'next year' mean, after all? What does 'next week' mean? What does 'day after tomorrow' mean?" The only date he can count on in this situation is the self-imposed deadline for honor: "Tomorrow is the day of my death—April 5."

Overexcited by this storm of thoughts, Lieutenant Gustl finally falls asleep on a park bench in the Prater. When he awakens, dawn is already breaking. From the eight hours of narrated time preceding the deadline, the reader must subtract a few hours of unconscious lifetime that the hero has spent sleeping or dozing. Thus the narrative and reading time of this story almost coincides with that of the waking time recounted.

Like the hero on his park bench, the reader awakes with a start: only a few minutes are left before the deadline. The remaining amount of time is barely enough for a quick stop in a coffee house that has just opened. The morning newspapers have already been set out. The waiter blurts out the exciting news: at precisely midnight, the baker Habetswallner had a stroke "and died on the spot!"

Lieutenant Gustl quickly recovers himself. He has only to reason that between the event at the concert hall and Habetswallner's sudden death so little time passed that the baker cannot have spread word of his disgrace. But a disgrace that no one knows about is not a disgrace, for honor exists entirely in the eyes of others. Consequently Lieutenant Gustl is still in full and undiminished possession of his honor. There is no longer any reason to put a pistol to his head. The lieutenant can hold his head high as he returns to the barracks. On the duty roster for the day: eight o'clock, rifle practice; nine-thirty, drill. And at four in the afternoon, the duel with the professor is scheduled. In thinking about the latter, the lieutenant speaks his internal monologue out loud: "Just wait, my man, just you wait! I'm in fine fettle. I'm going to cut you up like horse-radish!"

A SHORT TIME TO BE HUMANE

García Márquez, *Chronicle of a Death Foretold*

At the end of the nineteenth century, the era of honor was coming to an end. In Hermann Sudermann's play *Honor* (*Die Ehre*, 1899), a clear last word is spoken by a count and former military officer who calmly observes: "Just between you and me, there isn't any such thing as honor" ("Im Vertrauen gesagt: Es gibt gar keine Ehre").[10] While it is true that from time to time honor still provides a strong impulse for narrative and dramatic literature (Fontane, Schnitzler), honor is no longer among the ideas that most move the twentieth century. Only occasionally does some story of honor, disgrace, and vengeance appear in the papers under the rubric "news in brief," but even then these usually proceed from the margins of Europe and are perceived only as exotic.

Much the same seems to hold for Latin America. In a few areas in this part of the world we have to turn the clock back if we want to follow the Colombian author Gabriel García Márquez (b. 1927). In the short novel (which one might also call a long novella) Garcia Márquez published in 1981 under the title *Chronicle of a Death Foretold* (*Crónica de una muerte anunciada*), the characters are people of the twentieth century, but all the unenlightened ideas about honor current in earlier centuries still flit through their heads.[11] They live in a "forgotten village" (*pueblo olvidado*) whose backwardness is shown above all precisely by the fact that the old conception of honor has not been forgotten, as it has in the rest of the world. They are governed by a particularly rigid code of honor, which according to the logic of the narrative is doubly founded, because it is based to an equal extent on the Spanish and Arabic traditions.

In this Colombian village, whose name the author apparently does not wish to remember, the following happened: A young man of mysterious ancestry, but handsome and wealthy, has settled in the village and married the young and beautiful Angela Vicario. A splendid wedding party is held. But even before the wedding night is over the groom sends the disgraced bride back to her parents' house: she is no longer a virgin. Soon it becomes known in the village that Santiago Nasar, a man with a Spanish-Arabic name, has seduced her. A case of honor has arisen, and the deadline is short. For the bride's brothers, the twins Pedro and Pablo, it is clear that they have to immediately avenge the disgrace that has fallen upon their family. Santiago Nasar must die.

Recounted in this summary way, the action might be that of a play by Lope de Vega, Caldéron, or Tirso de Molina. We are confronted by a "classical" drama of honor whose pathos is based on the representation of honor as a drive of elemental power. Since a question of honor has been raised and become public, its burden weighs like a dark myth over the Colombian village and transforms the latter into a stage for a fateful tragedy. For the reader, this dramatic situation is produced chiefly by the foreknowledge the narrator provides at various points in the text. This foreknowledge is either conveyed directly, as for instance when on the first page of the book Monday is said to be the day of the passive hero's death, or transmitted through the awareness of the residents of the village, who play the role of chorus in this narrative tragedy. All this makes it clear at the beginning of the narrative that Santiago Nasar not only *should* but *will* die, in fact, *is* already dead. For those with foreknowledge, he is only wandering through life like a "ghost"; in their eyes, his face is already marked by death. Thus he has only a short time to live, which more or less coincides with the reading time of this (short!) novel.

Here, we would like to examine in detail the extremely limited time frame within which the action of this narrative takes place—just as the narrator, during his later investigations in the village, delimits with great precision the temporal protocol of the occurrence. In detail, these temporal data diverge slightly, just as the statements of witnesses on which they are based are never entirely reliable. But in the time of the action as a whole, there is a highly dramatic intensification measured at first in hours, then in minutes, and finally in seconds.

For the twenty-one-year-old Santiago Nasar, the critical period begins on a Monday, at 3 a.m.—so long has the Sunday wedding feast lasted—with the discovery of the "disgrace." It is only a little while before the whole village knows about it. And thus the villagers are also aware that the bride's brothers will grant the agent of the disgrace only a short time before they take their revenge on him for the shame he has brought on their family. The twins Pedro and Pablo make no attempt to keep their murderous intentions secret. They let everyone know that they want to kill Santiago and are only waiting for a favorable opportunity to carry out the murder. They do not even hide the butcher knives whose blades they are already sharpening.

Only Santiago Nasar, who has also attended the wedding feast and is returning home tired out, knows nothing about the short time that remains for him to live. Unsuspecting, he takes time to rest for a good hour. But he has a headache and gets up at 5:30. At 6:05—so precisely is the time indicated—he goes out of the house. However, he has left his watch on the bedside table. From then until his death shortly after 7 a.m., Santiago Nasar no longer knows what clock (public) time—*his* time—it is. Is it still possible for the village to stop or avert this fate? Among the many people who know what is going on, doesn't anyone try to prevent the brothers from carrying out their murderous act? In fact, a small effort to do so is made. Since the brothers seem to be drunk, and probably are, their knives are taken away from them. They promptly obtain other knives, and hone their blades in front of everyone. Then they go to sleep sitting up, holding their knives in their hands. People in the house hold their breath so as not to awaken them for their act. But soon the twins are awake again, and they tell everyone again that they are just waiting for Santiago Nasar, so they can kill him.

Do they really want to kill him? The narrator has his doubts, for as time goes on, he notices certain signs that the twins' resolution is waning. They flaunt themselves as avengers a little too conspicuously and declare their murderous intentions a little too clearly to anyone within earshot, whether or not he wants to hear about them. It might even turn out that ultimately they will do only unwillingly what they have decided and proclaimed that they will do. Perhaps they are waiting not for a chance to kill Santiago Nasar but rather for someone to prevent them from committing that crime. So if the whole village is aware of the danger, won't anyone get involved and at least warn the intended victim?

No, no one acts to forestall the prospective crime. Most of the villagers don't believe the danger to Santiago Nasar is real, or simply close their eyes to it. That is their policy in this situation. Although here and there good intentions, half-hearted attempts, or timid hints appear, in every case some fateful accident causes an interruption or distraction that prevents these from constituting an effective warning. Hence within the limits of the time preceding the murder, all these attempts remain abortive. For example, someone writes an anonymous message of warning giving full details and slips it under the door of Santiago's house. But Santiago has left home some time before, and no one happened to notice the message. Another resident of the village goes off in search of the unsuspecting Santiago, missing him by a few minutes at various places. Finally, when Santiago is already fleeing from his murderers, he lacks only a few seconds' time to get his gun, with which he could save himself; the "fateful door" is locked too early. Thus destiny makes use of many heads and hands in the village in order not to change its course in the slightest. For Santiago Nasar, time now consists only in a short and inalterable deadline-period: that is the rigorous "unity of time" in this tale, and the irony of this tragic fate.

The "death foretold" occurs at 7:05. The twins slaughter the unarmed Santiago Nasar "like a swine." They immediately turn themselves in to the police and are taken to the judge in charge of investigating the crime. They confess their crime and regret nothing. Nonetheless, they spend three years in prison while their case is investigated. That is the long period of time that the judicial system takes for itself. Then comes the trial, and the murderers are acquitted because their act is deemed a "legitimate defense of their honor" (*legítima defensa del honor*). Nor is any other person in the village held responsible for what happened. They have all failed only by a moment in carrying out their well-intentioned plans to save the victim. Thus they also have nothing to regret. The narrator himself comes from the village. He, too, failed to warn Santiago Nasar. But more than twenty years after the crime was committed, he recalls it. He returns to his village and begins to look into the precise facts regarding what happened so long ago. The result is this "novel." For all who are willing to read it, it is the warning for which there was no longer enough time in that Colombian village.

FIFTEEN MINUTES' DELAY FOR DEATH · Blaise Cendrars

Blaise Cendrars (1887–1961), born Frédéric Louis Sauser, came from a French-speaking Swiss family. He fought in the French army during the First World War, was seriously wounded, and in 1916 acquired French citizenship. After the war, he led an eventful life and made adventurous trips in many countries. He wrote poems, novels, travel literature, and newspaper articles. In 1948 he published half-autobiographical, half-fictional notes under the title *Bourlinguer* (*Globetrotting*).[12] This book, with its rapidly changing settings, shows us that the author was always living and writing in haste: "I have no time. . . . Life carries me along and my writing hurries me" ("Je n'ai pas le temps. . . . La vie m'emporte et mon écriture me presse"). In another passage he quotes with approval Benjamin Franklin: "Time is money." Thus many of Cendrars' books were written as if he were using a still camera or a movie camera.

In his memoir *Bourlinguer*, Cendrars focuses his camera for a few pages on an event that he witnessed as a child in Naples,[13] where his family lived from 1894 to 1896. During these years, his father was a close friend of a Neapolitan photographer, who in this memoir goes under the appropriate name of Ricordi ("memories"). One night the two men decide to take the nine-year-old boy with them as they join a great crowd of other curious people climbing up to the fortress, where the following morning a public execution is to be carried out.

A soldier who had committed some crime whose precise nature they do not know is to be shot by a military firing squad. Ricordi, the photographer, even has an important role to play in this execution. He is supposed to or wishes to record the whole "ceremony" in a series of photographs that will serve to document it for all time. Thus the two men and the nine-year-old boy are given front-row seats for the show.

I will allow the author himself to speak here by quoting at length from the short account of this event that he gives in *Bourlinguer*. The central passage in the report goes as follows:

The photographer took pictures of the whole ceremony as it unfolded: reading the death sentence, stripping the soldier of his rank, selecting at random the firing squad, loading the weapons, tying the condemned man to a post set up in a ditch, putting a blindfold on him—all this photographed with flashes of magnesium, the early dawn being slow in coming and the light being poor for taking photos, Ricordi explained, completely absorbed in his work, which led him to go ask the governor of the fortress who was presiding over this demonstration of social justice to delay the execution for a few minutes and await the first rays of the sun that would lend the whole scene a sort of halo and make it look grandiose with the dark post back-lit; and the governor granted his request, on condition that the officer commanding the troops agreed, and the latter agreed, so long as the officer commanding the firing squad didn't have any objection, and the latter went to meet the photographer, who we saw run forward with his camera and tripod; and the two men began to gesticulate, and Ricordi set up his camera, and the officer consulted his watch, and Ricordi examined the sky and made his adjustments, and the sky grew pink, and the first ray of sunlight fell like a golden arrow, and Ricordi made a sign, and the officer drew his saber, and there was a muffled beating of the drums that rolled and grew louder and louder, and a command rang out and a salvo, followed by an isolated shot; and the wretched little soldier crumbled, his tongue hanging out, half strangled by the ropes that held him to the pole; and the troops marched past the corpse of the executed man . . . , all this at least a quarter of an hour behind schedule, because of the photographer.

Le photographe prit des photos de tout le déroulement de la cérémonie, la lecture du verdict de mort, la dégradation du militaire, le tirage au sort du peloton, le chargement des arms, l'attachage du condamné au poteau planté dans un fossé, le bandage des yeux, tout cela photographié avec des éclairs au magnésium, le petit jour étant lent à venir et la lumière étant mauvaise pour la photo, expliquait Ricordi tout à son affaire, ce qui le poussa à aller demander au gouverneur de la place de Naples qui présidait à cette manifestations de justice sociale de bien vouloir reculer de quelques minutes l'exécution et d'attendre les premiers rayons du soleil qui donneraient une auréole à toute la scène, ce qui ferait grandiose avec le poteau noir à contre-jour; et le gouverneur accéda à sa demande, à condition que l'officier

commandant les troupes fût d'accord, et celui-ci fut d'accord, à condition que l'officier commandant le peloton d'exécution n'y vît aucun
inconvénient, et ce dertnier se porta à la rencontre du photographe
que l'on voyait courir portant son appareil et son trépied; et les deux
hommes se mirent à gesticuler, et Ricordi braqua son appareil, et
l'officier consultait sa montre, et Ricordi inspectait le ciel et faisait sa
mise au point, et le ciel rosissait, et le premier rayon de soleil jaillit
comme une flèche d'or, et Ricordi fit un geste, et l'officier tira son sa-
bre, et les tambours se mirent à battre sourdement et à rouler de plus
en plus fort, et un commandement retentit et une salve sèche, suivie
d'un coup de feu isolé; et le misérable petit pioupiou s'était écroulé,
la langue pendante, à moitié garrotté par ses liens; et la troupe dé-
fila devant le cadavre du supplicié . . . , tout cela avec un grand quart
d'heure de retard sur l'heure légale, à cause du photographe.

This literary report concerning an execution delayed for a short time
is a moral text, although or perhaps because the morality—unlike that
in Schiller's "Bürgschaft," for instance—is not expressed explicitly in
maxims. In Cendrars, the morality is contained in his prose style. In
his commentary on Cendrars' text, Jérôme Thélot makes this clear by
relating the numerous phrases that are strung together paratactically
with the conjunction "and" (*et*) to the photographer Ricordi's activities.[14] Each phrase of this kind corresponds to one of the pictures in
which the photographer—"completely absorbed in his work"—is doc-
umenting the execution. The author's style is *his* camera, by which the
reader is so controlled that he must identify himself with the objective
work of the photographer. He is thus put in the wrong—backlit, so to
speak—along with the photographer.

As a literary historian, Thélot assigns this episode recorded by Cendrars an epochal significance for the history of the media's control over
society. Here we see documented for the first time how a society that
has everything important for living and dying subordinates itself to
the temporal requirements of the media, even if only for a quarter
of an hour. The media did not continue to limit their requirements
to a short amount of time, however, and from the twentieth century
on they have manipulated with increasing ruthlessness so-called "real
time" to the advantage of media time. Did the media age begin in Naples early one morning at the end of the nineteenth century?

Who bears the responsibility for this development? In Cendrars' work, the photographer Ricordi is only doing his job as a memory-man. And the judicial system in Naples is also only doing what was within its legal power under the given circumstances: it is authorized in using force to set a limit to a human life. But for the illegal delay granted at the photographer's request, a long chain of responsibility reaching from top to bottom is set in motion in the fortress at Naples: from the governor to the commander of the troops, from the latter to the commander of the firing squad, who finally lets the photographer do as he likes, even if he "gesticulates" about it. Ultimately, power falls to the man of the media, and all the others wait with him for favorable light: the solitary condemned man, the meticulously regulated judicial apparatus, and the gawkers in the sensation-seeking crowd. Here Cendrars announces a new time in which—after many detours—all social power ultimately falls into the hands of the media.

EVERYMAN'S LAST REPRIEVE · Hugo von Hofmannsthal

Hugo von Hofmannsthal's play *Everyman* (*Jedermann*, 1911), conceived on the model of an anonymous English morality play with the same title (1490), has been on the program of the Salzburg Festival ever since 1920. Chiefly in that way it has become known to a wider public as well.[15]

In this "play about the death of the rich man" ("Spiel vom Sterben des reichen Mannes")—the drama's subtitle—Hoffmannsthal's Everyman is a businessman who is very familiar with money matters and payment periods, and who is always on the lookout for ways to gain an advantage. As a successful businessman, haste is his element. Time is short even for his mother:

> EVERYMAN
> Really haven't much time.
> MOTHER
> I'm happy to see you, my son,
> My heart aches so to find
> that your worldly occupations
> leave you little time for me.

JEDERMANN
Hab aber wahrlich nit viel Zeit.
MUTTER
Bin froh, mein Sohn, daß ich dich seh,
Geschieht mir so im Herzen weh,
daß über weltlich Geschäftigkeit
Dir bleibt für mich geringe Zeit.

Both Everyman himself and his wealth are in a hurry: "My money has to work and run for me" ("Mein Geld muß für mich werken und laufen"). Hoffmannsthal's contemporaries already saw the play in an economic perspective, as a dramatization of Georg Simmel's *Philosophy of Money* (*Philosophie des Geldes*, 1900).

As a good businessman, Everyman is caught up in all sorts of affairs involving appointments and deadlines, and complains that he himself can hardly keep up with all his payments:

The money's no longer mine at all.
Has to be delivered no later than today
As full payment for a pleasure garden.
I've given the buyer my word for it,
He won't wait any longer for his money.

Das Geld ist gar nit länger mein.
Muß heut noch abgeliefert sein
Als Kaufschilling für einen Lustgarten.
Ich steh dem Verkäufer dafür im Wort,
Er will aufs Geld nit länger warten.

Thus it is also part of his role as a rich man to demand that the payment deadlines for all the money he has himself lent out be scrupulously respected. For example, a poor man who has borrowed from Everyman and is not able to repay him by the deadline is thrown into the debtor's prison. Everyman has no mercy to spare for such failings, and in Simmel's manner he admonishes:

Who told you to borrow money at interest?
Now you have your just reward.

My money knows nothing about you or me,
And nothing about a person's reputation.
Time's up, due date's here.
Take your complaint to them.

Wer heiß dich Geld auf Zinsen nehmen?
Nun hast du den gerechten Lohn.
Mein Geld weiß nit von dir noch mir
Und kennt kein Ansehen der Person.
Verstrichne Zeit, verfallner Tag
Gegen die bring deine Klag.

The poor debtor appeals to Everyman's sympathy in vain, but the rich man at least still has a heart for his wife and child, whom he protects from the worst kind of wretchedness. He doesn't want to be inhumane, he says.

For some time the rich man's business affairs have been going just as he wants them to, and he is content with himself and with the world. This is the right moment for him, together with his mistress, to celebrate their "liaison" (their *Buhlschaft*, as Hoffmannsthal calls it somewhat archaically) with a glittering party. And then, right in the middle of the party, Death appears to take away the rich man. For Everyman, time has run out.

But Hoffmannsthal's play does not end so simply and casually as that. Now the rich man resorts to begging and pleading. He is still young, barely forty years old, and entirely "unready" to provide an account of his life for all eternity. Death listens, and grants him a final reprieve, but only for "a short hour's time" (*ein Stündlein Zeit*), with the stern warning: "Don't waste this reprieve!"

The rich man takes Death's advice to heart during his last—short enough!—hour. And so Mammon appears a final time in vain. Supported by his good Catholic friends "Faith" and "Works," Everyman goes repenting to meet his salvation and redemption. His remaining debt, which he incurred on Earth, has already been paid in advance, as we learn at the end of the play:

God has cast into the balance pan
His sacrificial death and martyr's pain.

And Everyman's debt has been paid
In advance for all eternity.

Gott hat geworfen in die Schal
Sein Opfertod und Marterqual.
Und Jedermannes Schuldigkeit
Vorausbezahlt in Ewigkeit.

A SHORT EPILOGUE IN THE EMERGENCY ROOM · Tabucchi

The Italian author Antonio Tabucchi (b. 1943), whose novels and stories can in many respects be read as variations on the theme of time, has written a short dialogue entitled "Time is Tight" ("Il tempo stringe").[16] Put more precisely, this is—according to the author's declared intention—a "dialogue manqué" (*dialogo mancato*). It takes place in an emergency room. One of the patients, fifty-four years old, has just died after a traffic accident, with his younger brother Enrico's name on his lips, as the nurse heard. His body now lies wrapped in bandages on the hospital bed, one leg suspended in traction. This is how he is found by his brother Enrico who, knowing nothing about the accident, has just traveled a long distance to meet with him. Enrico arrives a few minutes too late, and there is little time for even a mute dialogue with his dead brother, for the corpse has to be taken to the morgue. The hospital room is needed.

However, Enrico can remain with the dead man for a few minutes, barely enough time for a "dialogue manqué" in which he bitterly settles accounts with the big, strong brother who was able to deal with life, and who was loved and admired by everyone, and most of all by their father, who had always wanted such a splendid fellow for a son, and not a weakling like his second-born, "little Enrico" (*Enrichetto*). And so the elder son had always looked down on the younger, given him condescending advice, and pitied him just like everyone else. Enrico has had to swallow all this his whole life. But today, at his brother's deathbed, he can for the first time talk to his brother without being immediately interrupted and corrected. Thus this monologue, which is a furious complaint and accusation, is at the same time the first real dialogue between two unequal brothers, who distantly recall Cain and Abel.

They are an unequal pair because Enrico writes verse and his brother does not. Thus the highpoint of the younger brother's speech is a fictive birthday oration in the form of an Orphic ode to a happy future, seen from the point of view of the father. Only one of his sons, the elder, will have a future that the father can be proud of. For futuristic expectations one must be strong, sure, and confident, not shy and weak, like the little brother, whose life will run through his fingers.

But now the time of the future has run out, and the time of the present is short. The nurse appears and urges the visitor to finish up his "meditation." The employees want to go home. The brother is granted a few more minutes, which are just enough for a complaint about time: "It seems that not much time remains. Unfortunately, in life one never has much time. . . . Time is tight, my dear" ("Pare che non ci sia molto tempo. Purtroppo nella vita non c'è mai molto tempo. . . . Il tempo stringe, mio caro").

With this thought in mind, Enrico thinks about how his brother probably ended up in the emergency room and then in the morgue. He was always short of time. Therefore he liked fast cars, expensive ones, with which he could make time. So his brother, always in a hurry, was probably driving his convertible much too fast again, and finally crossed the finish line (*fine di corsa*).

The dialogue manqué ends with a dramatic reversal. The frame of the hospital bed, from which the brother's leg was suspended in traction by means of a weight, suddenly begins to creak, and the weight comes crashing down on the bed, causing the corpse to rear up as if alive. This threatening sight terrifies the visitor, and in this moment of terror his dialogue with his brother comes to an end.

. . .

In another of the dialogues manqués, entitled "Mr. Pessoa is Wanted on the Telephone" ("Il Signor Pessoa è desiderato al telefono"),[17] Tabucchi has the Portuguese poet say: "And in this hypothetical stage, which is called the interim, we seek poetry" ("E in questo ipotetico stadio che si chiama frattempo cerchiamo la poesia"). The interim; that's not a bad synonym for poetry.

A RACE AROUND THE WORLD
Jules Verne, *Around the World in Eighty Days*

Compared with the preceding centuries, the nineteenth changed most as a result of its technological mastery of locomotion. Machine-driven vehicles moved much faster than horse-drawn ones on land or vessels driven by wind and sails on the seas, and in their temporal feats travelers were able roam the globe ever more boldly. How long a time—or rather, how short a time—is still required to go around the whole earth? That question was first answered by the imagination of science fiction.

The French novelist Jules Verne's *Around the World in Eighty Days* (*Le tour du monde en quatre-vingts jours*) is set in 1872 and was published as a book in 1873.[18] The story begins in London. Phileas Fogg is an impeccable gentleman whose sole occupation is whiling his time away at the Reform Club. One day there is a debate about how much time one "still" needs to travel around the world. Spontaneously, the gentleman chosen as the hero of the story bets everything he owns that he can travel around the globe in no more than eighty days. The bet is taken, and Phileas Fogg, whom no one has ever seen in a hurry, immediately sets out, accompanied by his French servant Passepartout, on a trip around the world.

Jules Verne is a brilliant storyteller. He has divided the roles according to the well-known national stereotypes, the always imperturbably correct and absolutely punctual Englishman and the constantly nervous, worried Frenchman, who is rather unreliable in matters concerning time. The story is further enlivened by a subplot the author skillfully weaves into the main plot. A bank robbery in London has attracted much attention, and suspicion immediately falls on the worthy gentleman Phileas Fogg, who has left the city in a hurry and apparently has enough money to take a trip around the world. A detective named Fix is assigned to track him down, and he sets out on the same race around the world in order to put his bank robber behind bars. He is the source of not a few of the obstacles that throughout the story make it uncertain whether Fogg will win his bet.

At first, the journey over three continents and the seas separating them proceeds in accord with a travel plan that leaves nothing to be desired in terms of precision. Yet there are, or course, numerous incidents and "retarding elements," which Verne relates with relish, that defer Fogg's arrival and constantly interfere with his very tight schedule.

The travelers encounter many problems and delays occasioned by the rigors of the weather and the vagaries of machines, so that Fogg is soon forced to add plus and minus signs to his time calculations. But as a true Englishman he remains completely unruffled by these adversities; he had taken such things into account from the outset, and if the train fails to run, he continues his journey on skis, on the back of an elephant, or on foot.

The most serious obstacle arises in India. Fogg wastes no time on sight-seeing, but he witnesses preparations for the ceremonial immolation of a widow—a "Sutty," as the narrator tells the reader, displaying his knowledge of foreign customs. A beautiful young woman is expected to follow her deceased husband onto the funeral pyre. Will she also die, then? Or can Phileas Fogg still save her, though time is short? Is this phlegmatic gentleman a "man with a heart" (*homme de coeur*) after all? Yes, sometimes, Phileas Fogg says in answer to his servant's worried question, "when I have time for it." And he has this time. By means of a ruse, the beautiful widow, Mrs. Aouda, is in fact saved and the travelers must care for her until they reach London again. Does this foreshadow a further obstacle to the timely completion of their journey? Readers of the novel may well think so. But nothing happens between Mrs. Aouda and her savior, although she gives him many signs of her gratitude and admiration. In this respect, the expectant reader must wait patiently for a long time yet. The journey goes on, and the time lost in thwarting the "Sutty" is rapidly made up. However, the suspense regarding whether Fogg will win his risky bet or lose it is maintained until the end of the story.

Two of Fogg's adventures deserve closer examination because of their exemplary character. The first occurs on land, the other at sea. On land, while crossing the American continent by rail, the travelers arrive at a ramshackle bridge over which the train cannot safely pass. Or can it, perhaps? If it can get up enough speed, the train just might make it over the rickety bridge before it collapses. And that is what happens. The train roars over the bridge at a hundred miles an hour. The experiment is successful, "and we got through." The train engineer's superior technological knowledge has worked this miracle, which in this novel is not a miracle at all but rather the result of a law of physics, according to which the weight of the train is reduced (really?) by its high speed: "The speed ate up the weight" ("La vitesse mangeait la pesanteur"). In a risky way, even the laws of physics help the English gentleman win his bet.

Another great adventure still awaits the travelers as they cross the Atlantic from America to Europe. They miss the ship on which they had planned to take passage. As a result, they are in danger of losing a whole week. Fogg rents a fast steamboat with sails, but its captain—his name is "Speedy"—refuses to take the ship to Liverpool. He is imprisoned in the cabin. Fogg—he can do this, too—sails the ship himself. But he runs out of coal, and they cannot keep up their speed with sails alone. Fogg simply buys the whole boat from its captain and gives orders that everything on board that can be burned be used to fire the boiler. The *Henrietta* sails into Liverpool's harbor, a naked hull that looks as if it has been shaven, a pure time machine.

But all their haste seems to be in vain. Phileas Fogg, who is briefly detained by Fix, the detective, arrives in London a few hours too late. Nothing more urgent remains for him to do than to marry the beguiling Mrs. Aouda at the nearest registry office. And in that way the story comes to a satisfactory conclusion, with a *deus ex calendis* having the last word. To the astonishment of the world travelers, it turns out that their time-accounting is off by one day. Since they traveled from west to east, crossing twenty-four longitudes, they have gained a whole day of calendar time. So Phileas Fogg hastens to the Reform Club, arriving precisely three seconds before the deadline set by the wager, which is won by a matter of moments.

SHORT TIME, COMIC STYLE · Camoletti, *Boeing-Boeing*

The comedy *Boeing-Boeing* (1960) by the French dramatist Marc Camoletti is one of the most successful of recent "Boulevard" farces.[19] As of 2004, it has been performed some eighteen thousand times all over the world, and many further productions are planned. Outside France, it is the most often performed French play. The comedy has also had great success as a film.

In 1960, when Camoletti wrote his comedy, it was already clear to all global travelers that worldwide air traffic was suffering from a shortage of short time. Larger and faster airplanes were needed, and the

Boeing aircraft company in Seattle produced the jet airliner and then the jumbo-jet, replacing a successful model with a super-successful model. This development results in serious problems for a young man in Paris who has signed a clever pact with short time, but in the pre-jumbo era, when flights still took quite a long time. The happiness of the young man, whose name is Bernard, depends on this precisely calculated length of time, because he specializes in love affairs with stewardesses (today called "flight attendants"). He is "engaged" to three very attractive stewardesses: an American named Janet, a German named Judith, and a French girl named Jacqueline. All three are sure that Bernard loves them and is faithful to them, and they feel "at home" in his apartment when they are in Paris for a short time between international flights.

All this amazes Robert, Bernard's best friend. Berthe, his cook and housemaid, is less amazed, because "maids understand everything and never say anything" ("les bonnes, ça comprend tout et ne dit jamais rien"). Bernard's discreet conversations with his faithful friend Robert soon reveal to the audience the "system" on which his risky love life is based. He has become an expert on international flight schedules and has so perfectly organized his Parisian "polygamy" that Janet has always just left when Jacqueline arrives in Paris, and Jacqueline's schedule forces her to fly off just in time to prevent Judith from finding her in "her" apartment when she lands in Paris.

Thus each of Bernard's three fiancées stays with him for only a short, carefully calculated amount of time, which is, however, quite enough for the young man, since he has tripled his pleasure. However, he has to keep a very sharp eye on the clock and the calendar, because his schedule has no leeway for dealing with unforeseen events. Hence at breakfast time Bernard often has to advise Janet not to eat another yogurt. He is obliged to tell Judith that redoing her makeup is quite unnecessary. And he finds it prudent to cut short Jacqueline's cheery chatter by replying in monosyllables. In no case must one of his stewardesses miss her flight and return unexpectedly to his apartment.

Robert, who quickly grasps his friend's system, is astonished and a little scared by it: "You're cutting it close, damned close!" ("Mais c'est juste, juste, ça dis donc!"). Bernard doesn't share his concerns. He has complete confidence in the mathematical and technological exactitude of his schedule, because airplanes have to fly on time: "Schedules are schedules" ("Les horaires sont les horaires"). And just as Boeing airplanes circle the globe in precise accord with their schedules, so Judith, Janet, and Jacqueline arrive punctually at the apartment in Paris where Bernard is always waiting for them. Even Berthe the cook calculates the arrival and departure times so exactly that she can always put the meal on the stove and on the table at the right time, following Bernard's motto: "Precision makes you strong" ("La précision fait la force").

But of course fate will have its say in this comedy as well. This time it lies in the hands of the engineers who are always making planes bigger and faster. How happy Janet, Judith, and Jacqueline are when the new planes make it possible for them to arrive in Paris at 17:08 instead of 19:06, and perhaps even, for once, to spend a whole three days with Bernard! Earlier and earlier, the stewardesses phone him or appear unexpectedly at his door. For a while, he is able, with Robert's not entirely selfless help, to keep the three fiancées from meeting, but finally time becomes so hopelessly short for everyone involved that Bernard's system breaks down. What combination of ruses makes it possible to salvage a comic ending to this turbulence, with two monogamous marriages and a still independent and not unhappy Janet, we need not explain here, since reading time is short.

A TWENTY-MINUTE DEADLINE: LOLA RUNS
Tom Tywker, *Lola rennt*

Since its premiere (1998), Tom Tykwer's film *Lola rennt* (*Lola Runs*), with Franka Potente and Moritz Bleibtreu in the starring roles, has acquired cult status among film buffs.[20] In this film, two kinds of shortages coincide: a shortage of money and a shortage of time. Money: A young man named Manni leaves in the subway a plastic bag containing a hundred thousand German marks, and a homeless man picks it up without any idea of what's in it. Time: Manni is under the greatest pressure; within twenty minutes he has to hand the money over to a fairly shady business partner. Otherwise, he will face a threat that in the film remains hazy and unexplained. Lola, his girlfriend with bright red hair, wants to help him get out of this fix and tries to get the money from somewhere within the short period of twenty minutes. Thus she has to run, run, run.

I've used the verb "run" three times here because a "running time" of twenty minutes as the deadline for getting hold of the money is not enough to make a full-length film. The filmmaker and director solved this problem by juxtaposing three slightly different versions, each of which is a little more than twenty minutes long and has the same characters and an almost identical action. The three versions differ only in the ways in which the money is found, among which the spectator can choose at the end.

The driving force behind Lola's running, which lasts throughout almost the whole film, is thus the money that has to be gotten within the shortest time, before the deadline at twelve sharp. The few resources that Lola can, with a bit of luck, tap for this purpose are the following: Her father is a bank president. He has a great deal of money in his safe. In the cash drawer at the supermarket, she thinks, there is also money lying around. And finally, there is also a lot of money to be won at the casino, if Lola, playing roulette and betting on the fateful number "20," gets lucky real quick. In any case, Lola has to run as fast as she can in every situation in the film, otherwise her friend won't get the money that he has to deliver punctually at noon.

So Lola breathlessly races through the streets to her father's bank, to the supermarket, to the casino. Everywhere, public clocks show her the time that is inexorably running along with her. Obstacles of all kinds ("delays," as the director calls them) confront her on her way: a dog that barks at her, a Citroën that has to brake abruptly ("that was close!"), an ambulance with a flashing blue light, and finally Herr Maier's elegant car, which hits Lola and makes her limp.

However, for a while Lola has access to a way of accelerating time: Manni's pistol. She uses it to threaten her father in the bank and the cashiers at the supermarket, but both attempts to make time fail, under tragic circumstances. Thus the first twenty-minute version of the film ends with Lola's death (she accidentally shoots herself with the pistol), the second with Manni's death (when he is hit by the ambulance).

At the beginning of the third "round" (we are in cyclical time here!) a parallel run is incorporated into the film. The bum, who in the meantime has acquired a bicycle, pedals past Manni with the plastic bag in his basket. So now Manni has to run after the fast-moving bum just as breathlessly as his girlfriend has been running (filmscript: "They sprint as if their lives were at stake"). Manni finally catches up with the homeless man, who readily returns the plastic bag with the money when Manni threatens him with the pistol: "Tough luck for him!"

In the end, the film paradoxically turns out well for both runners, though only in the third version of the hunt for money. In that version, two plastic bags full of cash come together in an ironic double happy end: one is the original bag of money that Manni has gotten back from the bum, and the other, also containing a hundred thousand marks, Lola has won in barely five minutes at the roulette table. Thus the two arrive punctually at the meeting point at the water tower, on the dot of twelve, with their virtually identical plastic bags. Both of them have won the race with time, and the whole fiasco with the deadline is resolved and vanishes into thin air, as if nothing had happened.

Epilogue on the Sense of Time

At the beginning of this book I said that in it time would be understood in Hippocratic, not Aristotelian terms. Hippocratic time is in principle strictly limited, because as human time it is in short supply. In the preceding chapters, this view of time has been illustrated by many examples. However, some further information regarding an explicit theory of time, which has up to this point been discussed only in an abbreviated form and from varying points of view, will be more explicitly presented in this epilogue. This information is to be gained above all from language and the history of language, and has heretofore attracted little if any attention from authorities on the philosophy of time. Nonetheless, we must examine it carefully and not hesitate to enter into detail.

First of all, open any Latin dictionary, where we will find the well-known word *tempus*, a neuter noun whose plural is *tempora*. It means "time." Immediately following this entry we find another, a precisely homophonic word *tempus/tempora* that means "temple" (that is, the flattened space on each side of the forehead). The question immediately arises: How are these two words related? Are they only accidental homophones, or is there some substantial connection between time and the temples? No, there is no connection, lexicographers of the Latin language unanimously reply, these are in fact two different and arbitrarily homophonic words.

If the reader, as a philologist, is not immediately satisfied with this answer, he will continue to inquire into linguistic history. If he specializes in Romance languages, the results of his inquiry seem at first to confirm the view of the Latin lexicographers. In the Romance languages, the Latin word-forms *tempus/tempora*, with their two different meanings—"time" and "temple"—correspond in fact to two words that differ not only semantically but also formally. In Italian, *tempo/tempi* ("time") is distinguished from *tempia/tempie* ("temple"), just as in French, *temps/temps* ("time") is clearly differentiated from *tempe/tempes* ("temple").

However, closer examination of the history of these words shows that these word-forms have become differentiated phonically only because in Romance languages the words for "time" (Italian *tempo* and French *temps*) are derived from the Latin singular *tempus*, while the Romance words for "temple" (Italian *tempia* and French *tempe*), as well as English "temple," which derives from the Old French form, are derived, via various intermediate stages, from the Latin plural *tempora*. This is on the whole logical, since as an abstraction, the word "time" is normally used in the singular and thus can continue the Latin form *tempus*, while the word for "temple," since this part of the body comes in pairs, usually appears in the plural "temples," and can thus be explained as an elaboration, in accord with the rules of historical phonetics, of the Latin plural *tempora*.

If we now consult a German etymological dictionary, we find that the word for "temple" (*Schläfe*) is derived from an old plural of the word for "sleep" (*Schlaf*). This leads to a further question: what do temples have to do with sleep and what does sleep have to do with time?

We may pursue our inquiry by examining linguistic atlases.[1] In an Italian linguistic atlas we discover, in the entry for *tempia* ("temple"), that in southern Italy and in Sicily there is a circumscribed linguistic area in which the temple is referred to by a form *sonnu* (or something similar), which clearly goes back to Latin *somnus* ("sleep"). Even more striking is the fact, documented by various linguistic atlases, that in another large linguistic region of Europe stretching from northern Italy through southern France and as far as Catalonia, the temples are indicated by a form *pols* (or something similar), which goes back to Latin *pulsus* and originally meant "pulse beat." When this detailed information is taken into account, the question from which we started acquires an even more confusing form: What do time, temples, sleep, and the pulse have to do with each other? Is there perhaps a theoretical common denominator for this jumble of contingencies?

There is in fact a clear and simple answer to the whole series of questions we have asked here, an answer that at the same time opens up a broad horizon of cultural history. The answer we are looking for comes to us from the most ancient period of European medical history and begins with the physician Hippocrates, who has been repeatedly mentioned in this book.[2] Already in Hippocrates and several of his successors in the art of medicine, starting especially with Herophilos of Chalcedonia (c. 300 BC), we find numerous testimonies to the theory and practice of a regular "pulsology" developed by physicians. This remained widespread in Europe well into the modern age, being used primarily as a diagnostic tool—just as today many physicians still occasionally "take the pulse" of a patient and in some cases draw conclusions from it as to the nature of the disorder involved.

However, since ancient times physicians have been aware that the diagnostics of the pulse involves not only counting and measuring the rapidity or slowness of the pulse beat but must also pay at least as much attention to the latter's rhythm. Thus the Greek physician Rufus of Ephesus (first century AD) categorized pulse rhythms according to the meters of poetry and music, and drew diagnostic conclusions from the different meters. Many centuries later an Italian physician, Michele Savanarola (seventeenth century) advised his students to learn to play a musical instrument, in order to hone their feeling for metrics and rhythm as practicing pulsologists. This clearly shows that the art of a prosodically sensitized pulsology is closely related to the fine arts of poetry and music, insofar as the latter are also essentially based on rhythm, scansion, and prosody.

In this historical context the question, much debated among lexicographers, of the etymology of such central cultural words as *tempus*, *time*, and *Zeit* can be raised anew.[3] Is it really plausible to argue that a Latin word such as *tempus* is related to the Greek verb *temnein* ("to cut")? What is there in time that can be cut—except perhaps the thread of life that the Fates cut at the end of a lifetime? A far more plausible hypothesis is that *tempus*, *time*, and possibly also *Zeit* (Low German *Tied*) were originally onomatopoeic words that with their *tam/tem/tim/tom/tum* were modeled on a rhythmically beaten percussion instrument (drum, timbal, cymbal, etc.) whose sounds are transmitted to our senses via the "ear drum" ("typanum"). In such a context, a continually flowing time as a shapeless "duration" (Bergson's *durée*) is inconceivable.

Now, in the context of older pulsology it was appropriate to view the pulse beat, with its specific meter and rhythm, as an event that concerns the body as a whole. Today, the pulse is usually taken, if at all, only at the wrist (Italian *polso*), at the point where the wristwatch (Italian *orologio da polso*) is worn. However, as has been demonstrated in many documents from medical history, in earlier times physicians regularly took the pulse at various points on the body (and measured it, for the most part, with a clepsydra), not only at the wrist (*in carpo*) but also and especially at the temple, or more precisely at the temples (*in temporibus*).[4] Only when the English physician William Harvey—a practicing pulsologist—discovered the circulation of the blood (1628) could the pulse be redefined as follows: "The pulse . . . is nothing other than the blood stream impelled by the heartbeat" ("pulsus . . . nil nisi sanguinis a corde impulsus").[5] Thus the heartbeat sets a uniform rhythm for the whole body. This conception also made it plausible that to judge the pulse beat it suffices to take the pulse at one point on the body, preferably at the easily accessible and less intimate wrist. That is why physicians eventually ceased to see the temples as a part of the body particularly relevant for diagnostic purposes.

Nonetheless, even after Harvey's discovery the temple was still occasionally considered important for pulsological diagnostics, especially in feverish conditions where the arteries in the temples swell and protrude. In such cases the pulse beat, accelerated by the fever, can not only be felt but also seen and, particularly in phases of nighttime sleeplessness, heard. For the patient this is often an upsetting experience that shows him in his own body how much his life depends on the beating of his heart and pulse. In the "crisis," which in earlier times could not be broken as it now can by the use of antibiotics and other drugs, illness could therefore be associated with a new awareness that life-time sooner or later runs out, and that in general human existence is, to use Heidegger's expression, a being toward death (*Sein zum Tode*).[6]

When an ill person gets well, however, he immediately forgets time and pulse beat, his temples and sleeplessness. Nevertheless, physicians have continued to reflect on these connections and they have developed a theory of time based on such observations. This theory holds that the temples (*Schläfen*) are the place in the body where time normally "sleeps" (*schläft*). But if time is reawakened by a serious illness, it immediately manifests itself as a life-maintaining function, and in the form of an accelerated pulse beat attracts the concerned attention of the patient. Only then does the latter anxiously or hopefully notice life-time, which has become conspicuous in his own body. Suddenly, life-time can be felt, seen, and heard in the feverishly accelerated pulse; in short, it is (still) present to the senses. Thus life-time is most clearly experienced in the symptoms indicating that it is in short supply. It is a kind of time from whose *conditio humana* we can draw the existential certainty that it is limited—though perhaps not yet exhausted, so that "one" (Heidegger: *man*) can still forget time again.

Among the foregoing observations on philology and medical history, for a theoretical understanding of time and life-time we should above all keep in mind that in contrast to all mechanical or physicalistic concepts of time, time is here understood basically as "the sense of time," not very different from the other senses—in the classical canon, the senses of sight, hearing, smell, taste, and touch.[7] All these "external" senses and their specific functions are represented by sense organs on the surface of the human body: eyes, ears, nose, palate/tongue, skin. We normally use these "tools" without thinking about them. However, when the body is disturbed by internal or external factors, we become conscious of the activity of the senses. Suddenly, we become "all eyes," "all ears," and so on, even including the heightened sense of our own skin that Nietzsche called *Hautlichkeit*.[8] Time is also perceived by all these organs, so that the first "meaning of time" (*Sinn der Zeit*) can be said to be its sensory nature (*Sinnlichkeit*).

Considered in relation to the body, the sense of time can be either added to the canon of the five senses as a "sixth sense" with the same status as the others, or identified as a superior "common sense" (*sensus communis, bon sens*) that is the psychic coordinator of all the other senses. In either case the sense of time is a "real," that is, corporeal, sense, because it has its own bodily organ—according to the older view, the temples, and according to the modern view, the circulation of the blood and its rhythmical pulse beat. Although we generally remain unaware of it, like the other senses, in crises it will be perceived beating on the surface of the body. However, since evenly flowing circulation of the blood is its condition, the sense of time takes on a special anthropological status insofar as it is at the same time an internal sense, as the only one that determines the beginning and the end of human life-time. To that extent we can say of the sense of time, and of it alone, that it creates or abolishes the presuppositions not only for itself, but also for all the activities of the other senses.

. . .

The question is now whether the observations based on philology and the history of medicine that we have applied to the sense and pulse of time are in accord with the philosophical views of time and short time associated with the great names in the history of philosophy. I will limit myself here to the doctrines of three great philosophers of time, Aristotle, Kant, and Heidegger, and at the same time review and summarize what has already been said regarding this question.

Aristotle is the first philosopher in the Western tradition to whom we owe an explicit theory of time (see above, chap. 1, sect. 1). We have already noted that this theory is based on space—just as in Aristotle's *Physics* the chapter on time immediately follows the chapter on space. In Aristotle's doctrine of categories as well, the discussion of the category "when" (*pote*) immediately follows that of the category "where" (*pou*). In Aristotle, the *tertium commune* between space and time is movement, which should be considered as the identity of a spatial movement between a point behind and a point ahead, and a temporal movement between an earlier point and a later one. This pairing of space and time is supported by many other spatial metaphors in Aristotle's work. Among them, the movements of the stars—whether their itineraries through the firmament are observed by amateurs using the naked eye or by astronomers using special instruments—are particularly convincing or persuasive.

It is clear that the conception of the sense and pulse of time proposed in this book is incompatible with the Aristotelian theory of time. Human time, which derives its rhythm from the regular or irregular beating of the pulse, cannot be understood as a movement in space, or if so, at most as the circulation of the blood flowing through the arteries and veins. But since the circulation of the blood was discovered two thousand years after Aristotle's death, during this long period of time the temple (*tempus*) was considered, along with a few other places on the body where the pulse could be measured, as the corporeal "seat" of the sense of time—and that is a very different kind of place from those that geometers and astronomers can observe and calculate.

Thus I can hardly fail to endorse Bergsonian critique of Aristotle's "spatialization" of the concept of time. I cannot help but insist, like Bergson and his followers, that time is to be understood in temporal and not spatial terms. This is particularly true when the time that is granted humans to live is short or very short. For this reason we should see in Hippocrates' first aphorism, together with the "pulsology" he also founded, an implicit anticipatory criticism of Aristotle.

• • •

Secondly, the view of the sense of time and the pulse of time defended here can be compared with Immanuel Kant's "critical" theory of time.[9] In his *Critique of Pure Reason* (*Kritik der reinen Vernunft*) Kant broadens the theories of time he found in the history of pre-critical philosophy to include a specific dimension of depth. In particular, through dialogue with Aristotle and his followers he dissociates time from the physics of moving bodies as well as from the catalogue of categories ("When?"), and by defining it as a "pure form of internal appercep-tion" he gives it an unprecedented metaphysical dignity as the a priori condition of sense experience. However, he granted the same dignity to space, which was also made an a priori condition of sensation and dissociated from the geometers' field of experience as well as from the catalogue of logico-ontological categories. Thus despite this tremen-dous upheaval, the familiar pairing of time and space—which Bergson disapproves of in this philosopher as well—is maintained.

Hence there is an irreducible difference between the internal (and in Kant, that always means a priori) sense of time and our concep-tion of a sense and pulse of time that can be experienced in the body. Does this mean that we have fallen back into pre-critical thinking? Certainly not, since the sense of time, insofar as it is corporeally mani-fested in the rhythmical beating of the pulse, represents a special kind of a priori condition: that of corporeality, in which the shortness of life, together with the good or bad health of the body, has a worthy place. This sense of time, as "internal," remains clearly distinct from the "ex-ternal" senses, which Kant calls a posteriori. In my view, the sense of time alone is entitled to the a priori dignity of indicating through its rhythm the fundamental condition of human beings who know (but do not always want to know) that their days are numbered.

. . .

The third and last of the great philosophers of time who remains to be discussed in this short review is Martin Heidegger (see above, chap. 8, sect. 4). In his *opus magnum*, *Being and Time* (*Sein und Zeit*), Heidegger sets thinking about time on entirely new paths that cannot be ignored. This also holds for the concept of time in limited supply that we identified as the center of thinking about time, and to which "philological" disputes about such temporal phenomena as the pulse and the temples belong. Only if the time of human existence is moving toward an inevitable end, death, is it fundamentally short. All the small shortages and their temporal limits that restrict and pressure us in everyday life derive from the most extreme and "existential" shortness of a time that is rushing toward its end. Thus we can here declare our fundamental agreement with Heidegger's philosophy of time and use it to justify the following aphorism: Someone who has not internalized what makes time short does not yet know what time is.

But there remains one possible reservation about Heidegger's view: does "one" (*man*) have to know what time is at all? Hasn't everyone a perfect right to let time, in its everyday inconspicuousness, take care of itself and "sleep" in the temple (*in der Schläfe schlafen*)? I think there are basically two favorable circumstances that readily legitimate this *incuria*: youth and good health. Someone who is young and healthy does not need—whether questioned or not—to know or even to sense what time is and how short the limits set on existence are. Under such conditions, even the pulse beat can be disregarded and for the time being counted among the things taken for granted in life. Only when—usually at an "untimely" moment—the pulse (or some other sign of corporeality) announces that the pleasant carelessness of youth and good health has become fragile, does the "true time in which we live and which is our inner measure" (Carlo Levi) make an uncalled-for appearance and disturb our previously so robust idea—which was in fact a lack of awareness—of time. Then we may still not know precisely what time *is* in its essence, but we see ever more clearly what it *does* with us and what we can still provisionally do with it. However, perhaps this is the starting point for the philosopher's "fore-running" (*Vor-laufen*) whose path (*Weg*)—which may lead to a dead end (*Holzweg*)—Martin Heidegger marked out (see above, chap. 8, sect. 4).

. . .

After these philosophical considerations it seems to me fair to give the last word to an artistic voice in which time as life-time and thus as short time is once again expressed with poetic and musical emphasis. The occasion for this reflection on time is not an illness but "only" the simple contrast between youth and age, which suffices to produce an irresolvable conflict between two people who love each other. That is what we read and hear in *Der Rosenkavalier* (1911), a "comedy for music" whose text was written by Hugo von Hofmannsthal and which became famous chiefly as an opera by Richard Strauss.[10]

Among the characters, the Marschallin has always enjoyed the audience's special sympathy. She is to be imagined as being about forty years of age, which since Balzac is no longer considered that old. But it is a critical age for a woman if she loves a very young man, Octavian (nicknamed "Quinquin"), and if in addition another, very young woman, Sophie, becomes her competitor. As a result, the Marschallin is forced to recognize that an unconquerable enemy has arisen to oppose her love: time. This painful recognition finds its poetic and musical expression in the turbulent rhythms of her great monologue and aria on time, which also represents the highpoint of the opera from an artistic point of view:

> Really, Quinquin, time
> doesn't change things a bit.
> Time is a strange thing.
> If you just live along, it's nothing at all.
> But then suddenly
> You're aware of nothing else.
> It's all around us, and also inside us.
> It trickles on faces, it trickles in the mirror.
> In my temples, I feel it flowing.
> Between you and me it's flowing again,
> As soundlessly as an hourglass.
> Oh, Quinquin!
> Sometimes I hear it flowing—incessantly.
> Sometimes I get up in the middle of the night
> And stop the clocks, all of them.
> Nevertheless, one must not fear it.

It is also a creation of the Father
Who has created us all.

Die Zeit im Grund, Quinquin,
die Zeit, die ändert doch nichts an den Sachen.
Die Zeit, die ist ein sonderbar Ding.
Wenn man so hinlebt, ist sie rein gar nichts.
Aber dann auf einmal,
da spürt man nichts als sie.
Sie ist um uns herum, sie ist auch in uns drinnen.
In den Gesichtern rieselt sie, im Spiegel rieselt sie.
In meinen Schläfen, da fließt sie.
Und zwischen dir und mir da fließt sie wieder.
Lautlos wie eine Sanduhr.
Oh, Quinquin!
Manchmal hör ich sie fließen—unaufhaltsam.
Manchmal steh ich auf mitten in der Nacht
Und laß die Uhren alle, alle stehn.
Allein man muß sich auch vor ihr nicht fürchten.
Auch sie ist ein Geschöpf des Vaters,
der uns alle erschaffen hat.

Thus her concern about losing her very young lover, and perhaps already the imminent danger of this painful loss, triggers in the Marschallin an awareness of time that is entirely based on the aspects of time that are dwindling and flowing away. She first feels this "flowing" time in her temples. She has now understood in her own body what time is for her. It is her life-time. Time in short supply.

Notes

The epigraph to this book is taken from Hugo von Hofmannsthal, *Die Gedichte und kleinen Dramen*, 5th ed. (Leipzig: Insel Verlag, 1919), 79.

Chapter 1
LIFE IS SHORT, ART IS LONG

1. Hippocrates, *Works*, ed. and trans. W. H. S. Jones et al., Loeb Classical Library (Cambridge, Mass.: Harvard University Press, 1957–). On the Aphorisms, see Josef-Hans Kühn and Ulrich Fleischer, *Index Hippocraticus* (Göttingen: Vandenhoeck & Ruprecht, 1989). See also Stephanos of Athens, *Commentary on Hippocrates' Aphorisms*, part 2, ed. Leendert G. Westerink (Berlin: De Gruyter, 1985; 2d ed. 1998) (= *Corpus Medicorum Graecorum* 10.1.3.1).
2. Molière, *Monsieur de Pourceaugnac*, 1.8.
3. Martin Heidegger, *Holzwege*, 8th ed. (Frankfurt/M: Klostermann, 2003), 48.
4. See Hans Blumenberg, *Lebenzeit und Weltzeit* (1986; Frankfurt/M: Suhrkamp, 2001), 69.
5. Galen, *Aphormismi Hippocratis, graece et latine, unacum Galeni commentariis* (Lyon, 1668). See also *Corpus Galenicum*, ed. Kühn, 20 vols. (Leipzig, 1821–33).
6. Aristotle, *Physics*, book 4, chaps. 10–14, trans. R. P. Hardie and R. K. Gaye, in *The Basic Works of Aristotle*, ed. R. McKeon (New York: Random House, 1941). Cf. Aristoteles, *Traité du temps* (Greek and French texts), introduction, translation, and commentary by Cathérine Collobert (Paris: Kimé, 1995). On Aristotle, see also Ueberweg's *Grundriß der Geschichte der Philosophie*, the volume

entitled *Die Philosophie der Antike, 3: Ältere Akademie—Aristotles—Peripatos*, ed. Hellmut Flashar.

7. Aristotle, *Physics*, trans. Hardie and Gaye, p. 293.—Translator's note: Weinrich cites Martin Heidegger's translation, "Das nämlich ist die Zeit, das Gezählte an der im Horizont des Früher und Später begegnenden Bewegung," in Martin Heidegger, *Sein und Zeit* (1927; Tübingen: Niemeyer, 1986), 428. However, the following comment applies as well to the English translation cited here.

8. Aristoteles, *Physique (I–IV)*, ed. Henri Carteron (Paris: Les Belles Lettres, 2000), 150. Carteron translates the Aristotelian definition of time as follows: "Voici en effet ce qu'est le temps: le nombre du mouvement selon l'antérieur-postérieur" (*Physics* 219b).

9. Heidegger, *Sein und Zeit*, 428.

10. Goethe, *Dichtung und Wahrheit*, beginning of book 11. Hamburg edition, ed. Erich Trunz, vol. 9, p. 452.

11. Diogenes Laertius, *Leben und Meinungen berühmter Philosophen* (Hamburg: Felix Meiner, 1998), book 5, chap. 2, "Theophrast," pp. 261–74.

12. La Bruyère, *Les Caractères*, introduction and notes by Louis Van Delft (Paris: Imprimerie Nationale, 1998); paperback, ed. Emmanuel Bury (Paris: Librairie Générale Française, 1995), 12:102.

13. Lucius Annaeus Seneca, *Philosophische Schriften lateinisch und deutsch*, 5 vols. (Darmstadt: Wissenschaftliche Buchgesellschaft, 1987–95). There are many complete and selected separate editions of the various writings, dialogues, and letters. For the text on the brevity of life, we may mention *De brevitate vitae—Die Kürze des Lebens*, ed. Franz Peter Waiblinger (Munich: dtv, 1998). The *Letters to Lucilius* are found in Latin and German in the Reclam Universal-Bibliothek (Stuttgart: Reclam, 1997–99).

14. Theophrastus: "That time is a costly expenditure" (cf. Büchmann, *Geflugelte Worte*, 204). In France, La Bruyère adapted Theophrastus's formula as follows: "La plus forte dépense que l'on puisse faire est celle du temps" ("The most costly expenditure one can make is time"); *Les Caractères*, ed. Van Delft, 73.

15. Translator's Note: *Lebenzeit*. Since this is a key term throughout, I am using the subtly awkward rendering "life-time." "Lifetime" is not an acceptable translation because the reference is not to the lifespan but rather to time considered as life, and life experienced as or in time. In this context, *Lebenszeit* needs to be treated as a kind of technical term.

16. See Helga Nowotny, *Eigenzeit: Entstehung und Strukturierung eines Zeitgefühls*, 2d ed. (Frankfurt/M: Suhrkamp, 1990).

17. Jean Racine, preface to his tragedy *Britannicus*.

18. See Manfred Fuhrmann, *Seneca und Kaiser Nero: Eine Biographie* (Berlin: Alexander Fest, 1997). Fuhrmann thinks Seneca may have been born in year "zero" (p. 10).

19. Aristoteles, *Economics (Oikonomike)*. Greek and French bilingual edition under the title *Économiques*, ed. B. A. van Groningen and A. Wartelle, with

an introduction and notes by Emmanuel Dauzat (Paris: Les Belles Lettres, 2003).

20. See Theo Semmler, *Ökonomie: Sprachliche und literarische Aspekte eines 2000 Jahre alten Begriffs*, Mannheimere Beiträge zur Sprach- und Literaturwissenschaft 6 (Tübingen: Narr, 1985).

21. See Gerhard Dohrn-van Rossum, *Die Geschichte der Stunde: Uhren und modern Zeitordnung* (Munich: Hanser, 1992).

22. Jacob Burckhardt, *Die Kultur der Renaissance in Italien: Ein Versuch* (1860; rpt. of 1860 ed., Köln: Phaidon, 1956), 71ff.

23. Friedrich Kittler, in the *Suddeutsche Zeitung*, February 14, 2004.

24. Leon Battista Alberti, *I Libri della famiglia*, ed. Ruggiero Romano and Alberto Tenenti, revised Francesco Furlan, Nuova Universale Einaudi 102 (Turin: Einaudi, 1994). The most important statements about time management are found in book 3, lines 689ff. (pp. 216ff. in this edition). On this subject, see also the editor's introduction, esp. x–xv.

25. Leon Battista Alberti, *Vita*, Latin-German edition by Christine Tauber (Frankfurt/M: Stroemfeld, 2004). Note especially the editor's introduction, 7ff.

26. *Lord Chesterfield's Letters,* ed. David Roberts (Oxford: Oxford University Press, 1992).

27. Rainer Maria Rilke, *Die Aufzeichnungen des Malte Laurids Brigge*, in *Werke in Drei Bänden* (Frankfurt/M: Insel Verlag, 1966), 2:107–346, esp. 265–70. See also Rainer Warning, "'Nervenkunst' bein Rilke: Malte und die Geschichte seiner Nachbarn (49.-53. *Aufzeichnungen*)," in Rainer Warning and Winfried Wehle, eds., *Fin de siècle* (Munich: Fink, 2002), 401–28.

Chapter 2
THE MIDPOINT OF LIFE

1. Dante Alighieri, *Convivio* 4.23.7 and 9. Cf. also *Purgatorio* 13.114: "l'arco d'i miei anni." The passage in the Psalms on which this doctrine is based is found in Psalm 89:10. See also Lichtenberg's brief work "Discourse on the Number 8," in which he takes the age of eighty to be "the probable limit of human life" (*Schriften und Briefe* [Darmstadt: Wissenschaftliche Buchgesellschaft, 1972], 3:460).

2. The Holy Year (Luther: *Halljahr*) is based on the Old Testament, Leviticus 25, and the New Testament, Luke 4:19. I deal with this subject in greater detail in my book *Lethe: The Art and Critique of Forgetting*, trans. Steven Rendall (Ithaca: Cornell University Press, 2004), chap. 8, sect. 4, "Amnesias, Amnesties, and the Unfathomable *Halljahr*."

3. On Petrarch's life and work we now have Karlheinz Stierle's book *Francesco Petrarca*, (Munich: Hanser, 2004). In the following sections I will use this book as my point of reference in several respects. Documentation regarding the poetic crowning in Rome is found chiefly in Petrarch's volume of letters,

Familiares (in *Opera omnia*, vol. 4). The quoted term *immaturus* is in Petrarch's Letter 17.2, in *Opera omnia*, 2:1069.

4. Francesco Petrarca, *L'Afrique*, 1338–74, ed. Rebecca Lenoir (Grenoble: Jérôme Millon, 2002). On Robert of Anjou, canto 9, verses 421ff. and 439f. On the triumph of Scipio Africanus, canto 9, vv. 387 and 398.

5. The year 1300 was a leap year in the Julian calendar then in use (it would not be one in the Gregorian calendar).

6. Francesco Petrarca, *Canzionere,* introduction by Roberto Antonelli, essay by Gianfranco Contini, notes by Daniele Ponchiroli, Einaudi Tascabili Classici 104 (Turin: Einaudi, 1964). On the problem of time in Petrarch, see also E. Taddeo, "Petrarca e il tempo," *Studi e problemi di critica testuale* 25 (1982): 53–76.

7. The preceding quotations are to be found in Petrarch's *Canzionere* in the following poems: Song 71, Sonnet 263, Song 30, Sonnet 284, Sonnet 244, Sonnet 197, Sonnet 249—note especially the oxymoron *dolci durezze* ("sweet/soft hardness," in Sonnet 351).

8. On the laurel motif, see Sara Sturm-Maddox, *Petrarch's Laurels* (University Park: Pennsylvania State University Press, 1992).

9. *Canzionere*, Sonnet 61.

10. *Canzionere*, Song 268.

11. Francesco Petrarca, *De vita solitaria*, 1346–66, Latin and French, ed. Christophe Carraud (Grenoble: Jérôme Millon, 1999), 1.2.1 and 2; 1.2.21, 1.5.7.

12. Friedrich Hölderlin, *Werke und Briefe*, ed. Friedrich Beißner and Jochen Schmidt (Frankfurt/M: Insel, 1969), vol. 1, *Gedichte*, "Hyperion," pp. 36–37, 134–35. On the interpretation of the poem "The Midpoint of Life" ("Hälfte des Lebens," lit. "Half of Life"), see Luciano Zagari, *La città destrutta di Mnemosyne: Saggi sulla poesia di Friedrich Hölderlin* (Pisa: Edizione PTS, 1999), 140ff. See also Ernst Jandl's interpretaton in *Deutsche Gedichte und ihre Interpretationen*, ed. Marcel Reich-Ranicki (Frankfurt/M: Insel, 2002), 3:180ff.; and in the same volume, Marcel Reich-Ranicki's interpretation of the ode "An die Parzen" (126–29).

13. Seneca, *De brevitate vitae*, 2. Quoted in Goethe, *Textdatei Goethe: Sprüche in Prosa*, ed. Harald Fricke (Frankfurt: Insel, 2005), 13. I thank Harald Fricke for bringing this to my attention in a letter.

14. Goethe, *Briefe aus Italien 1786–1788*, ed. Peter Goldammer (Munich: C. H. Beck, 1982), and *Italienische Reise 1786–1788*, ed. Christoph Michel and Hans-Georg Drewitz, 2 vols. (Frankfurt/M: Deutscher Klassiker Verlag, 1993). I quote according to Goethe's dating.

15. The quotation about language: September 11, 1786; about the boots, September 17, 1786.

16. Regarding Goethe's feelings on arriving in Rome, see Harald Weinrich, *Kleine Literaturgeschichte der Heiterkeit* (Munich: C. H. Beck, 2001), 16f.

17. Quotations: "very happy," September 28, 1787; "share my joy," letter of September 6, 1787; "I can say this much," March 22, 1788; "school," Naples March 22, 1787; "constant pleasure," September 6, 1787.

18. Quotations: "youthful dream," July 3, 1787; "rebirth," December 3, 1786; "in Rome," March 14, 1787; "born again," August 23, 1787; "I am very well," letter of June 16, 1787.

19. Quotation: *Wilhelm Meister*, "grant me," June 5, 1787.

20. Quotations: All Saint's Day, "so late," November 1, 1786; "change his mind," report from October 1787; "I am not here," November 10, 1786.

21. Goethe, *Wilhelm Meisters Lehrjahre*, chap. 7, 9, in *Goethes Werke in 14 Bänden*, ed. Erich Trunz (Hamburg edition), 7:496.

22. Goethe, *Wilhelm Meisters Wanderjahre*, chap. 3, 11, Hamburg ed., 8:405.

23. Christoph Wilhelm Hufeland, *Makrobiotik oder die Kunst, das menschliche Leben zu verlängern* (Jena, 1797; rpt. of the 5th Berlin edition, 1823, ed. by K. E. Rothschuh [Stuttgart: Hippokrates Verlag, 1975]). The quotations, with page references: "longevity," 146; nutrition and care for the body, 387ff.; wine and smoking, 394f.; "overworking," 261; "the more a person," 142; Francis Bacon, 20; "it fills," 50; life force, 49 ff.; "consumption," 65 ff.; "a certain degree of culture," 149; a serene nature, 185; a day in the country, 416. On Hufeland's medical views, see also Klaus Bergdolt, *Leib und Seele: Eine Kulturgeschichte des gesunden Lebens* (Munich: C. H. Beck, 1999), esp. 177ff.

24. Goethe, *Dichtung und Wahrheit*, Hamburg edition, vols. 9 and 10. "Hippocratic method," beginning of book 11, Hamburg edition, 9:452; "a star," 9:66. See also Dieter Borchmeyer, *Goethe: Der Zeitbürger* (Munich: Hanser, 1999).

25. I quote Goethe's *Faust* and its earlier version (*Urfaust*) by verse number in the critical and annotated edition by Albrecht Schöne, 2 vols. (Frankfurt/M: Deutscher Klassiker Verlag, 1994). "Dear me!," *Urfaust* v. 205f. (cf. *Faust* 521); "and long before," *Urfaust* v. 211f.; "dry pedant," *Urfaust* v. 168 (cf. *Faust* 521). On the problematics of time in *Faust*, see especially Peter Matussek's article "Faust I" and Gert Mattenklott's article "Faust II" in *Goethe-Handbuch*, ed. Bernd Witte et al., vol. 2, *Dramen*, ed. Theo Buck (Stuttgart: Metzler, 1997), 352–477. On *Faust* see also Jane K. Brown, Meredith Lee, and Thomas P. Sayne, eds., *Interpreting Faust Today* (Columbia S.C.: Camden House, 1994). In addition, see Ortrud Gutjahr, ed., *Westöstlicher und norsüdlicher Divan: Goethe in interkultureller Perspektive* (Paderborn: Schöningh, 2000).—Translator's note: When quotations from *Faust* are given as complete verse lines, I have used Walter Arndt's English verse translation (New York: Norton, 1976). When quotations are not given as whole verses and are integrated into the body of the text, I have translated directly from the German to ensure that the sense and syntax fit into the context in which they are cited. Translations of passages quoted from *Urfaust* are my own.

26. On the famulus Wagner, "die Kunst, die man," v. 1058f.; "It's true that I know," v. 600f; "the most learned," v. 6644.

27. On his introductory complaint, see especially the scene "Night." The quotation "cured of the thirst," v. 1768.

28. On Faust's "break-out" (*Ausscheren*)—though without this term—see Hans Blumenberg, *Lebenszeit und Weltzeit* (1986; rpt. Frankfurt/M: Suhrkamp,

2001), beginning of part 2, "The Opening of Time's Shears," 69ff. See also Marianne Gronemeyer, *Das Leben als letzte Gelegenheit: Sicherheitsbedürfnisse und Zeitknappheit* (Darmstadt: Primus Verlag, 1993; 2d ed., Darmstadt: Wissenschaftliche Buchgesellschaft, 1996), esp. 122–24.

29. Goethe, *Briefe aus Italien 1786–1788*, and *Italienische Reise 1786–1788* See also Nicholas Boyle, *Goethe: The Poet and the Age* (Oxford: Clarendon, 1991), vol. 1.

30. "About sixty," Thomas Mann, *Gesammelte Werke*, 9:600.

31. On Mephistopheles' "arts": v. 1443; "several thousand years," v. 1776; "itinerant scholar," vv. 1321–24; "from afar," v. 3094; "I fear just one thing," vv. 1786f.

32. On the witches' kitchen: "swill-cookery," vv. 2341f.; "balm," vv. 2346ff.; "nature's way," v. 2348; "go back to witching," v. 2365. Regarding the "advertisement" for Hufeland's book, Schöne's commentary allows us to note that chronologically it is a "pre-publication advertisement." The lines in question were already in print in 1790, whereas Hufeland's *Makrobiotik* was not published until 1796. However, Hufeland, whom Goethe knew well, had been working on his book since 1785. On the witches' kitchen, see also Jochen Schimidt, *Goethe's Faust: Erster und Zweiter Teil. Grundlagen—Werk—Wirkung* (Munich: C. H. Beck, 1999).—Translator's note: *Margarete*: In most English translations, "Gretchen" is used throughout to avoid confusion.

33. On speed and novelty: "the rush of time," v. 1754; "novelty," v. 4113; "wager," vv. 1698–1707.

34. On Faust's old age: "greatest age," stage directions to the "Palace" scene (preceding v. 11,142); "highest moment," v. 11,586 (Mephistopheles comments: "The final moment, worthless, stale, and void"); "one hundred years," *Conversations with Eckermann*, June 6, 1831. On the problem of time in *Faust II*, see Jane K. Brown, *Faust, Theater of the World* (New York: Twayne, 1992), esp. 88–92. On the concept of *kairos*, see below, chap. 4,sect. 1, with additional bibliography.

35. Vittorio Alfieri, *Vita scrissa da esso*, vol. 1, critical edition of the final draft by L. Fassò (Asti: Casa d'Alfieri, 1951). On this subject, see Carlo Ossola, "Sur le vif: *Paris débastillé* by Vittorio Alfieri," in Carlo Ossola, *L'avenir de nost origines: Le copiste et le prophète* (Grenoble: Jérôme Millon, 2004), 125–49, esp. 132, with a French translation of the sonnets.

36. I refer here particularly to Schiller's *Kallias* and *Briefe zur ästhetischen Erziehung der Menscheit* (*Letters on the Aesthetic Education of Mankind*), *Schillers Werke*, Nationalausgabe, 20:333 ("son of his time"), 23:120 ("everything mortal"), and also his letter to Körner, November 28, 1796 ("beautiful tragedy").

37. Friedrich Schiller, Prologue to *Wallenstein*, *Sämtliche Werke*, ed. Gerhard Fricke and Herbert G. Göpfert, 2:270–74. On the final verse of the Prologue, see especially Norbert Oellers, "Die Heiterkeit der Kunst: Goethe variiert Schiller," in G. Martens and W. Woesler, eds., *Edition als Wissenschaft: Festschrift für Hans Zeller* (Tübingen: Niemeyer, 1991), 92–103. See also Dieter Borchmeyer, *Macht und Mélancholie: Schillers Wallenstein* Athenäum Monografien Literaturwissenschaft 91 (Königstein: Athenäum, 1988), and Sigbert

Latzel, *Der ernste Mensch und das Ernste: Eine sprachbezogene Analyse* (Munich: iudicium, 2001).

38. Honoré de Balzac, *La Peau de chagrin*, in *La Comédie humaine. Études philosophiques I*, ed. Marcel Bouteron, Bibliothèque de la Pléiade (Paris: Gallimard, 1950), 11–249; I quote the paperback edition by S. de Sacy (Paris: Gallimard, 1974).

39. Goethe: "It is an outstanding work in the most recent style, which nonetheless distinguishes itself by the way it moves back and forth, with energy and taste, between the possible and the unbearable, and is able to make very consistent use of the marvelous and the most remarkable convictions and events, about which much good could be said in detail." Conversation with Eckermann, October 11, 1831.

40. See Gertrud and Helmut Denzau, *Wildesel* (Stuttgart: Jan Thorbecke, 1999).—Translator's Note: The French word *chagrin* means both a wild ass and sorrow or grief. A "shagreen" is "an untanned leather covered with small round granulations" (Webster 10).

41. "Pact," Balzac, *La Peau de chagrin*, 66.

42. "Live excessively," 64

43. "Time-miser," 246; "mask of an old man," 267.

44. Academy, 295.

45. Will, power, and knowledge, 61ff.

46. Honoré de Balzac, *La Femme de trente ans*, in *La Comédie humaine*, ed. Pierre Citron, Bibliothèque de la Pléiade (Paris: Gallimard1979), 10:47–294.

47. Pierre Barbéris, *Balzac et le mal du siècle: Contribution à une psychologie du monde moderne*, 2 vols. (Paris: Gallimard, 1970), chap. 9, "La peau de chagrin," 2:1415–1613.

48. Honoré de Balzac, *Physiologie du mariage*, ed. Samuel de Sacy (Paris: Gallimard, 1971).

49. Oscar Wilde, *The Picture of Dorian Gray and other Writings,* ed. Richard Ellman (New York: Bantam, 1982), 1–193.

50. See Richard Ellmann's biography, *Oscar Wilde*, esp. chap.12. Also see Hiltrud Gnüg, *Kult der Kalte: Der klassische Dandy im Spiegel der Weltliteratur* (Stuttgart: Metzler, 1988), 292–312.

51. Oscar Wilde, *De profundis and Other Writings*, introduction by Hesketh Pearson (London: Penguin, 1986). "The Ballad of Reading Gaol," 229–52 (the quotations in sections 3 and 5).

52. Friedhelm Kemp on Goethe's three lives, in *Johann Wolfgang Goethe: Leben und Welt in Briefen*, collected (and continuously commented upon) by Friedhelm Kemp (Munich: Hanser, 1996).

53. Reinhart Koselleck, *Zeitschichten: Studien zur Historik* (Frankfurt/M: Suhrkamp, 2000), 97.

54. Alfred de Vigny, *Oeuvres completes*, vol. 1, *Poésie, Théâtre*, ed. François Germain and André Jarry, Bibliothèque de la Pléiade (Paris: Gallimard, 1986). The play *Chatterton* is found on pages 747–869.

55. John Keats, *Selected Poems* (New York: Gramercy Books, 1993), 30. The poem "Chatterton" is on p. 14. In it, see also the line "A half-blown flow'ret which cold blasts amate."

56. Gottfried Benn, "Altern als Problem für Kunstler," in *Gesammelte Werke in 8 Bänden*, ed. Dieter Wellershof, vol. 4, *Reden und Vorträge* (Wiesbaden: Limes, 1968), 1116–46. Cf. Norberto Bobbio, *De senectute e altri scritti autobiografici* (Turin: Einaudi, 1996).

57. See Frank Schirrmacher, *Das Methusalem-Komplott* (Munich: Karl Blessing, 2004).

58. August von Platen, *Gedichte*, selected, with an afterword, by Heinrich Henel (Stuttgart: Reclam, 1968). Cf. Hans Christoph Buch's interpretation in *Deutsche Gedichte und ihre Interpretationen*, ed. Marcel Reich-Ranicki (Frankfurt/M: Insel, 2002), 4:42–44.

59. Thomas Mann, "Tod in Venedig" ("Death in Venice"), in *Gesammelte Werke in 13 Bänden*, vol. 8, *Erzählungen* (Frankfurt: Fischer, 1990), 444–525. On the uncompleted "carpet-novel," see also Christophe Pradeau, "Le roman a le temps," *Poétique* 132 (2002): 387–400.

60. Ingeborg Bachmann, *Gedichte*, in *Werke*, 3d ed., vol. 1, ed. Christine Koschel, Inge von Weidenbaum, and Clemens Münster (Munich: Piper, 1993). Both poems discussed appear on 36f.

61. See Sigrid Weigel, *Ingeborg Bachmann: Hinterlassenschaften unter Wahrung des Briefgeheimnisses* (1999; rpt. Munich: Deutscher Taschenbuch Verlag, 2003). On "time by the hour," see esp. 565f. See also Hilde Spiel's interpretation of this poem in *Deutsche Gedichte und ihre Interpretationen*, ed. Marcel Reich-Ranicki (Frankfurt/M: Insel, 2002), 10:292f, and Christian Schärf's interpretation in *Interpretationen: Werke von Ingeborg Bachmann* (Stuttgart: Reclam, 2002), 27–42.

62. Ingeborg Bachmann, *Werke*, vol. 1; paperback edition in *Das Dreißigste Jahr: Erzählungen* (Munich: Piper, 2003), 17–60. See also the numerous comments on this story in Sigrid Weigel's book, as well as Bettina Bannasch's interpretation in *Interpretationen: Werke von Ingeborg Bachman*, 140–55.

Chapter 3

LIMITED TIME IN THIS WORLD AND IN THE NEXT

1. Psalm 89:10 (Vulgate); 90:10 (RSV). I give here, and for all quotations from the Jewish Bible in this section, the text of the *Tanakh* (Jewish Publication Society, 1985), Psalm 90:l, 10. In this case, however, I have modified the text (to make it correspond to the German) in that I have substituted for "and we are in darkness" the alternative translation "and we fly away," which is mentioned in a footnote to this text.

2. Quotations from Koheleth (= Ecclesiastes) 3:1; 5:1–2; Daniel 7:1; 2 Maccabees 2:24–27.

3. Matthew 18:3; cf. Mark 10:15, Luke 18:17.

4. "Our Father," Matthew 6:7; "idle word," Matthew 12:36.

5. "Time is fulfilled," Mark 1:15; "the kingdom of God is nigh," Luke 10:9 and John 17:1; "only a little while," John 7:33, following Isaiah 29:17.

6. The election of Peter and Andrew, Matthew 4:22; James and John, Mark 1:20; father's death, Matthew 8:21 and 10:37; Fourth Commandment, Matthew 15:4–6.

7. Workers in the vineyard, Matthew 20; on the "last called," see also Upton Sinclair's novel *One Clear Call* (New York: Viking, 1948).

8. Birds, lilies, Matthew 8:21 and 10:37; Fourth Commandment, Matthew 15:4–6.

9. 1 Corinthians, 7:29. RSV: "the appointed time is grown very short."

10. 1 Corinthians, 7:38. See Giorgio Agamben, *The Time that Remains: A Commentary on the Letter to the Romans*, trans. Patricia Dailey (Stanford: Stanford University Press, 2005).—Translator's note: Here the King James translation differs substantially from the RSV (which corresponds more closely to Luther). The RSV gives: "So that he that marries his betrothed does well; and he who refrains from marriage will do better."

11. 2 Peter 3:8.

12. Jacques Le Goff, "Au Moyen Âge: Temps de l'Église et temps du marchand" (1960). In Le Goff, *Pour un autre moyen âge: Temps, travail, et culture en Occident. 18 essais* (Paris: Gallimard, 1977), 46–65.

13. Jacques Le Goff, *La Naissance du Purgatoire* (Paris: Gallimard, 1981). English: *The Birth of Purgatory*, trans. Arthur Goldhammer (Chicago: University of Chicago Press, 1984).

14. Dante Alighieri, *La Divina Commedia,* Testo critico della Società Dantesca Italiana, revised by Giuseppe Randelli (Milan: Ulrico Hoepli, 1955). The quotation "Il tempo è caro in questo regno" is from *Purgatorio* 24.91. See also Andreas Kablitz's important article, "Zeitlichkeit und Ewigkeit in Dantes Purgatorio: Das Fürstental am Fuß des Läuterungsberges" (Dante, *Divina Commedia*, *Purgatorio* VII-VIII)," in *Werk und Diskurs: Karlheinz Stierle zum 60. Geburtstag*, ed. D. Ingenschay and H. Pfeiffer (Munich: Fink, 1999), 33–72.—Translator's note: All quotations from Dante's *Commedia* are taken from Charles S. Singleton's translation (Princeton: Princeton University Press, 1970).

15. Jacques Le Goff, *La Naissance du Purgatoire*, 388.

16. On qualitative retribution in Dante ("qual io fui vivo, tal son morto"): *Inferno* 14.51. On quantitative retribution (temporal retribution): *Purgatorio* 4.130f. See also *Purgatorio* 23.84: "dove tempo con tempo si ristora." I deal with this subject at greater length in *Lethe: Die Kunst und Kritik des Vergessens*, 3d ed. (Munich: C. H. Beck, 2000), chap. 2, sect. 5; English: *Lethe: The Art and Critique of Forgetting*, trans. Steven Rendall (Ithaca: Cornell University Press, 2004).

17. Dante to Forese Donati: *Purgatorio* 23.40–93. In verse 89 Ante-purgatory is described as "la costa ove s'aspetta" (Singleton: "the slope where they wait").

18. Dante to Belacqua: *Purgatorio* 4:97–139. The quotation "Chè perder tempo . . ." is from a different canto: *Purgatorio* 3:78.

19. Dante to King Manfred (Manfredi): *Purgatorio* 3:103–45. The two verses quoted ("Ma la bontà . . .") are in *Purgatorio* 3:122–23. On multiplication by thirty: "For the time he remained in it [the state of excommunication], thirty" ("per ognun tempo ch'elli è stato, trenta"), *Purgatorio* 3:139.

20. H. W. Brands, *The First American: The Life and Times of Benjamin Franklin* (New York: Anchor, 2002). See also Edmund S. Morgan, *Benjamin Franklin* (New Haven: Yale University Press, 2002). On the historical context, see Ralf Dahrendorf, *Die angewandte Aufklärung: Gesellschaft und Soziologie in Amerika* (Frankfurt/M: Fischer, 1968).

21. Leonard W. Labaree and Barbara B. Oberg, eds., *The Papers of Benjamin Franklin* (New Haven: Yale University Press, 1959–.) See also Rudolf Wendorff, *Zeit und Kultur: Geschichte des Zeitbewußtseins in Europa* (Opladen: Westdeutscher Verlag, 1980), esp. 278f.

22. Benjamin Franklin, "Necessary Hints to Those that Would be Rich," in *The Papers of Benjamin Franklin*, ed. Labaree and Oberg, 3 (1961), 306.

23. Benjamin Franklin, *The Autobiography and Other Writings*, ed. with an introduction by Peter Shaw (New York: Bantam, 1982). See also Jochen Hörisch, *Kopf oder Zahl: Die Poesie des Geldes* (1996; rpt. Frankfurt/M: Suhrkamp, 1998); also Jean Chesneaux, *Habiter le temps* (Paris: Bayard, 1996), esp. 33f.

24. Translator's Note: *die Eintagsfliege*. I've followed here the English translation published by The American Museum at Philadelphia in 1790.

25. The fable of the ephemera or may-fly: The original was written in French. For an English translation, see Peter Shaw's edition of the *Autobiography*, 255f.

26. *Poor Richard's Almanac*, in Peter Shaw's edition of the *Autobiography*, 181–93.

27. Father Abraham: in the selection from *The Way to Wealth* (1758) presented in Peter Shaw's edition of the *Autobiography*, 191.

28. Street-cleaning in London: Peter Shaw's edition of the *Autobiography*, 114ff.

29. Max Weber, *Die protestantische Ethik und der Kapitalismus* (1905), in Weber, *Die protestantische Ethik I: Eine Aufsatzsammlung*, ed. Johannes Winckelmann, 8th ed. (Gütersloh: Güterslohe Verlagshaus Mohn, 1991).

30. Ibid., 40ff.

31. Jean Calvin, *Institutio Christianae religionis*, 1536. English: *Institutes of the Christian Religion*, trans. Ford Lewis Battles, 2 vols., 1960. On Purgatory, see especially chap. 3, sect. 5.

32. Heinrich Heine, *Sämtliche Schriften in 12 Bänden*, ed. Klaus Briegleb, vols. 5 (text) and 6 (commentary), ed. Karl Pörnbacher (Frankfurt/M: Ullstein, 1981). All quotations from Heine cite this edition. The quotation regarding the "pacific mission" is from a letter to Friedrich Merckel written in the spring of 1833.

33. The "thought-action model" was first developed by Heine in *Kahldorf über den Adel in Briefen an den Grafen M. von Moltke aus dem Jahr 1831* (Heine, *Sämtliche Schriften*, 2:655). I offer a more detailed description of this doctrine in my article "Heinrich Heines deutsch-französische Parallelen," *Heine-Jahrbuch* (1990): 111–28.

34. "World revolution": *Lutetia: Berichete über Politik, Kunst, und Volksleben*, part 2, chap. 46 (December 7, 1892), in Heine, *Sämtliche Schriften*, 9:406. On this subject, see Dolf Sternberger, *Heinrich Heine und die Abschaffung der Sünde* (Hamburg: Claassen, 1972), chap. 11: "Absage an die Adresse Hegels," 259–83.

35. Heinrich Heine, *Zur Geschichte der Religion und Philosophie in Deutschland*, concluding section, in *Sämtliche Schriften*, 5:505–641, esp. 636ff.

36. Heinrich Heine, *Deutschland—Ein Wintermärchen*, caput 6 (1844), in *Sämtliche Schriften*, 4:591f.

37. See Wolff A. von Schmidt, "Marx und Heine," *Archiv für Kulturgeschichte* 54 (1972): 143–52.

38. Karl Marx, *Zur Kritik der Hegelschen Rechtsphilosophie*, in Karl Marx, *Die Frühschriften*, ed. Siegfried Landshut (Stuttgart: Kröner, 1971), 207–24, esp. 223.

39. *Deutsch-französische Jahrbücher*, ed. Karl Marx and Arnold Ruge (1843; only two issues appeared). Rpt. ed. Joachim Höppner (Leipzig, 1981). The quotations are taken from the "Plan" (83–96).

40. The thunder-and-lightning metaphor is already found in Hegel, *Werke*, 2:458.

41. Karl Marx, *Zur Kritik der Hegelschen Rechtsphilosophie*, concluding section.

42. Heinrich Heine, Preface to *Lutetia*, in *Sämtliche Schriften*, 9:232.

Chapter 4
SHORT AND SHORTEST TIMES

1. Erwin Panofsky, "Father Time," in *Studies in Iconology* (New York: Oxford University Press, 1939). See also Lionello Gozzi, *Vivere nel presente: Un aspetto della visione del tempo nella cultura occidentale* (Bologna: Il Mulino, 2004).

2. Isidor of Seville, *Etymologiae* 8.11.31–34; Tiepolo's *Il Tempo* is in the Villa Valmarana, Vicenza; Goya's *Saturn Devouring his Children* is in the Prado, Madrid.

3. Isidor of Seville, *Etymologiae* 8.11.30.

4. Goethe, "terrible speed," *Italienische Reise*, ed. Christoph Michel and Hans-Georg Drewitz, 2 vols. (Frankfurt/M: Deutscher Klassiker Verlag, 1993), November 9, 1786; "everything velociferous," see Manfred Osten, *"Alles veloziferisch" oder Goethes Entdeckung der Langsamkeit* (Frankfurt-am-Main: Insel, 2003).

5. On Kairos, see also Erwin Panofsky, *Studies in Iconology*, and Giacomo Marramao, *Kairós: Apologia del tempo debito* (Rome: Laterza, 1992).

6. See Marianne Gronemeyer, *Das Leben als letzte Gelegenheit: Sicherheitsbedürfnisse und Zeitknappheit*, 2d ed. (Darmstadt: Wissenschaftliche Buchgesellschaft, 1993); on Kairos and Fortuna, see esp. 75.

7. On Kairos in Hippocrates, see above, chap. 1, sect. 1.

8. Note how Galen, in his commentary on Hippocrates, raises this adjective to the superlative: *oxyatos*. Its Latin equivalent is (*maxime*) *praeceps* (Galen, *Aphormismi Hippocratis, graece et latine, unacum Galeni commentariis* [Lyon, 1668], 346, 353).

9. Cicero: "Occasio autem est pars temporis habens in se alicuius rei idoneam faciendi aut non faciendi opportunitatem" (*De inventione* 1.27). See especially Bruno Hillebrand, *Ästhetik des Augenblicks: Der Dichter als Überwinder der Zeit—von Goethe bis heute* (Göttingen: Vandenhoeck & Rupprecht 1999), and Christian W. Thomsen and Hans Hollander, eds., *Augenblick und Zeitpunkt: Studien zur Zeitstruktur und Zeitmetaphorik in Kunst und Wissenschaften* (Darmstadt: Wissenschaftliche Buchgesellschaft, 1984).

10. The quotations from Goethe, "Alexis und Dora," are of verses 15–16 and 101. On this poem, see especially Andreas Anglet, *Der "ewige" Augenblick: Studien zur Struktur und Funktion eines Denkbildes bei Goethe* (Köln: Böhlau, 1991), esp. 114–20, and Albrecht Schöne, *Götterzeichen, Liebeszauber, Satanskult* (Munich: Hanser, 1999), esp. 262–70.

11. See Karl Heinz Bohrer, *Plötzlichkeit: Zum Augenblick des ästhetischen Scheins* (Frankfurt/M: Suhrkamp, 1981), and *Ekstasen der Zeit: Augenblick-Gegenwart-Erinnerung* (Munich: Hanser, 2003).

12. Bruno Hillebrand, *Ästhetik des Augenblicks*, 34, 45.

13. Schiller, *Maria Stuart*, 3.6 and 4.4.

14. Schiller, *Don Carlos*. The dialogue with the king, 3.10; the quotation "One must take advantage," monologue in 3.9; the quotation "O Carl," 5.3.

15. Schiller, *Wallenstein* trilogy. In *Sämtliche Werke*, ed. Gerhard Fricke and Herbert G. Göpfert (Darmstadt: Wissenschaftliche Buchgesellschaft, 1981), 2:269–547. See also Dieter Borchmeyer, *Macht und Melancholie: Schillers Wallenstein* (Frankfurt/M: Athenäum, 1988). "Old luck," *Wallensteins Tod*, 3.3; "opportunity," *Wallensteins Tod*, 1.7; "the moment has come," *Piccolomini*, 5.6; "The time has not yet come," *Wallensteins Tod*, 1.7.

16. Schiller, *Wallenstein* trilogy. "Now we must act," *Wallensteins Tod*, 1.1; "lucky star," *Wallensteins Tod*, 5.2; "It is a great moment," *Piccolomini* 4.4; exchange between Gordon and Buttler, *Wallensteins Tod*, 5.6; "On this moment," *Wallensteins Tod*, 5.9. See Dieter Borchmeyere, *Macht und Melancholie*; also, Peter-André Alt, *Friedrich Schiller*, 2 vols. (Munich: C. H. Beck, 2004).

17. Stefan Zweig, *Sternstunden der Menschheit: Vierzehn historische Miniaturen* (Frankfurt/M: Fischer Taschenbuch Verlag, 2002).

18. Emile Zola, *L'Argent*, vol. 5 of *Les Rougon-Macquart*, Bibliothèque de la Pléïade (Paris: Gallimard, 1967).

Chapter 5
THE ECONOMY OF LIMITED TIME

1. Homer, *Odyssey*, trans. Robert Fagles (New York: Penguin, 1996). The "treatise" on hospitality stretches from book 6 (arrival in Phaeacia) to book 13 (arrival in Ithaca); books 9–12 are devoted to Odysseus's long narrative. Quotations: "What *are* they," *Odyssey* 6.132–33; "Every stranger," 6.227–28; supplementary budget, 13.1–17. On Homer, see Joachim Latacz, *Homer: Der erste Dichter des Abendlands*, 2d ed. (Munich: Artemis, 1989), esp. 182–86.

On Greek hospitality, see René Schérer, *Zeus l'Hospitalier: Éloge de l'hospitalité* (Paris: Armand Colin, 1993).

2. The Polyphemus episode is part of Odysseus's narrative: 9.170–566.

3. Denis Diderot and Jean le Rond d'Alembert, *Encyclopédie ou Dictionnaire raisonné des sciences, des arts, et des métiers* (1751–72), art. "Hospitalité."

4. Friedrich Adolph Freiherr Knigge, *Über den Umgang mit Menschen* (1788; rpt. Darmstadt: Wissenschaftliche Buchgesellschaft, 1967, 2nd ed. 1976). See esp. chap. 2, sect. 9, "Über das Verhältnis von Wirt und Gast." The quoted passages are found in the first section of this chapter, except for the last (about fish), which is in section 3.

5. Bernhard Laum, *Heiliges Geld: Eine historische Untersuchung über den sakralen Ursprung des Geldes* (Tübingen: Mohr, 1924). Georg Simmel, *Philosophie des Geldes* (1900), ed. David P. Frisby and Klaus Christian Köhnke (Frankfurt/M: Suhrkamp, 1989).

6. Aristotle, *Nicomachean Ethics* 1133a.30.

7. Quintilian, *Institutio oratoria* 1.6.3.

8. Francis Bacon, *The Advancement of Learning*, ed. Michael Kiernan (Oxford: Clarendon, 2000).

9. Leibniz, *Unvorgreifliche Gedanken, betreffend die Ausübung und Verbesserung der deutschen Sprache*, in *Zwei Aufsätze*, ed. Uwe Pörksen (Stuttgart: Reclam, 1983).

10. Goethe, *Werke*, Weimarer Ausgabe, Abteilung 2, Band 11 (Weimar, 1893), 167.—*Faust* II, Act 1, "Pleasance" (vv. 6055–6130).

11. Plutarch, *The Lives of the Noble Grecians and Romans*, trans. John Dryden, revised Arthur Hugh Clough (New York: Modern Library, n.d.), 898.—Cato, *Disticha Catonis*, ed. M. Boas (Amsterdam: North Holland, 1952).

12. Nicolas Boileau, "Art poétique" 1, v. 186.—Dominique Bouhours, *Entretiens d'Ariste et d'Eugène* (1671; rpt. Paris, 1947), 92.—Claude Favre Vaugelas, *Remarques sur la langue française* (1647), ed. Chassang (Versailles: Cerf, 1880), 2:276.

13. François de La Rochefoucauld, *Maximes et réflexions*, nos. 250 and 142. See Louis Van Delft, "La Rochefoucauld: Le style 'soldat,'" in *Thèmes et genres littéraires aux XVIIme et XVIIme siècles: Mélanges I. Truchet* (Paris: Presses Universitaires de France, 1992), 173–78.

14. Georg Christoph Lichtenberg, *Sudelbücher*, Heft G, no. 215 (Promies numbering), in *Schriften und Briefe*, ed. Wolfgang Promies, 6 vols. (Munich: Hanser, 1968–74), quoted in Albrecht Schöne, *Aufklärung aus dem Geist der Experimentalphysik* (Munich: C. H. Beck, 1982), 120.—Arthur Schopenhauer, "Über Schriftstellerei und Stil," in *Parerga und Paralipomena: Kleine philosophische Schriften* (Munich, 1977), 1:585–641, esp. 610.—Nietzsche, *Götzendämmerung*, ed. Schlecta ed., vol. 2 (Darmstadt, 1960).

15. André Gide, "Billets à Angèle" (1921), in *Incidences* (Paris: Nouvelle Revue Française, 1924), 40.

16. Jean Paul, *Vorschule der Ästhetik: Kleine Nachschule zur Ästhetischen Vorschule*, ed. Norbert Miller (Munich: Hanser, 1963). See especially IX. Programm, §45, "Sprachkürze," 175–78.

17. Germaine de Staël, *De l'Allemagne*, ed. Simone Bakyé, 2 vols. (Paris: Garnier-Flammarion, 1968), 1.1, 1.2. 1.11, 1.12, 2.1, 4.10–12.

Chapter 6
THE DRAMA OF TIME IN SHORT SUPPLY

1. Aristotle, *Poetics*, ed. and trans. W. Hamilton Fyfe, Loeb Classical Library 22 (Cambridge, Mass., 1932). See the extensive commentaries in Roselyne Dupont-Roc and Jean Lallot, eds., Aristote, *La Poétique* (Paris: Seuil, 1988).
2. Aristotle on epic: *Poetics*, chap. 24 (59b17)
3. Aristole on drama (tragedy): *Poetics*, chap. 5 (49b).
4. On the three unities: Pierre Corneille, *Discours des trois unités*, in Corneille, *Théâtre complet*, ed. Pierre Lièvre and Roger Caillois, Bibliothèque de la Pléïade (Paris: Gallimard, 1950), 1:65–82.
5. Aristotle, *Poetics*, chap. 5 (49b).
6. Pierre Corneille, *Le Cid*, in *Théâtre complet*, 1:693–776. See Marc Fumaroli, *Héros et orateurs: Rhétorique et dramaturgie cornéliennes* (Geneva: Droz, 1990).
7. Chimène: "Va, je ne te hais point!" (3.4). The litotes here is famous.
8. "Lofty soul," 2.4.
9. "On both sides," 1.6.
10. "Blood for blood," 2.8.
11. "Time has often . . . ," 5.7.
12. Corneille, *Théâtre complet*, 700–706, esp. 703.
13. William Shakespeare, *Hamlet*, ed. George Lyman Kittredge (1939; rpt. New York: Ginn-Blaisdell, 1967). See Harold Bloom, *Hamlet: Poem Unlimited* (New York: Riverhead Books, 2003).
14. On the concept of " soul murder," see the commentary in Holger M. Klein's edition of *Hamlet*, 2 vols. (Stuttgart: Reclam, 2000), 2:368.
15. First scene with the ghost, 1.5.
16. Claudius's speech and shortening of time, 1.2 and 2.2.
17. According to current scholarship the source for Shakespeare's knowledge of humoral pathology and the theory of melancholy is Timothy Bright's *A Treatise of Melancholy* (1586). See John Dover Wilson, *What Happens in Hamlet?* (1935).
18. Hamlet's suspicion, 1.5.
19. Hamlet's duty to exact revenge and his complaint against time, 1.5.
20. Distractions, 2.1; reading, 2.2; pastimes, 3.1; play within the play, 3.2.
21. A room in the castle, 3.3. In this scene, Claudius cries, "O, my offence is rank, it smells to heaven; / It hath the primal eldest curse upon't / A brother's murder!" (allusion to Cain's fratricide).
22. Laertes plot, 4.7.
23. Voyage to England and the fatal letter, 3.1; 3.3; 4.3; 5.2.
24. "The interim is mine," 5.2; "I am but hurt," 5.2.
25. Gotthold Ephraim Lessing, *Nathan der Weise: Ein dramatisches Gedicht in fünf Aufzügen*, in Lessing, *Werke und Briefe in 12 Bänden*, vol. 9, ed. Klaus Bohnen

and Arno Schilson (Frankfurt/M: Deutscher Klassiker Verlag, 1993). On the parable of the ring, 3.4–7.

26. Marcel Proust, À la recherche du temps perdu, ed. Pierre Clarac and André Ferré, 3 vols, Bibliothèque de la Pléïade (Paris: Gallimard, 1954). The seventh part, Le temps retrouvé, is in vol. 3.

27. More details regarding the sense of history and the "lower senses" will be found in my article "Memoria corporis—mit Blick auf Proust," in Esprit civique und Engagement: Festschrift für Henning Krauß zum 60. Geburtstag, ed. Hanspeter Plocher et al. (Tübingen: Stauffenberg, 2003), 693–98.

28. See Bruno Hillebrand, Ästhetik des Augenblicks.

29. The theme of the time-novel to be written by the narrator: À la recherche du temps perdu, 3:1032–48. All quotations from Proust's work quoted in this section appear in this passage, with the exception of "the artist Time" ("l'artiste, le Temps"), 2:936. An interesting criticism of Proust's novel is provided by his fellow novelist Anatole France: "Life is too short and Proust is too long" ("La vie est trop courte et Proust est trop long"), quoted in Christophe Pradeau, "Le roman a le temps," Poétique 132 (2002): 393.

Chapter 7
FINITUDE, INFINITY

1. Hans Blumenberg, "Der Prozeß der theoretischen Neugierde," in Blumenberg, Die Legitimität der Neuzeit (Frankfurt/M: Suhrkamp, 1966). English: The Legtimacy of the Modern Age, trans. Robert M. Wallace (Cambridge, Mass.: MIT Press, 1983), part 3, chaps. 9–10. See also André Labhardt's very informative article on the history of the concept of curiosity, "Curiositas: Notes sur l'histoire d'un mot et d'une notion," Museum Helveticum 17 (1960): 206–24. See also Nicole Czechowski, ed., La curiosité: Vertiges du savoir (Paris: Autrement, 1993), which includes important articles by Judith Schlanger (50–64) and Bernard Beugnot (101–119); Odo Marquard, "Neugier als Wissenschaftsantrieb oder Die Entlastung von der Unfehlbarkeitspflicht," in Marquard, Glück im Unglück: Philosophische Überlegungen (Frankfurt/M: Fischer, 1995), 75–91.

2. Aristotle, Metaphysics, book A, 980a21: Πάντες άνθρωποι τού ειδέναι όρέγοται φύσει. Often translated in English as "All men by nature desire knowledge." In our own time, Isaiah Berlin has noted that "only barbarians are not curious" (The Crooked Timber of Humanity: Chapters in the History of Ideas, ed. Henry Hardy [London: J. Murray, 1990], 2).

3. Cicero: "insatiabilis quaedam e cognoscendis rebus voluptas" (De Finibus bonorum et malorum 4.12).—Seneca: "curiosum nobis natura dedit ingeniam" (De otio 5.3).

4. Tertullian, De praescriptione haereticorum 8.1.—Augustine: "vana curiositas" (Confessiones 5.3–6 and 10.35).

5. Dante, Divina Commedia, Purgatorio 21.1–4.

6. Knigge, *Über den Umgang mit Menschen*, chap. 5, "Über den Umgang mit Frauenzimmern," 10 (cf. above, chap. 5, n. 4).

7. Judith Schlanger in *La curiosité*, ed. Czechowski, 50ff. See also Schlanger, *La vocation* (Paris: Seuil, 1997).

8. On the "gigantic" hunger for knowledge in Rabelais, see Jean Starobinski, "L'ordre du jour," *Le Temps de la réflexion* 4 (1983): 101–25, and Harald Weinrich, *Lethe*, chap. 2, sect. 1.

9. Torquato Tasso, *Il Porzio ovvero de le virtù*, in Tasso, *Dialoghi*, 3 vols., ed. Ezio Raimondi (Florence: Sansoni, 1958). See also Giacomo Jori, *Per evidenza: Conoscenza e segni nell'éta barroca* (Turin: Marsilio, 1998), chapter "Incertezza," 255f.—In the Italian word *il fine* (the goal) an echo of the feminine word *la fine* (the end) may be heard.

10. Leibniz, *De arte inveniendi*, in *Opuscules et fragments inédits*, ed. Louis Couturat (Paris, 1903; rpt. Hildesheim: Olms, 1961, 2nd ed. 1988), 167–70. The synthetic art of finding or invention was also called by Leibniz the art of combination (*ars combinatoris*). He uses the verb *indagare* ("look for") as a synonym of *invenire*.

11. Blaise Pascal, *Oeuvres complètes*, ed. Jacques Chevalier, Bibliothèque de la Pléïade (Paris: Gallimard, 1954). The order and numbering of the *Pensées* is a matter of debate, and differing orders are found in other editions. However, for our purposes here these differences are not very important, especially since almost all editions have concordances that allow the reader to locate a given passage in another edition.

12. *Pensées*, fragment no. 84, p. 1107. (Here I have corrected a typographical error in the Pléïade edition: "en" insted of "et"). On this fragment, see Giacomo Jori, *Per evidenza*, 257. See also Arnaldo Pizzorusso, "Conferenza Rajna: Pascal et la letteratura," *Atti della Academia Nazionale dei Lincei* 396 (1999): 145–57.

13. *Pensées*, fragment no. 203, p. 1138 (*nous ne cherchons*) and no. 444, p. 1211 (*infiniment à savoir*).

14. *Pensées*, fragment no. 84, pp. 1105–12.

15. *Pensées*, fragment no. 88, p. 1112 (*petite durée*); no. 334, p. 1171 (*instant*). See also Pascal's "L'Art de persuader," in Blaise Pascal, *L'Art de persuader précédé de l'Art de conférer de Montaigne* (Paris: Rivages, 2001): *Néant du temps*.

16. On the "wager," see *Pensées*, fragment no. 451, pp. 1212–16.

17. Paul Valéry, *Cahiers*, ed. Judith Robinson, Bibliothèque de la Pléïade (Paris: Gallimard, 1974), 2:1195ff.

18. The *Mémorial* appears at the beginning of the *Pensées* in Léon Brunschvicg's edition (*Pensées et opuscules* [Paris: Hachette, 1897]). Cf. Dominique Descotes' edition (Paris: Garnier-Flammarion, 1976), 43f.

19. *The Complete Poems of Emily Dickinson*, ed. Thomas H. Johnson (Boston: Little, Brown, 1960), poem no. 301, p. 142. This poem was written in 1862 but first published after 1890.

20. Hans Blumenberg, *Lebenszeit und Weltzeit* (Frankfurt/M: Suhrkamp, 1986), esp. part 2, "The Time-Shear." Particularly important here are chapters 1 ("Apokalypse und Paridies") and 13 ("Zeiterfüllung und Erfüllungszeit").

21. Reinhart Koselleck, *Zeitschichten: Studien zur Historik* (Frankfurt/M: Suhrkamp, 2000), chap. 2, "Verschränkung und Wandel der drei Zeitdimensionen."—Hermann Lubbe, *Im Zug der Zeit: Verkürzter Aufenthalt in der Gegenwart*, 2d ed. (Berlin: Springer, 1994).

22. Hans Blumenberg, *Das Lachen der Thrakerin: Eine Urgeschichte der Theorie* (Frankfurt/M: Suhrkamp, 1987). See also Harald Weinrich, "Thales und die thrakische Magd: allseitige Schadenfreude," in Wolfgang Preisendanz and Rainer Warning, eds., *Das Komische*, Poetik und Hermeneutik 7 (Munich: Fink, 1978), 435–37.

23. Hans Blumenberg, *Lebenzeit und Weltzeit*, chap. 2, 2: "Die Kongruenz von Lebenzeit un Weltzeit as Wahn," 80–85, with reference to a brief remark made by Sebastian Heffner, *Anmerkungen zu Hitler* (Frankfurt/M: Fischer, 2003), 25ff., 125.

24. Odo Marquard's most succinct statements regarding "the experience of shortage" as one of man's most primal temporal-anthropological experiences are found in his article "Zeit und Endlichkeit" (1991), which is now included in the volume *Zukunft braucht Herkunft: Philosophische Essays* (Stuttgart: Reclam, 2003), 220–33, esp. 231.

25. Other books by Marquard: *Abschied vom Prinzipiellen: Philosophische Studien* (Stuttgart: Reclam, 1986); *Apologie des Zufälligen* (Stuttgart: Reclam, 1986); *Philosophie des Stattdessen: Studien* (Stuttgart: Reclam, 2000).

26. Marquard on Blumenberg, especially in the article "Entlastung vom Absoluten. In Memoriam Hans Blumenberg," in *Philosophie des Stattdessen*, 108–20, esp. section 4, "Endlichkeit," 217ff.

27. Odo Marquard, "Über die Unvermeidlichkeit von Üblichkeiten," in *Glück im Unglück*, 62–74.

28. See especially Hermann Lubbe, *Zeit Erfahrungen: Sieben Begriffe zur Beschreibung moderner Zivilisationsdynamik* (Stuttgart: Franz Steiner, 1996).—Reinhart Koselleck, *Zeitschichten*.

29. Odo Marquard, *Temporales Doppelleben: Philosophisches Bemerkungen zu unserer Zeit*, Jahrbuch 1990 der Deutschen Akademie für Sprache und Dichtung (Wiesbaden: Luchterhand, 1990), 69–76. See also Peter Borscheid, *Das Tempo-Virus: Eine Kulturgeschichte* (Frankfurt/M: Campus, 2004).

Chapter 8
LIVING WITH DEADLINES

1. See Gerhard Dohrn-van Rossum, *Die Geschichte der Stunde: Uhren und moderne Zeitordnung* (Munich: Hanser, 1992).

2. Translator's Note: *Frist*. This is a used as a technical term throughout this chapter, with the meaning of "a determinate period of time ending in a deadline." I use the term "deadline-period" to render it.

3. Niklas Luhmann, "Die Knappheit der Zeit und die Vordringlichkeit des Befristeten," *Verwaltung* 1 (1968), quoted in Helga Nowotny, *Eigenzeit: Entstehung*

und Strukturierung eines Zeitgefühls, 2d ed. (Frankfurt/M: Suhrkamp, 1990), 136, 171.

4. See Hans Maier, *Die christiliche Zeitrechnung* (Freiburg: Herder, 1991).

5. See Rudolf Wendorff, *Zeit und Kultur: Geschichte des Zeitbewußtseins in Europa* (Opladen: Westdeutscher Verlag, 1980), 32.

6. Gustav Muthmann, *Rückläufiges deutsches Wörterbuch,* 3d ed. (Tübingen: Niemeyer, 2001), 894.

7. The indifference to the problem of deadlines that is found in legal literature is a further indication of the "extraordinary poverty of the legal perception and working-out of time" which Mireille Delmas-Marty complains about, and which she—no doubt correctly—traces back to the tendency to procrastination prevalent in the legal system. As a remedy for this unfortunate tendency, she recommends a legal "rhythmology." See Mireille Delmas-Marty, *Le flou du droit: Du code pénal aux droits de l'homme* (Paris: Presses Universitaires de France, 1986), 79, 82, 258.

8. See Günther Jakobs, *Staatliche Strafe: Bedeutung und Zweck,* Nordrhein-Westfälische Akademie der Wissenschaften, Vorträge, G 390 (Paderborn: Schöningh, 2004).

9. With regard to § 218a, the administration of justice makes a sharp distinction between an interruption of pregnancy that is not unlawful according to the so-called broader medical-social grounds for abortion and that does not depend on time limits (paragraph 2), on the one hand, and, on the other hand, an interruption of pregnancy of the kind examined in detail here, which is in fact, according to a judgment of the Federal Constitutional Court (*Bundesverfassungsgericht*), unlawful, but which if carried out before certain deadlines is not subject to penalty (paragraph 1).

10. Matthew 25:13 (King James version).

11. Martin Heidegger, *Sein und Zeit,* (1927; Tübingen: Niemeyer, 1986), chaps. 1–6.

12. George Steiner, *Martin Heidegger* (New York: Viking, 1979), 111.

13. Martin Heidegger, *Holzwege,* ed. Friedrich W. von Hermann (Frankfurt/M: Klostermann, 2003).

14. Odo Marquard, "Zeit und Endlichkeit," 220–33.

Chapter 9
SHORT STORIES ABOUT SHORT DEADLINES

1. The stories from the *Arabian Nights* are cited according to the original Arabic text translated by Enno Littmann (Frankfurt/M: Insel, 1976). See Claudia Ott's translation based on the oldest (but incomplete) Arabic manuscript by Muhsin Mahdi (Munich: C. H. Beck, 2004). Here I quote the Insel edition. The episode of the merchant and the demon: vol. 1, esp. 32ff. The thousand-and-first night is in vol. 4, esp. 631ff.

2. See Ernst-Peter Wieckenberg, *Johann Heinrich Voß: "Tausend und eine Nacht" und einige vergessene Gedichte* (Saarbrücken: Lichtenberg Jahrbuch, 2000), 97–126.

3. Shakespeare, *The Merchant of Venice* (Cambridge: Cambridge University Press, 1987). "This devil," 4.1; "the honest Antonio," 3.1; "I stay here," 4.1; "I'll torture him," 3.1.

4. Friedrich Schiller, "Die Burgschaft," in *Sämtliche Werke*, 8th ed. (Darmstadt: Wissenschaftliche Buchgesellschaft, 1987), 1:352–56.

5. Adelbert von Chamisso, *Peter Schlemihls wundersame Geschichte*, in *Sämtliche Werke in 2 Bänden*, ed. Werner Feudel and Christel Laufer (Leipzig, 1980; Munich: Hanser, 1982), 2:15–79, esp. chap. 4, p. 47.

6. Gustave Flaubert, *Madame Bovary: Moeurs de province*, in *Oeuvres complètes*, ed. A. Thibaudet and R. Dumesnil, Bibliothèque de la Pléïade (Paris: Gallimard, 1952), 1:325–27. Quotations: "fantaisies," 557; "Et avec la date," 574; "une forte longue échéance," 573; "une procuration,," p. 557f.; "Pensiez-vous, ma petite dame," 592; "I beg you," 594; "abyss," 609; "la sérénité," 613.

7. Guy de Maupassant, "La parure," in *Boule de Suif* (Paris: Albin Michel, 1957), 146–58.

8. Theodor Fontane, "Schach von Wuthenow: Erzählung aus der Zeit des Regiments Gensdarmes," in *Werke in 3 Bänden*, ed. Kurt Schreinert (Munich: Nymphenburger Verlagshandlung, 1968), 1:5–140.

9. Arthur Schnitzler, "Leutnant Gustl," in Schnitzler, *Casanovas Heimfahrt: Erzählungen* (Frankfurt/M: Fischer Taschenbuch, 1973).

10. Hermann Sudermann, *Die Ehre*, 2.1, in *Dramen des Naturalismus*, ed. A. Müller and H. Schlien (Emsdetten, 1962), 285. See also Harald Weinrich, "Die Mythologie der Ehre," in Manfred Fuhrmann, ed., *Terror und Spiel: Probleme der Mythenrezeption*, Poetik und Hermeneutik 4 (Munich: Fink, 1971), 341–56 and 669–86 (discussion).

11. Gabriel García Marquez, *Cronica de una muerte anunciada* (1981; rpt. Barcelona: Random House Mondadori, 2003).

12. Blaise Cendrars, *Oeuvres complètes*, ed. Claude Leroy, vol. 9 (Paris: Éditions Denoël, 2004; paperback ed., Paris: Denoël 1948), 259 and 138.

13. Ibid., 202–204.

14. Jérôme Thélot, *Les inventions littéraires de la photographie* (Paris: Presses Universitaires de France, 2003), 3–5.

15. Hugo von Hofmannsthal, *Jedermann: Das Spiel vom Sterben des reichen Mannes*, ed. Andreas Thomasberger (Stuttgart: Reclam, 2000).

16. Antonio Tabucchi, "Il tempo stringe," in Tabucchi, *I dialoghi mancati* (1988; Milan: Feltrinelli, 2002), 47–75. On Tabucchi's conception of time, see Anna Dolfi's commentary on Tabucchi in *Notturno indiano* (Turin: Società Editrice Internazionale, 1996), chap. 1, "La correzione del definitivo," esp. 4–6.

17. Antonio Tabucchi, "Il signor Pessoa è desiderato al telefono," in Tabucchi, *I dialoghi mancati*, 30.

18. Jules Verne, *Le tour du monde en 80 jours* (Paris: Librairie Générale Française, 2000).

19. Marc Camoletti, *Boeing-Boeing: Comédie en trois actes* (Paris: Librairie Thèâtrale, 1995).
20. Tom Twyker, *Lola rennt*, ed. Michael Töteberg (Reinbek bei Hamburg: Rowohlt, 1998).

Chapter 10
EPILOGUE ON THE SENSE OF TIME

1. My main source here is the *Sprach- und Sachatlas Italiens und der Südschweiz* (AIS), ed. Karl Jaberg and Jakob Jud (Zofingen: Ringier, 1928–40), especially the map *La tempia*.
2. For editions of Hippocrates, see chap. 1, n. 1. On Herophilos, see Heinrich von Staden, *The Art of Medicine in Early Alexandria* (Cambridge: Cambridge University Press, 1989), 352–55. On Rufus of Ephesus, *Rufus d'Ephèse: Traité abrégé sur le pouls* (Greek and French), in *Oeuvres*, ed. Charles Darember and Émile Ruelle (Paris: Imprimerie Nationale, 1879), 219–32. See also R. Brückle, *Die Pulschrift des Rufus von Ephesos* (Munich, 1939), 12ff.—Werner Friedrich Kümmel, "Der Puls und das Problem der Zeitmessung in der Geschichte der Medizin," *Medizin-Historisches Journal* 9 (1974): 1–22. On the background in the history of time, see Rudolf Wendorff, *Zeit und Kultur: Geschichte des Zeit- bewußtseins in Europa* (Opladen: Westdeutscher Verlag, 1980), esp. 205. Also, Gerhard Dohrn-van Rossum, *Die Geschichte der Stunde: Uhren und moderne Zeitrechnung* (Munich: Hanser, 1992), esp. 263.
3. On the unresolved problem of the etymology of the word *tempus*, see Giacomo Marramao: "E necessario tornare a riflettere sul linguaggio, prendendo in esame . . . il mistero delle origini del latino tempus" ("We must reflect once again on language, taking as our example . . . the mystery of the origin of the Latin word *tempus*") (*Kairos: Apologia del tempo debito* [Rome: Laterza, 1992], 98f.). On the etymology of words for the temple, see Hjalmar Frisk, *Quelques noms de la tempe en indo-européenne* (1951), rpt. in Frisk, *Kleine Schriften zur Indogermanistik und zur griechischen Wortkunde* (Göteborg: Wettergren und Kerber, 1966), 83–101.
4. See Antonius de Haen, *Ratio medendi*, 12 vols. (Vienna, 1768). On pulsology, see esp. part 12, chaps. 1–4.
5. William Harvey, *Exercitatio anatomica de motu cordis et sanguinis in animalibus* (1628), in William Harvey, *Movement of the Heart and Blood in Animals* (Latin and English) (Oxford: Oxford University Press, 1957), esp. chaps. 5 (where the passage quoted occurs) and 18.
6. On Heidegger, see above, chap. 8, sect. 4.
7. A more detailed discussion of the "sense" of time in the context of the canonical five senses and the common sense will be found in my article "Memoria corporis mit Blick auf Proust," in *Esprit civique und Engagement: Festschrift für Henning Krauß zum 60. Geburtstag*, ed. Hanspeter Plocher et al. (Tübingen: Stauffenberg, 2003), 693–98.

8. Translator's note: *Hautlichkeit,* "skinness," an abstract noun derived from *Haut* ("skin").

9. Immanuel Kant, *Critique of Pure Reason,* trans. Norman Kemp Smith (London: Macmillan, 1958), 1.1, Transcendental Aesthetic, § 1 (space) and § 2 (time).

10. *Der Rosenkavalier: Komödie für Musik in drei Aufzügen von Hugo von Hofmannsthal, Musik von Richard Strauß* (Mainz, 1987), 49.

Index